Personal Boundaries

by Victoria Priya, LCSW, SEP

for dummies®
A Wiley Brand

Personal Boundaries For Dummies®

Published by: **John Wiley & Sons, Inc.,** 111 River Street, Hoboken, NJ 07030-5774, www.wiley.com

Copyright © 2024 by John Wiley & Sons, Inc., Hoboken, New Jersey

Published simultaneously in Canada

Contents at a Glance

Table of Contents

CHAPTER 9: **Sexual Boundaries: Yes and No Are Complete Sentences**

CHAPTER 10: **Boundaries for Speaking: Filtering Your Thoughts before Sharing Them**

Introduction

Your personal boundaries — your ability to set limits with yourself and others — determine not only the quality of your emotional and mental health, but also the quality of all your relationships.

At their most basic and fundamental level, boundaries are a source of safety and freedom. You make countless decisions every day that keep you physically safe and protect you. You exercise your freedom every time you make binary *yes* or *no* choices, which are expressions of your boundaries.

You may be feeling clueless about boundaries. Or maybe you've recently realized that your current skill level isn't up to the task of helping you resolve a challenging new situation or navigate a difficult relationship.

This book gives you a solid foundation of knowledge about how personal boundaries work and reveals the blind spots that can trip you up as you're discovering or leveling up your boundaries. You may see — maybe for the first time — how parts of your personal history negatively impact your ability to set boundaries, and what to do about it. One of the most widespread misconceptions about boundaries is that you need different categories of boundaries for the various relationships, roles, or situations you encounter in your everyday life.

The truth is, creating boundaries in adult relationships works the same way every time — whether the boundary is with your spouse, your boss, a family member, or a friend. Once you understand the principles and the steps, boundary setting becomes simpler, easier, and sometimes even fun! No kidding.

I'm admittedly biased, but I wholeheartedly believe that boundaries are the most underrated life skill any person can possess. Clients, readers of my first book, and podcast listeners have told me countless times over the past two decades that having better boundaries changed not only their lives, but also their children's lives.

Let that sink in. Your boundaries not only improve your life, but also impact all your relationships — creating a legacy that benefits future generations. Yes, boundaries really are that powerful.

About This Book

Whether you consider yourself a boundaries novice or a boundaries ninja, this book gives you new ways of thinking about and setting boundaries.

Here's just a sampling of the information this book provides:

>> What personal boundaries are and how they help you establish order, safety, and protection

>> How to avoid unnecessary mistakes by knowing the common misperceptions people have about setting boundaries

>> How to navigate the inevitable pushback and resistance to your boundaries

>> How to recognize the signs that you may need to set a boundary

>> How to work the six steps for identifying, creating, and maintaining effective personal boundaries

>> How to figure out why a boundary didn't work or was unsuccessful, and what to do next

What you find here that you won't find in any other book on boundaries is an easy-to-follow, step-by-step process that shows you how to set a boundary in any context or relationship, including with yourself.

If you're new to personal boundaries, this book outlines the fundamentals, and explains why you may not have learned about personal boundaries when you were growing up. If you already have a good working understanding of boundaries, this book takes your current knowledge and skill set to the next level.

Disclaimer: Stories and examples presented in this book are fictional or composite nonidentifiable factual events that have been edited to protect confidentiality. This book is not intended as a substitute for professional mental health treatment or medical advice.

Foolish Assumptions

Having worked for decades with people who struggle with boundaries, I'm going to assume that you fall into one of three categories:

>> You've recently become aware that personal boundaries are a "thing" after years or even decades of having little or no information about how boundaries work, and you're ready to find out more. Congratulations, and welcome!

>> You have a pretty good understanding about how personal boundaries work, but you've discovered that your current knowledge and skills aren't adequate for a challenging new situation or a difficult, troubled relationship you're trying to navigate.

>> You're a life coach, psychotherapist, or other mental health treatment provider who has struggled to find a high-quality resource you feel comfortable giving to clients or patients who need good information about personal boundaries.

No matter which category you're in, this book meets you where you are. And I believe you have a hunch, or maybe even an unshakable conviction, that leveling up your boundaries can improve some aspect of your life — personally or professionally. It most certainly can, and I'm honored to have the privilege of sharing some life-changing information with you.

Icons Used in This Book

Throughout this book, icons in the margins on the left side of the page highlight certain types of valuable information I want to bring to your attention. Here's a brief description of each icon:

TIP

The Tip icon marks tips, shortcuts, and additional information that supplements or provides a deeper understanding about that section's subject matter.

REMEMBER

Remember icons mark information I want to make sure you have to help you better understand a concept that relates to a topic explained or presented in another part of the book.

TECHNICAL STUFF

The Technical Stuff icon includes information to clarify and expand your understanding of specific concepts or terms.

WARNING

The Warning icon tells you to watch out! It marks important information that can help you avoid unnecessary mistakes, relationship conflict, wasted time, or other missteps as you're improving your boundary-setting skills.

THINK ABOUT IT

The Think About It icon alerts you to information that has a bit of a philosophical basis and may need some mulling over in your spare time.

Beyond the Book

In addition to the abundance of information and guidance I give you in this book to help you identify, create, and maintain effective personal boundaries, you can access even more help and information online at Dummies.com. To check out this book's online Cheat Sheet, just go to www.dummies.com and search for "Personal Boundaries For Dummies Cheat Sheet."

Where to Go from Here

Like all *For Dummies* books, this book is designed in a way that doesn't require you to read it chapter by chapter, or cover to cover. That means some information may be repeated in more than one chapter to provide context (or emphasis) since the book may be read out of order. You can start by reading any chapter you're curious about, or zeroing in on a chapter that addresses a problem or issue you're struggling with right now. If you're the type of person who enjoys the order created by reading a book from beginning to end, go for it! Ultimately, it doesn't matter where you start. It only matters that you do. Setting boundaries is a learned skill, and you can do it.

REMEMBER

For even more boundaries goodness, go to www.victoriapriya.com/boundaries clarifier to get the 6-Step Boundaries Clarifier eWorkbook.

1

Defining Personal Boundaries

IN THIS PART . . .

Discover what personal boundaries are and how they help you establish order, safety, and protection.

Avoid unnecessary mistakes by knowing the common misperceptions about setting boundaries.

Decide who gets to know what about you by understanding the relationship between privacy, secrecy, and intimacy.

IN THIS CHAPTER

» Defining boundaries

» Recognizing that boundaries are inescapable

» Appreciating the benefits of boundaries

» Understanding the extremes of boundaries

» Realizing boundaries vary from culture to culture

Chapter **1**

Creating Order, Safety, and Protection with Boundaries

Chances are very good that you picked up this book because you're feeling curious, confused, mystified, or completely clueless about personal boundaries. If you relate to any of these emotions, you're far from alone. I can't count the number of times adults in their 30s, 40s, or 50s have told me, "I didn't even know what boundaries were."

Not knowing where to start or what to do when you think you need to set a boundary is frustrating. Sometimes it's even frightening. Boundaries, at their most basic level, are about protection. And when you don't feel confident about your ability to protect yourself emotionally, physically, or sexually, you're more likely to feel anxious, suspicious of others, or unnecessarily defensive as you try to create a sense of safety.

You may have tried in the past to set a boundary that didn't work. Or maybe you set an excellent boundary, but the backlash you got from other people made you think you were wrong or made a mistake. These are exactly the kinds of experiences you can expect when you start implementing or leveling up your boundaries skills.

The good news is you can find simple principles, tools, and skills in this book that will take you from feeling like a boundaries bumbler to a boundaries ninja. I give you six steps for creating boundaries of all kinds (see Chapter 13) and show you what to do when a boundary isn't successful (see Chapter 18). Having these tools and knowing how to respond to people who are less than thrilled about your new boundaries skills will provide the kind of clarity and confidence that makes boundary setting easy — and maybe even fun!

In this chapter, I define what personal boundaries look like and expand your vocabulary by giving you additional words for describing boundaries. You begin to see that boundaries are simply a fact of life that's present throughout your day — creating safety, order, and calm. The boundaries running in the background of your everyday experience, along with the boundaries you create for your self-protection and self-care, support and improve your life in ways you may never have imagined.

Despite having a reputation for being harsh, rigid, and selfish, boundaries actually create space and freedom. I show you a simple way to think about your boundaries on a continuum from too little to too much, so you can visualize boundaries when they're operating at the extremes and when they're in balance.

Your family's cultural or ethnic background and the area of the world in which you spent the formative years of your life play an important role in what you know and believe about boundaries. And while different cultures have different ideas and beliefs about boundaries, ultimately you get to decide which boundaries are right for you and how you put your own personal boundaries into practice.

You're the ultimate decider of every boundary you create.

Knowing What Boundaries Are

Before you can set personal boundaries, you must know what boundaries are — how to describe them, what their functions are, and how they show up in your life.

Some people think boundaries are unnecessary, unkind, or manipulative. Some people believe that setting a boundary means telling another person what to do. Healthy, effective boundaries are none of these.

Personal boundaries serve two primary functions:

>> Your boundaries protect you and other people.

>> Your boundaries define who you are.

Protecting yourself and others

When you think about protecting yourself or another person, here are a few examples that may come to mind:

>> You understandably want to avoid being hurt or injured, or you want to make sure other people aren't hurt or injured.

>> You've experienced an emotional, physical, or sexual trauma, and you need to temporarily guard or shield yourself so that you can take care of yourself and heal.

>> You care about or love someone (including yourself), and you don't want them to suffer.

Protecting yourself includes a wide range of mundane, everyday actions. Occasionally, you encounter unexpected (and usually unwanted) events that require you to defend or protect yourself. Everything from putting on your shoes before you go outside, to locking your front door at night, to defending yourself against an armed attacker belongs under the banner of protection.

The four primary categories of boundaries for how you protect yourself and others are:

>> Physical

>> Sexual

>> Speaking

>> Listening

TIP

Physical, sexual, and speaking boundaries include both self-protection and protecting others, while the listening boundary is primarily one of self-protection. For a detailed discussion of each of these boundaries, see Chapters 8 to 11.

Here's a brief overview of what it looks like when you're protecting yourself in the four categories of boundaries. Think of these examples as self-protection north stars or aspirations for your healthy, effective boundaries:

>> When you protect yourself with physical boundaries:

- You're aware of how close you want to be to others physically. Your preferences are based on your chosen standards rather than on others' standards or any other external factor that doesn't align with your preferences or values.

- You're able to maintain the physical closeness or distance you want. This means you're able to stop someone when they get too close to you.

- You're aware of how much access to your personal belongings you want to give to others.

- You're able to maintain the access to your personal belongings that feels comfortable for you. You stop others when they take or use your personal belongings without your permission.

>> When you protect yourself with sexual boundaries:

- You're aware of how close you want to be to others sexually. Your preferences around closeness are based on your chosen standards rather than on others' standards or any other external factor that doesn't align with your preferences or values.

- You're able to maintain the sexual closeness or distance you want. This means you're able to stop someone when they get too close to you sexually or when they touch you sexually in a way you don't want to be touched.

>> When you protect yourself with speaking boundaries:

- You understand that in personal (rather than casual or professional) conversations, the primary role of speaking or talking is to be known by the other person.

- You know how to determine who gets to know what about you. You match your private information with the level of connection or intimacy you have with the other person. (See Chapter 3 for more information about matching your private information with the people you want to share it with.)

- You understand that speaking clearly, respectfully, and coherently not only protects others but also protects you from unnecessary conflict, disconnection, or future regret.

>> When you protect yourself with listening boundaries:

- You understand that the primary role of listening is to discover or understand who the other person is.

- You actively assess what you're hearing to avoid taking on blame or shame, or agreeing with another person's perceptions that don't match what you believe to be accurate or true.

- You understand that what other people say is a description of their reality — their thoughts, beliefs, opinions, judgments, and so on. What they say isn't a description of you unless you agree that it is. For example, if someone tells you that you're rude, that's their opinion about you. It's not a fact or the truth. You get to decide whether you share their perception that you're rude.

TIP

If you want to maximize the chances of being heard by another person, avoid common patterns of communicating that imply blame. For example, don't make statements that describe another person, such as "You're being (mean, rude, ridiculous, and so on)," or ask *why* questions, like "Why are you talking to me like that?"

The following describes what it looks like when you're protecting others in the four categories of boundaries. Just like the examples of self-protective boundaries above, these are descriptions of excellent boundaries that develop as your boundaries skills improve:

>> When you protect others with your physical boundaries:

- You respect their nonnegotiable right to decide how close they want to be to you or if they want to be touched.

- You respect the physical closeness or distance another person wants from you. You stop yourself when someone tells you that you're getting too close to them.

- You respect their right to choose how much access they give you to their personal belongings, and you abide by the limits they set.

>> When you protect others with your sexual boundaries:

- You respect their nonnegotiable right to decide how close they want to be to you sexually or if they want to be touched.

- You accept *no* as a complete sentence and a final answer. After receiving a *no,* you don't attempt to negotiate, persuade, manipulate, or pressure the other person to engage sexually with you.

- You respect the sexual closeness or distance the other person wants. You stop yourself when the other person tells you that you're too close to them sexually or when they tell you they don't want a certain type of sexual touch or contact.

WARNING

Physical and sexual boundaries are nonnegotiable. That means when someone says *no* to physical or sexual touch, their *no* isn't open to interpretation, persuasion, manipulation, or negotiation.

>> When you protect others with your speaking boundaries:

- You understand that in personal (rather than casual or professional) conversations, the primary role of speaking or talking is to be known by the other person.

- You think about what you're getting ready to say before you speak so that your words are as clear, respectful, and coherent (understandable) as possible.

- You have a filter between your thoughts and the words you speak because you know that not everything you think or feel needs to (or should) be spoken. You think about how to say what you need to say in a way that can be received or taken in by the other person. You understand that to be truly heard, you must speak in a way that makes your words easier to receive or hear.

- You speak clearly, respectfully, and coherently and avoid using words or a tone of voice that's disrespectful, blaming, shaming, or abusive.

>> When you protect others with your listening boundaries:

- You listen to discover or understand who the other person is rather than to judge, blame, or shame.

- You strive to maintain an attitude of curiosity while listening.

- You actively monitor your thoughts, body sensations (such as heart racing or sweating), and emotions as you listen to avoid reacting or becoming defensive.

If this sounds a bit complicated, that's because it is! But before you become overwhelmed thinking that boundary work is too confusing or difficult for you, here's what you need to know: Your journey to healthier, more effective personal boundaries is a series of baby steps, one after the other. Where you are right now is the perfect place for you to be.

TIP

Begin your boundaries journey by using the information, skills, and tools in this book. Then go out into the world and experiment by putting into action what you've discovered. When you want to go deeper or need to figure out how to fix a boundary that didn't work, read the chapters in Part 5 or revisit any concepts that are unclear or challenging.

You can do it!

Seeing how your boundaries define who you are

When I tell people that the second function of boundaries is to define who you are, I often see a puzzled expression on their faces. Here's a simple way to think about it: If you build a fence around the perimeter of property that rightfully and legally belongs to you, you're defining what's yours and what's not.

REMEMBER

Every choice you make is a boundary. When you say *yes*, you're actually saying *no* (placing a limit or boundary) to something else or to many other things. For example, when you say *yes* to marrying someone, you just said *no* to the billions of other people you could have married!

Here are just a few ways that your boundaries define who you are:

>> You choose what to wear or not wear. The terms *fashion statement* and *statement piece* perfectly illustrate the concept that people define (or make statements about) themselves through the way they dress.

>> You determine what or how much to share about yourself with others.

>> You choose the topics or areas of interest you want to explore, research, study, or talk about.

>> You establish your level of physical health through your choices about nutrition, the quantity of food you eat, how much you move your body (exercise), how much sleep you get, and whether you maintain your health by having annual exams or health screenings, for example.

>> You identify your level of mental health in large part by what you choose to pay attention to and your willingness to explore new ideas and think critically. You define the quality of your mental health by choosing to experiment with new behaviors or by taking actions that improve your mental health, such as addressing compulsive/addictive behaviors or seeking mental health treatment.

>> You determine your level of financial health by your choices about how you manage your money, your approach to work, and your willingness to change unsuccessful money habits or to ask for what you need or want.

>> You understand that the overall health of your relationships is determined by your choices, including what you will or won't accept in a relationship. You decide how you want to stay connected to and respectful of other people even when they're not behaving the way you'd like them to.

Describing Boundaries

Believe it or not, there are many ways to describe boundaries. *Merriam-Webster* defines *boundary* as "something that indicates or fixes a limit or extent." For example, fixing a limit or extent may be exactly what you'd like to do the next time your friend asks if you want to hang out at the mall. And if you're wondering, "Can I really choose to say *no* to a friend?" the answer is an unequivocal *yes*. (Keep reading to discover how!)

Finding words for boundaries

When you think of a boundary, you may think of a property line or another type of border. Having a variety of words and terms to describe boundaries gives you more options for talking about them and more freedom to express them.

Here are some of the most common words to describe boundaries:

>> **Containing:** Containing is a fancy term (most likely invented by a psychotherapist) that describes how you protect other people from you. For example, when you protect people from your boundaryless, offensive, or even boundary-violating behavior or language, that's containing. Containing means you're placing limits or boundaries on yourself in the interest of being respectful, relational, and protective of others.

TIP

Throughout this book I use the word *relational* to describe a set of healthy relationship skills that includes being respectful and transparent (open), using healthy personal boundaries, and demonstrating through your behavior that no person is better than or less than another person.

>> **Fence:** Fence is a common word for boundary. A fence defines what's your space or property and what's another person's space or property.

- » **Limits:** Limits can apply to almost anything, including what you're willing to do or not do, how much you eat, or how close you allow others to get to you physically.

- » **Parameters:** Parameters define the scope or bounds of a behavior, project, or agreement.

- » **Proximity:** Proximity has to do with how close someone or something is to you. Proximity relates to physical and sexual boundaries, as well as how close you allow a person to get to you emotionally or intellectually (knowing what you think or your opinions).

- » **Standards:** Standards can be thought of as minimum requirements for what you want or need, or whom you choose to be in a relationship with.

- » **Walls:** Walls are sometimes a legitimate and necessary form for boundaries. However, walls should be used sparingly as boundaries. Creating walls as a form of boundaries is typically reserved for extremely difficult people, boundary pushers, boundary violators, or people who engage in illegal activities. However, some types of walls can come in handy in certain situations. For example, you can use a *wall of pleasant* (see the following Tip) to manage a difficult person you can't (yet) avoid having contact with.

TIP

Using a wall for a boundary isn't just for bad actors. If you need to endure a particularly difficult person in your life for a limited period of time, you can use a wall of pleasant. A *wall of pleasant* is a façade (mask) of pleasant neutrality where communication is limited to what is necessary or useful. It's an intentional (and I would say respectful) way to interact with a person in order to get through a time-limited situation.

Discovering that boundaries expand and contract

Many people think of boundaries as harsh and rigid. But the truth is, boundaries both expand and contract.

Expansion and contraction can be positive or negative. For example, sharing too much personal information about yourself with another person (expansion) may not be the best choice. On the other hand, limiting another person's access to you (contraction) because they've been disrespectful or abusive is healthy and positive.

Other examples of expansion and contraction of personal boundaries include:

>> When your children get older, they need fewer boundaries (contraction), and they have more freedom (expansion).

>> When you get to know someone and want to get closer to them, you share more personal information about yourself. This illustrates a movement from contraction to expansion.

>> When someone breaks an agreement with you or violates a boundary, you may restrict or eliminate their contact or proximity to you. This example illustrates the need for contraction (restricting or eliminating contact) as a form of self-protection and self-care.

>> When you're tense or anxious, your boundaries tend to become rigid or less fluid (contract). When you're relaxed, your boundaries tend to soften or become more fluid (expand).

REMEMBER

Recognizing the fluid nature of personal boundaries expands your options and supports the notion that boundaries aren't as harsh or rigid as many people believe.

Seeing that Boundaries Are Everywhere

Right now, you're reading this book in a particular place at a certain time of day, and you may be sitting, lying down, standing, or walking on a treadmill.

You decided to pick up this book, you chose a place to read, and you settled into the posture or body position you prefer. Each of these decisions is a boundary because decisions and choices are limits you place on what you will or won't do.

This simple example of how, when, and where you happen to be reading this book right now illustrates that the more you know about boundaries, the more you see that they're ubiquitous — meaning they're everywhere.

Getting dressed for the day

I don't recommend you make a habit of getting this granular about the details of your morning routine, but when you get up every morning, these are just a few of the boundaries you set that you probably never think about:

- » You choose to wear clothes (unless you have to wear a work uniform or live in a clothing-optional community).

- » You decide whether you need to wear clothes that keep you cool or clothes that keep you warm.

- » You may choose clothes based on your mood at the time you're getting dressed. (I had no idea this was a thing until a personal shopper introduced me to the term *emotional dresser* many years ago. I instantly recognized myself as someone who dresses according to mood — I just didn't have the name for it.)

- » You choose the shoes you want to wear.

- » Socks or no socks? You decide.

You haven't even made it out the door, and you've already gone through a complex process of ruling in and ruling out (your limits) how you want to clothe and adorn yourself for the day ahead.

Stopping at a red light

I don't know about you, but I've been irritated by more red lights than I can count. Given my genuine appreciation of boundaries, it's embarrassing to admit that I've run a few red lights in my life. And for that I stand guilty as charged: a boundary violator.

Every time you see a red light, you're seeing a boundary. It's telling you to stop (which can be considered a twin to saying *no*), and for safety's sake I hope you do. If you don't, you may face consequences.

Traffic lights are one example of the ways in which boundaries are at the root of many laws and regulations designed to protect you and others.

Screening calls

When I was growing up in the 1960s, we had a pale yellow rotary dial phone that hung on the wall in the kitchen. When you wanted to talk to someone, you had to either pull a chair close to the phone or sit on the floor right under it, because the curly cord would stretch only so far. The thought that one day I'd drive around in my car with a phone that tells me who's calling and shows the caller's face on a mini display screen would've no doubt elicited a "No way!" response from me.

Thanks to the miracle of technology, you can now see who's calling you every time (unless the caller uses the magic code for blocking their number or has fraudulent intentions). The beauty of having this amazing technology to screen calls is that it gives you an opportunity to make an informed decision to say *yes* or *no* (both are boundaries) to answering the call.

TIP

If someone calls you and doesn't leave a message, their call doesn't imply they want you to call them back, and it doesn't obligate you to do so (unless you have an agreement that you will). Many people feel compelled to call someone back even when the caller doesn't leave a message. It's always your choice.

Closing the door

For as long as I can remember, I've absolutely loved the feeling of closing and then locking a door. Closing a door is a beautiful boundary in and of itself, and locking a door takes the boundary to the next level.

Closing a door serves at least two important functions in the world of boundaries:

>> Closed doors create privacy that protects you and others.

>> Closed doors serve as barriers that keep other people out so you can feel safe, work, or take a time-out.

Placing your wallet in your pocket

One of the many funny stories I've heard about boundaries over the years came from a colleague and fellow boundaries nerd, Sheri Winston, an author and sexuality educator. Sheri told me about a time when she was teaching a class on boundaries and a guy in the class told her that he didn't believe in boundaries. Without missing a beat, she said, "Okay, give me your wallet." He (not surprisingly) replied, "Absolutely not! I'm not going to give you my wallet." Just like that, Sheri converted him to a boundaries believer!

I probably don't need to tell you that you have a right to keep your wallet in your pocket or handbag. And furthermore, no one has a right to take your wallet unless you give it to them — thanks to boundaries.

TIP

You naturally create more boundaries around what you value. People go to great lengths to protect their wallets and credit cards because they want to protect their money. Hidden travel pouches and wallets with credit card chip protectors are just a few examples. If you want to find out what's important to you, notice where you create the highest level of protection.

Avoiding TMI (or oversharing)

I discuss oversharing and knowing how much to share in Chapter 3, but for now I propose that it's best to avoid sharing too much information (TMI) with others — especially others you don't know well.

Here are a few examples of sharing TMI:

>> Revealing intimate details about your illnesses or injuries, especially to people who aren't in your close circle of family or friends

>> Giving an exhaustive (and exhausting) monologue about your meals for the day, starting with what you had for breakfast

>> Sharing intimate details about arguments or conflicts you're having with your partner with anyone other than a close friend or therapist

>> Having loud conversations containing personal information in restaurants or other settings where people nearby can hear you

>> Sharing personal or private information about a relative, spouse, or child

EVERY CHOICE YOU MAKE IS A BOUNDARY

It's impossible to calculate how many choices and decisions you make in a given day. Every choice is a *yes* or a *no*, which makes choosing and deciding a key element of your overall personal boundary system.

Here's a short list of everyday choices you make dozens of times in a week:

- What you're going to say
- What you're going to do
- Where you're going to go
- Whom you're going to go with
- When you'll leave
- How long you'll stay

Remember: When you say *yes* to something, you're actually saying *no* to everything else that's automatically eliminated by your decision. And every time you say *no*, you're creating a limit or a boundary.

Understanding the Benefits of Boundaries

Personal boundaries have more benefits than you can imagine. Helping you create order so you can feel calm and getting clear about whether a relationship will work are just two powerful examples. You can't develop high-quality self-care practices or feel safe or protected without good boundaries. Boundaries also significantly improve your communication skills, which naturally impacts the quality of your relationships.

Creating order

Here are just a few of the ways your boundaries create order:

>> When you need to focus on work, you choose not to get distracted by checking your email and text threads every two minutes.

>> You set your alarm clock so you can get your kids to school on time.

>> Every physical queue you get in is a boundary that creates order so that the first person (or people) in line are the first to get served.

Protecting yourself from others

You can protect yourself from others with your boundaries in the following ways:

>> You create the physical distance or space you need.

>> You limit or eliminate another person's access to you.

>> You don't allow someone to touch you when you don't want to be touched.

>> You choose not to engage with someone who is verbally or emotionally abusive.

REMEMBER

At their core, boundaries are about protection.

Protecting others from you

As they say, what's good for the goose is good for the gander! If you have a right to protect yourself from others, they also have a right to be protected from you.

Here's what it looks like when you're protecting others from you:

>> You're respectful of others when you're speaking and listening.

>> You refrain from being verbally or emotionally abusive to others.

>> You don't touch others without first asking if you can touch them and getting their permission.

>> You honor boundaries other people set with you.

Gaining clarity in relationships

One of the best-kept secrets about boundaries is that they help you know if a relationship is viable or if it can survive after a serious crisis.

Here are just a few of the ways boundaries give you clarity in relationships:

>> When you create agreements with someone, you observe whether they can uphold agreements they make.

>> When you make a request, you observe how they respond.

>> When you create a limit like "I can't talk on the phone after 9:30 p.m.," you observe whether the other person honors your boundary.

These situations give you valuable information about whether a person is relationship ready.

TIP

Your boundary work in relationships helps you get a very clear picture of who the other person is. Then you get to decide if they are someone with whom you want to have a close relationship.

Practicing self-care

Boundaries, as self-protection, are a form of self-care. Wanting to protect yourself (or anyone else) demonstrates that you value and care about yourself.

REMEMBER

People who practice good self-care and self-protection naturally care for and protect others. When you protect others from your boundaryless behavior, you feel good about yourself and avoid experiencing future regret or guilt. That's why protecting others takes care of and protects you.

Boundaries can support your self-care when:

>> **You carve out time and space for self-care.** To practice self-care, you must create parameters around your time and the access to you that others get.

>> **Other people try to prioritize you taking care of them over taking care of yourself.** Again, you need to create time and space boundaries so that you can prioritize yourself and practice self-care.

TIP

Over the years I've noticed that women struggle more with pleasurable self-care than do men. For example, most women would never dream of leaving their family for multiple weekends a year to engage in a fun hobby (the way men go hunting or fishing) or spend the day in front of the TV watching their favorite sports team. One of the reasons most women struggle to practice high-quality self-care is that it requires both prioritizing themselves and setting limits on other people's access to them. When your boundaries improve, so will your self-care.

Improving communication

When you level up your boundaries, your communication — both speaking and listening — will be clearer and more effective. And when your communication skills improve, so does the quality of your relationships.

The following are four ways that boundaries improve communication:

>> You're more curious, which helps you avoid making assumptions. Assumptions cause you to believe things that aren't necessarily true. Believing you know the truth when you don't is dangerous not only for your communication but also for your emotions.

>> You're less reactive because you know how to thoughtfully reflect on what you hear before you respond.

>> You know how to replace the ineffective strategies of hoping, wishing, manipulating, or demanding to get what you want by making clear, effective requests.

>> When you need to make an agreement with someone, your agreements are clearer and more specific, improving the likelihood that they'll be successful.

BOUNDARIES CREATE SPACE

Because the word *boundaries* is synonymous with limits, it may be hard to understand how boundaries create space.

One of my favorite stories about the hidden power boundaries have for creating space is in Greg McKeown's book *Essentialism: The Disciplined Pursuit of Less* (Crown Currency).

In his book, McKeown tells a story about an urban school with a playground bounded on at least one side by a busy street. When the children went outside for recess, the teachers had to stay extremely vigilant to make sure the kids didn't get too close to the street. You can imagine that every time a child got even 10 feet from the street, one of the teachers screamed (more than once, I'm sure) at the top of their lungs, "Not so close to the street!"

Eventually the school was able to install a fence, and that's when everything changed. After the fence was installed, the kids could go right up to the fence and even lean against it, within just a few feet of the street. They were perfectly safe. I can imagine the teachers sitting at a picnic table relaxing, drinking from their water bottles, and enjoying being outside and talking to one another.

What made the difference? The boundary of the fence created the opportunity for the children to experience more space, more freedom, and even more fun. The fence created even more space than the children had before, because their movement was rightfully restricted from the potential danger posed by the passing vehicles.

This is exactly what you experience with boundaries. Some boundaries, even simple ones like closing a door or telling your partner you'd rather not go to the demolition derby, can make you feel a level of space, freedom, and joy that may surprise you.

Remember: Every time you create a limit or boundary, you're creating space and freedom.

Seeing Boundaries at the Extremes

One of the simplest ways to think about any concept is to imagine it on a continuum — from one extreme to the opposite extreme. On one end of the continuum, you have one extreme, on the other end of the continuum you have the opposite extreme, and in the middle there is a balance between either extreme.

When it comes to personal boundaries, the two extremes are no boundaries on one end of the continuum and walled off on the other.

No boundaries or boundaryless means:

>> You're too vulnerable.

>> You're unprotected.

Walled off or having too many boundaries means:

>> You're not vulnerable (invulnerable).

>> You're too protected.

This doesn't mean that you're always either one or the other — no boundaries or walled off. At any given point in time, you're on the continuum.

REMEMBER

Not only are your boundaries on a continuum between no boundaries and walled off, but you're also on the same continuum for each of the four boundaries: physical, sexual, speaking, and listening. In other words, you can be either boundaryless or walled off in each of these four categories of boundaries.

Important facts to know about your boundaries on the continuum include:

>> Each of your four personal boundaries — physical, sexual, speaking, and listening — is located on a continuum between no boundaries and walled off. Where you are on the continuum of that particular boundary is personal and unique to you and corresponds to how that boundary typically operates in your life. Think of where you land on the continuum as a kind of boundaries "comfort zone." That doesn't mean you chose to be more boundaryless or more walled off, but it does mean your boundaries will tend to gravitate toward that point on the continuum.

>> Your *comfort zone* on the continuum between no boundaries and walled off can be different with different people or in different situations.

>> Your *comfort zone* on the continuum between no boundaries and walled off changes over time. For example, you may relax your physical or speaking boundaries as you become more comfortable with someone. Or your physical boundaries may move toward walled off after a crisis or injury.

REMEMBER

Your *comfort zone* on the boundaries continuum changes over time as your boundaries level up and improve.

Functional boundaries describe boundaries in balance:

>> **Functional physical boundaries:** You let others know how close they can get to you physically and determine the access others have to your personal possessions. You respect others' personal/physical space, and you don't touch other people without their permission.

>> **Functional sexual boundaries:** You decide with whom, when, where, and how you are sexual. You don't touch another person sexually without their permission. You have the ability to either refrain from or engage in sexual contact with another person.

>> **Functional speaking boundaries:** You share your thoughts (including perceptions and opinions) and emotions with others clearly and respectfully.

>> **Functional listening boundaries:** You listen to what others say, and you have the ability to see differences, if any, between what they say and what you perceive about what they say. In other words, you can understand that their reality may not be your reality. You maintain your own perceptions or truth even when the speaker says something different from what you believe or think.

TIP

The functional boundaries described in the preceding list are personal boundaries at their very best. When you're considering where your current boundaries belong on the continuum between no boundaries and walled off, choose which end of the continuum fits for you based on times when you're not at your best. Picking one as your default (which may also be your comfort zone) shows you where to focus your boundary work and helps you identify opportunities for growth.

When your personal boundaries are in balance, you're able to be vulnerable (to the extent that you want to be vulnerable) with another person while still feeling protected.

Notice in Figure 1-1 that the midpoint represents balance, which is marked with an oval. I prefer illustrating balance this way, rather than with a straight vertical line, because balance isn't something you achieve and then hold in any area of your life.

TIP

My favorite analogy for achieving balance comes from yoga poses, like tree pose, in which you stand on one foot for an extended period of time. In balance poses you never stand completely still. At a minimum, your foot and ankle make continuous micro-adjustments to keep you upright. Sometimes you lose your balance and have to start over. It's the same with boundaries. Don't aim for perfection. Aim for the very real messiness that true balance requires.

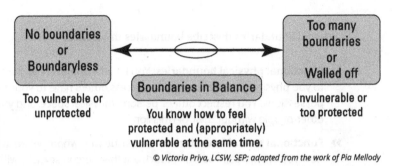

FIGURE 1-1:
Boundaries at the
extremes.

No boundaries
or
Boundaryless

Too vulnerable or
unprotected

Boundaries in Balance

You know how to feel
protected and (appropriately)
vulnerable at the same time.

Too many
boundaries
or
Walled off

Invulnerable or
too protected

© Victoria Priya, LCSW, SEP; adapted from the work of Pia Mellody

Acknowledging Cultural Differences

Different cultures have different ideas and perspectives about personal boundaries, and so do the individuals who belong to those cultures. No person or group of people can claim that their views on personal boundaries are the "right" boundaries or the boundaries everyone else should follow.

You, I, and every person who reads these words have preconceived concepts, opinions, and biases about what defines healthy, functional boundaries. These ideas are rooted in:

>> The family you grew up in

>> The cultural background(s) of your parents

>> The cultural background(s) of extended family members you came into contact with growing up

>> Your family's socioeconomic status and how you were taught to relate to others based on your status in your culture

>> The country (or region of the country) where you grew up

>> The cultural norms of the society you grew up in

REMEMBER

Cultural norms for boundaries are often different and distinct between various groups. However, it's a mistake to say that every person from a particular culture agrees with or observes the same personal boundaries.

Regardless of the culture or cultures that have had the most influence on you, ultimately you get to decide what boundaries make sense to you. You're not bound by what you were taught or what you learned about boundaries from your culture or your family of origin.

You may strongly disagree with certain principles, concepts, or tools I present in this book. What you get from these pages may make you rethink what you were taught and what you've believed until now. Some of what you discover here may catapult you to another level of empowerment and freedom.

I invite you to embrace what resonates and what feels true to you. The rest you can leave on the page. This simple exercise of taking what feels true and leaving the rest is an example of your personal boundaries at work!

TIP

I discovered during the many years I spent in close contact with the Vietnamese community that touching the top of another person's head (especially a child) is considered extremely rude by Vietnamese people. The head is considered the most sacred part of the body. This cultural norm illustrates how easy it is to unknowingly offend someone when having cross-cultural interactions. Grace, kindness, and understanding are invaluable qualities in all cross-cultural interactions.

Chapter **2**

Knowing What Boundaries Aren't

M ost people, through no fault of their own, fundamentally misunderstand how boundaries work. For example, I can't tell you how many times someone has told me (usually with a fair amount of righteous indignation) that they finally got fed up and set a boundary. They told old so-and-so what to do, how to do it, and when to do it. What they didn't realize is that they actually issued a demand, not a boundary.

Simply put, demands aren't boundaries. So, when you make a demand believing you've set a boundary, a whole cascade of frustration and misunderstanding will follow. Being told what to do is a sure-fire way to summon the inner toddler in most people, making them declare, "You're not the boss of me!

Getting clear from the beginning about what boundaries aren't saves you a ton of headaches, and maybe even a few heartaches. Plus, you'll know what doesn't work and what to avoid, even before you've mastered the nuts and bolts of how to identify, create, and maintain good personal and relationship boundaries.

This chapter covers some of the most common missteps people make when they *think* they're setting boundaries. I explain how expectations and *shoulds* have no place in the creation of healthy personal boundaries. This chapter also covers the finer points of ultimatums, which — believe it or not — can be appropriate and powerfully clear when they're issued in the right way.

I also let you in on a life-changing secret: You don't have to follow all the rules other people make for you, especially when they fail to explain those rules out loud! I give you permission to completely disregard boundaries that other people create for you — usually only in the privacy of their own mind — and expect you to follow. Doesn't that feel good?

Seeing That Demands Are Not Boundaries

You're going to be light years ahead of most people when it comes to personal boundaries if you understand this simple principle: You can create a boundary for yourself about what you will or won't do, but you can't set a boundary for another person.

When you tell another person what they will or won't do, you issue a demand, and demands can never be boundaries. Ever.

Demands aren't boundaries because you don't have control over what another person does (or doesn't do). You only have control over what you do (or don't do). And if you're courageous and brutally honest with yourself, you have to admit that sometimes you don't even have control over what you do (or don't do)!

REMEMBER

You have the power (and the right) to tell yourself what to do. When you tell another adult what to do, that's a demand, not a boundary. If you want to create a boundary with another person, you must create an agreement.

Here's a little pop quiz. (Don't worry — your grade won't be announced in front of the class.) Is the following statement a boundary?

You can't leave your socks on the floor anymore!

If you think that statement isn't a boundary, congrats — you get a 100 on the pop quiz!

I explain the nitty-gritty about why such a statement isn't a boundary in the next section when I show you the difference between making a demand and making a request. But the simple reason is that the person declaring an end to socks on the floor has absolutely no power to cause the sock-tosser to pick up their socks. The bottom line is that a boundary involving two people requires an agreement.

Distinguishing demands from requests

Merriam-Webster defines *demand* as "to call for something in an authoritative way." The Oxford Languages Dictionary defines *demand* as "an insistent and peremptory request, made as if by right." These definitions deserve a closer look because the word *request* in the *Oxford* definition implies asking a question. Demands are statements, never questions.

Both definitions of the word *demand* hint at an air of entitlement or unequal power. *Oxford* highlights the power imbalance of demands most plainly by saying that the request is made *as if by right*. Each definition suggests that demands are issued by a person who either has — or believes they have — more power than the person they're bossing around.

Merriam-Webster comes closer to capturing the true meaning and real-life experience of demands. By including the word *request* in the definition, *Oxford* seems to be suggesting that a demand could include a request or question, which is never the case.

Requests are questions that end with question marks. Demands are statements that end with periods (or exclamation points). Even if you placed a question mark at the end of a demand — for example, "You can't leave your socks on the floor anymore?" — I'm afraid the likely response you'd get would be a puzzled look on the listener's face, or maybe a barely concealed giggle. You certainly won't be setting a boundary. Like periods and question marks, demands and requests aren't the same, and they're not interchangeable.

REMEMBER

For the purposes of this book, I define a demand simply as a statement that tells another person (or group of people) what to do.

Admitting that demands are tempting

Even though no one likes to be told what to do, most people can't resist the temptation to boss others around.

Making demands is enticing because they're simple and straightforward. For example, if I'm in love with the $2 million house you just moved into, matter-of-factly saying "Give me your house" is easy enough. Four simple words, and your house is my house! Unquestionably, it takes a lot of nerve to ask for someone's $2 million house. But we've all been guilty of making demands like "Pick up some bread on the way home" or "Pull over — I'll drive now."

The other alluring feature of demands is that they require absolutely no vulnerability. Demanding that a person do this or that eliminates the inconvenient, humbling, and sometimes terrifying risk of receiving a *no*.

Imagine asking "Would you be willing to pick up some bread?" or "Would you give me your house?" instead. Notice the shift from steely invincibility to meek, mild vulnerability when you convert a demand into a request. This is exactly why many people are more comfortable making demands than requests.

TIP

If you grew up in a family where you observed adults making frequent demands of other adults like "Get me a glass of water" or "Do the dishes," you may think this kind of behavior is normal. (Chapter 5 explains how your childhood experiences and observations have a huge impact on your boundaries as an adult.) You can make great progress toward avoiding making demands by simply noticing when you're tempted to make one.

Spotting examples of demands

People react to upsetting or high-stakes situations differently. Sometimes, their gut reaction is to go straight into demand mode while feeling unashamedly entitled to do so.

For more than 15 years I worked primarily with women who had experienced chronic betrayal in a long-term relationship. As you can imagine, discovering you've been betrayed for months, years, or decades is devastating. It's common (and understandable) for the betrayed person to go into full-on detective mode and become extremely controlling immediately after discovering the betrayal in an effort to make sense of their new reality and to gain even a small sense of safety.

Because of the inherent trauma in these situations, making demands can easily and quickly become a first line of defense. Here are a few examples of the types of demands people make after discovering a betrayal:

>> You're going to get a therapist.

>> You're never going to travel again for work. Ever!

>> Give me the passwords to all your email accounts.

>> Tell the kids what you've done to me.

>> You can't go out with your buddies to play pool anymore.

>> You have to call me every day before you leave the office.

>> Stop drinking.

>> You're going to put a tracking app on your phone.

Given the circumstances, you may think, "Right on! Good for you!"

I think you can appreciate that a person who has been betrayed in a long-term relationship would want their partner to be in therapy and to be transparent about their whereabouts or online activities. But the fundamental problem with these kinds of demands — even in situations of betrayal — is that circumstances don't change the basic principle that adults don't have a right to tell other adults what they can or can't do.

REMEMBER

You can make requests, but you don't have a right to demand that another adult do anything.

Of course, making a request will feel more vulnerable than making a demand, and you may not get what you want in every instance. But the reality is that a person who obeys a demand is a person who hasn't agreed. And because there's no agreement, the person who received the demand usually has very low or no buy-in, which means they complied out of fear or pressure rather than to repair the relationship, change their behavior, or prove that they're sorry. If you want to get your needs and wants met in a relationship — even when your relationship is in shambles — master the skill of turning demands into requests.

TIP

You can find out more about crafting an effective request in Chapter 17.

Recognizing demands are harmful to relationships

Being *relational* means accepting and behaving as though other people have the same rights to their thoughts, beliefs, perceptions, emotions, and actions as you do. Being relational is respectful and collaborative. It means you have the ability to understand another person's perspective and you respect their right to think, feel, and behave differently than you do — even when you don't like or agree with their decisions.

Making demands of others isn't relational because demands assume you have the right to tell another person what to do. Making demands conveys to the other person that you don't care whether they want to do what you're demanding that they do. When you make demands, you're telling the other person that you care more about getting them to do what you want than you care about them doing what they want to do.

REMEMBER

Demands override and ignore another person's right to say *yes* or *no*, or to negotiate an alternative, mutually agreeable solution with you.

WARNING

Making demands is toxic to relationships. If you want to improve the quality of your relationships, you have to know how to make clear and effective requests. Chapter 17 shows you how.

Understanding Ultimatums

An *ultimatum* is a final proposition, condition, or demand. Ultimatums get a bad rap, and for good reason. When you don't understand the fundamental premise that without an agreement you can only set a boundary for yourself (a *self-boundary* for what you'll do), you also misunderstand the proper use of ultimatums.

Ultimatums have a reputation for being final, forceful, and often threatening statements. Here are four examples of ultimatums:

>> If you don't stop whistling, I'm going to move to a faraway country and never come back.

>> If you take money out of my purse again, I'm going to put superglue between all your fingers when you're asleep.

>> If you choose to spend the last $10,000 in our retirement account on cryptocurrency, I'm going to separate all my banking and investment accounts from yours.

>> If you feed the cat microwaved hot dogs again, you're going to take her to the vet when she gets sick.

Which one of these statements is not like the others? If you said the third one, your powers of observation are keen. Ultimately, most ultimatums are neither rational nor necessary. But the third ultimatum in the list is clean, effective, and likely reasonable. The first one is disproportional to the perceived offense, the second is a threat of physical harm, and the fourth isn't actionable because it requires the participation of another person who, for the time being, hasn't agreed.

In this section, I show you how to avoid creating meaningless ultimatums and how to issue ultimatums effectively.

Making an ultimatum a boundary, not a threat

There are two vital conditions that make an ultimatum a boundary:

» You have the power to create the boundary yourself, without the participation of another person.

» The ultimatum isn't an obvious threat, nor is it intended to be a threat.

Telling your partner you will divorce them if they rob another bank fulfills both conditions, provided you really do intend to divorce them. You have the power to file for divorce without the agreement or participation of another person, which satisfies the first requirement. Regarding the second condition, your ultimatum to divorce your partner can be considered a boundary as long as your intention was to give them vital information and not solely meant as a threat.

The second condition — that an ultimatum not be meant as a threat — requires rigorous self-honesty. You must have 100 percent confidence that you will follow through with what you say. Otherwise, it's likely a threat, and probably a hollow one.

TIP

Keep in mind that whether an ultimatum is perceived as a threat is in the eye of the perceiver.

Your partner may believe that you're threatening them when you say you will divorce them if they commit a future bank robbery. They're entitled to their perception, and you're entitled to yours. If you passed the self-honesty test of 100 percent clarity and confidence in the message of your ultimatum, you can have confidence that your statement is your true intention, not a threat.

On the other hand, telling your partner "If you rob another bank, you'll have to give me all the money" isn't a boundary for the simple reason that you can't tell another person what they can or can't do (and in this case, it's also illegal).

Knowing where to put the "you" in ultimatums

One of the easiest ways to avoid issuing worthless and meaningless ultimatums is by reviewing how your statement uses the word you. Boundaries, in the form of ultimatums, never include "you will . . .," but they often include "if you . . . ." The first phrase is a lead-in to making a demand, and the second describes a possible event in the future.

Ultimatums should only describe what you, as the speaker, will do in the future. Describing what another person will do in the future — as in "you will take the cat to the vet" — guarantees that your ultimatum isn't a boundary.

If you tell your partner, "I will divorce you if you rob another bank," the boundary is automatically and seamlessly created by the power you have to follow through with the action presented in the ultimatum. You are not telling your partner what they will do. In this case, you have the power to follow through and get a divorce if your partner robs another bank.

If you use the word *you* to describe what the other person will or won't do, you don't have a solid boundary.

Embracing the "I" in ultimatums

You can easily assess whether your ultimatum is a boundary by reviewing it for your use of *I*. An ultimatum that describes what you will do — as in "I will . . . ." or "I won't . . . ." — as a response to a future event is highly likely to meet the definition of a boundary. That's because you're describing what you have the power to do, and not what another person will do, which you have no power over.

For example:

>> I will leave for church 20 minutes before the service starts whether or not you're ready to go.

>> If you drive while under the influence with our daughter in the car one more time, I will either drive her myself or make arrangements for her to ride with someone else going forward.

>> If you call me names when we're arguing in the future, I will end the conversation.

Notice that each of these statements says *I will* — stating what you will do. None of them say *you will*. When you say "I" and what follows is a statement of what you know you'll do beyond a shadow of a doubt, you're good to proceed.

Checking your heart rate before issuing an ultimatum

The second condition that makes an ultimatum a boundary is that it isn't an obvious threat or intended to be a threat. Like demands, ultimatums can be extremely tempting to make because they're unilateral, or one-sided. You may hear an ultimatum flying out of your mouth before your rational mind has a chance to catch up with your blinding and overwhelming emotions.

REMEMBER

When emotions are running high, please, please, please don't issue ultimatums.

I know it's tempting to say, "If you scrape your teeth against that fork one more time, I'm going to make you eat with rubber chopsticks for the rest of your life!" But first, do what some couples' therapists recommend when conversations start to overheat: check your pulse. If your heart rate is above 100 beats per minute that means you're too emotional to continue the conversation. Take a walk around the block, turn on your favorite music or soundscape, pet your iguana, or do whatever you need to do, but don't utter an ultimatum.

Why? Because the chances are beyond high that the ultimatum you make won't meet the standards of a solid boundary (plus, rubber chopsticks may not match your fine china). But the worst part is that you'll lose credibility with yourself, and with the fork-scraping person who was on the receiving end of the rubber chopsticks ultimatum.

Erasing Expectations

Expectations are beliefs about how things should be in the present or the future. They can include how people should behave, how systems should work, or how events or situations should unfold. Expectations can range all the way from ordinary pet peeves, to somber and serious convictions.

Here are some examples of expectations:

- ❯❯ People shouldn't wear jeans to church.
- ❯❯ Girls shouldn't sit cross-legged.
- ❯❯ My spouse should know how I'd like to spend my birthday.
- ❯❯ Cashiers should smile when they're taking my money.
- ❯❯ Women should wear makeup when they go out in public.
- ❯❯ People should go to their grandmother's funeral.
- ❯❯ My best friend should host my baby shower.
- ❯❯ My parents should loan me money to go the salon when my roots start to grow out.

The list is endless!

So, what do expectations have to do with boundaries? If you have an entire fleet of unconscious expectations sailing through your head, your expectations may turn into something you'll mistake for boundaries.

Turning expectations into requests

For example, say your birthday is coming up in a few days. You expect your spouse to know how you want to spend your birthday, but you haven't told them. Your ideal day is breakfast in bed, followed by a fun day at the mall. Going to the mall is strategic because there's a big basketball game that day and you hate basketball. You want to make sure you'll have your spouse's undivided attention and they won't be glued to the TV.

Your birthday arrives, and your spouse tells you that they've planned something really special! They made a reservation at IHOP (because they know how much you love pancakes with raspberry eyes and a banana mouth drenched in warm maple syrup), and after that the two of you have courtside seats to Game 7 of the NBA finals!

If you've been in a relationship that lasted longer than a couple of weeks, you know that what happens next isn't going to be a happy birthday. When you're convinced that your unexpressed and unspoken expectations ought to materialize, you create a kind of one-sided agreement. And a one-sided agreement is nothing more than an *oxymoron* (a contradictory figure of speech that can't be true). You're in danger of believing — without any evidence or reason at all — that an agreement was broken or some kind of boundary was violated.

REMEMBER

If you want something from another person, you must ask. If you're unwilling to ask for what you want, you've decided it's more important that they read your mind than it is for you to get what you want. (Read that as many times as you need to deprogram your expectation habit and to fully understand what it means.)

Expectations are thoughts, plain and simple. And since they exist only in your mind, they can never create a boundary for another person.

Ignoring others' unspoken expectations

If you're highly sensitive or very *empathic*, you may be keenly tuned in to the needs and wants of other people, even when those needs and wants aren't verbally expressed. And even if you don't identify as highly sensitive or empathic, your history and experience with another person can give you reasonable certainty that they have specific expectations of you.

For example, say that your mother has an unspoken expectation that you'll call her at least once a week. In truth, you'd be happy talking to her once every two weeks, or even less than that.

In fairness to your mother, she may or may not be harboring unspoken expectations. What you believe about her expectations may be a figment of your imagination. Unless, of course, she told you (maybe more than once), "Honey, my friend Gertrude's daughter calls her every day. Isn't that sweet? I can only imagine how special and loved Gertrude must feel." Can you hear the nearly audible sigh at the end of that statement?

In this case, it's reasonable to go out on a very sturdy limb, based on keen deductive reasoning skills, and conclude that your mother wants you to call her . . . often. And if you don't feel comfortable making this assumption despite her praise of Gertrude's daughter, then ask her directly: "Mom, how often would you like me to call you?" She may not give you a straight answer. But at least you had the courage to ask, plus you've expanded your freedom to call her on your preferred schedule if she doesn't make a clear request.

TIP

My father liked to quote a profound yet profane saying on the dangers of making assumptions, which you may be familiar with: "Don't assume. It makes an ass of you and me." Keep that in mind the next time you're tempted to make an assumption about another person, or to assume that someone expects something from you.

Does your mother's unspoken expectation create an obligation on your part? Your logical mind may know that it doesn't, but you still may be battling a raging war within the very core of your being to call your mother on a schedule that feels right for you rather than the schedule you believe she wants. The good news is, doing what feels best for you gets easier with time — not just with your mother, but with everyone else.

REMEMBER

Unless you've willingly accepted the role of parent or caregiver to another person, you're not obligated to fulfill someone else's expectations, demands, or desires — or even their requests. Ever.

The bottom line is, you have permission to ignore other people's unspoken rules or expectations masquerading as boundaries — even your mother's! You're not a mind reader, and you shouldn't be expected to be one. Think of this permission slip like Dorothy's ruby slippers in *The Wizard of Oz*: You've had it the whole time, but now you know what it can do for you.

Eliminating Shoulds

You may have noticed that when discussing expectations, the word *should* comes up a lot. Saying "should" is a clue that you've got an expectation — not an established boundary — in mind.

TIP

Try this experiment: See if you can come up with a pretend expectation without using the word *should*. It's harder than you think!

Get in the habit of imagining a giant red flag waving in front of your face every time you hear the word *should*, especially when it's coming out of your mouth or hanging out in a thought bubble above your head. When you see this red flag, take a moment to ask yourself if you're expecting anything from anyone. And if you are, ask yourself if what you're expecting is in fact any of your business.

For example, is it really your business if your sister dyes her hair purple right before your son's wedding? You may shudder at the thought of how the wedding photos will turn out, but adults get to dye their hair whatever color they want.

Another question you can ask yourself when you see the waving red flag is whether you'd like to convert your expectation into a request, as in "Would you serve me breakfast in bed and take me to the mall on my birthday?" I know how painful this sounds, but if you really want breakfast in bed, don't rely on your partner's ability to read minds and predict Powerball numbers. You can do hard things! Just ask.

REMEMBER

Don't *should* on others. And don't *should* on yourself.

Realizing That Agreements Aren't One-Sided

Try for just a moment to imagine a world where there are no agreements about anything. It's safe to say that a world with no agreements would be utter chaos.

There are two types of agreements: those that are governed by cultural norms or laws, and those made between two or more people to define the terms of a business transaction, to create a partnership, or to formalize a commitment, for example.

TECHNICAL STUFF

There is a third kind of agreement: one that you make to another person, such as "I agree that I will be on time to the wedding." But for our purposes, we're going to consider this third type a promise, not a formal agreement.

Agreements governed by cultural norms or laws include waiting your turn in line to buy groceries, stopping at stop signs, and paying for your food after you've finished a meal at a restaurant. If only some people agreed to wait in line, stop at stop signs, or pay for food at restaurants, life as we know it would spiral into anarchy.

REMEMBER

Agreements are made between people, and it takes at least two people to create an agreement. One person can't enter into an agreement without the active participation of another person. And that's why agreements are never *unilateral* (one-sided).

Getting two "yeses" to create an agreement

Imagine that your Great Dane puppy has finally grown to his full height and you realize you need to move to a larger apartment. (Hopefully, your Great Dane isn't bigger than Zeus from Otsego, Michigan. According to Guinness World Records, Zeus was 44 inches tall and stood seven foot four on his hind legs!)

In search of the perfect new place, you go to several apartment complexes to tour their available units. The third one you visit has a very nice apartment that's plenty big for you and your Great Dane. The woman showing you the unit asks what you think — can you imagine how happy you and your Great Dane would be here? You like the place, so you say, "You know, I think we could be happy here." In that instant, she pulls a 120-page rental agreement out of her briefcase, plops it down in front of you, and says, "Perfect! We've already signed the rental agreement — you can move in today!"

Huh? "But I haven't signed it," you say. And she replies, "Oh, you don't have to sign it. It's all set."

If this story sounds unbelievable to you, it's not because you doubt that Zeus really did stand seven four on his hind legs. It's because you know instinctively that agreements require two *yeses*.

When creating an agreement with another person, you must say *yes*, and they must say *yes*. Otherwise, you've got a half-agreement, which is no agreement at all.

REMEMBER

If you don't receive a *yes* from another person when you make a request, you don't have an agreement. And when you don't have an agreement, you can't have a broken agreement or a boundary violation.

Telling versus asking

Some people have a habit of getting around the need to create an agreement by saying things like "Let's leave" or "Let's go to Spain for vacation this summer" or "We're going to the baby shower on Sunday." Then, after they issue a proclamation that involves the action and compliance of one or more other people, they proceed as if what they just said is the law of the land. Maybe they pick up their car keys and head to the van, or they start putting on their parka and snow boots while everyone else is sitting on the sofa watching the hockey game.

Telling people what's going to happen next when it involves their participation is a close cousin of issuing a demand, but with the subtle difference of declaring what two or more people (instead of just one) will do. Because multiple people are involved in this interaction, telling can masquerade as agreeing. But sorry — it's not.

Expressing desires doesn't create an obligation

I grew up in the Southern United States, so I know that Southerners are masters of subtle and indirect ways of communicating. Growing up, I quickly realized that remarks like "It sure is chilly in this room" or "Aren't you hot?" were thinly veiled assumptions that someone would either turn up or turn down the thermostat.

In this case, the way to create an agreement is to say something like "I sure am chilly in this room. Would you be willing to turn the thermostat up to 75?" And if the person receiving the request says *yes*, then an agreement is created and a warmer room is a few minutes away.

REMEMBER

I strongly encourage you to express all your desires. You never know when someone may give you exactly what you want. Just remember that desires are statements of wants and preferences. They don't create an obligation or duty on the part of anyone else.

TIP

Even if you have a longstanding pattern of automatically fulfilling other peoples' expressed (or unexpressed) desires, you can stop anytime if you want to. You can say, "I hear you're burning up in here. I'd be happy to turn down the thermostat for you if you ask me." They may not like you changing the dance steps they know so well. But if they want you to turn down the thermostat they'll learn to ask, provided you stand firm.

Chapter **3**

Exploring Privacy, Secrecy, and Intimacy

A client came into my office one day and told me a story that illustrates what happens when you're caught off guard and need to make a split-second decision about how much you're willing to share with another person.

The day before, he was driving to a 12-step meeting when his mother called him, just wanting to chat. To help you understand what happened next, I'll just say that his relationship with his mother is . . . strained. When she asked him where he was going, he did what most people do when they're caught off guard and don't want to tell the truth: He lied!

The fact that he was on his way to a 12-step meeting is his private information — full stop. It isn't a secret because his mother doesn't have a right to know where he was going or that he's part of a 12-step community.

If his relationship with his mother was close, he may have felt comfortable (or even proud) telling her where he was going. But in this case, he didn't want to give his mother this information. His preference for not sharing says something about the level of closeness, trust, and emotional intimacy he feels in that relationship. He exercised his right to not share his private information, but the way he did it is outside his value system because he lied to avoid telling the truth.

In his case, all he needed was a way to tell the truth while protecting personal information that he wants to keep private. We brainstormed his options, and he decided that if the same thing happens in the future, he'll tell his mother that he's on his way to hang out with friends or headed to a meeting. Both options are true.

In this chapter, I clarify the difference between what is private and what is secret, and how what you share should correspond to the level of intimacy — closeness and connection — you have with other people.

I define intimacy and explain that it applies to a broader experience of personal connection than you may have previously thought. You gain a better appreciation for the fact that not everyone gets to know everything about you — even friends and family members. I give you a simple four-question quiz you can use anytime you're wondering whether information you're holding is private or secret, and I also discuss why secrets are toxic to relationships.

Defining Private and Secret

Before I do a deep dive into the difference between secret and private, I want to begin with definitions. Here's how I define secret and private:

>> A *secret* is information intentionally withheld for the purpose of avoiding consequences.

>> *Private* information is information withheld intentionally for the purpose of creating safety or to protect yourself or others.

Generally speaking, thoughts (including fantasies) are always private information. Several years ago, someone shared with me that they believed they had a right to know all their partner's thoughts. Even if it were possible to see a person's every thought scroll across their forehead like breaking news (and thank goodness it's not!), no one has a right to this level of information about your thoughts or fantasies.

Here are some examples of secrets:

>> You have an agreement with your spouse that you won't spend more than $500 without talking to them first. You spent $700 on some new golf clubs and you're hiding them in the trunk of your car.

>> Your partner doesn't like it when you smoke cigarettes, and you told them you quit. However, you're still smoking several times a week, and you lie when your partner asks if you're smoking.

>> You're in a monogamous relationship and you had (or are having) an affair. Your partner doesn't know about the affair.

Here are a few examples of private information:

>> Your salary, income, or any specific information about your financial status

>> Problems you're having (or had in the past) in your marriage

>> Your contact information, including your telephone number or home address

>> Your sexual orientation or preferences

Looking at the definition of private, you can see it involves the use of healthy boundaries. That's because in some situations withholding private information protects you or others. Managing your private information means you get to decide with whom, when, where, and how you share the information based on how you want to be protected or how you want to protect others. I go deeper into how to decide who gets to know your private information in the section, "Connecting What You Know With Who You Know," but ultimately the decision is yours.

On the other hand, secrets replace a boundary of protection with a wall. The wall serves no other purpose than to avoid the consequences of the secret being found out. Walls of secrecy can manifest as silence, avoidance, anger, defensiveness, or any other means of blocking communication.

TIP

Protecting your private information is good boundary work. It's respectful and intimate. Secrecy, which is deception, is a violation of boundaries. Holding secrets harms intimacy and is self-serving.

Defining Intimacy

Intimacy is one of those words you may have heard repeatedly, but you're not sure exactly what it means. I want to begin by reviewing two dictionary definitions to give you a clear, solid definition you can use when you want to talk about intimacy.

The Oxford Languages Dictionary defines *intimacy* as "close familiarity or friendship; closeness," and the word *intimate* as "closely acquainted, or close; private and personal."

I've combined these two definitions to describe intimacy as:

> Private, personal, close familiarity with another person that can include physical, intellectual, emotional, sexual, or spiritual knowledge (information), connection, or interaction.

Knowing that intimacy doesn't (necessarily) mean sex

When you hear the word *intimacy*, do you immediately think sexy time? It's okay — most people do! However, intimacy is much broader than just sex. Intimacy includes all the ways you can know or interact with a person, including emotionally, intellectually, physically, and sexually.

It's interesting (and odd) that intimacy is often thought of as exclusively sexual even though sex can be completely free of intimacy. On the other hand, it can be one of the most intimate experiences two people have together. Just like intimacy doesn't mean sex, sex doesn't mean intimacy.

Whether a sexual experience is intimate or not is determined by the vulnerability and intention each person brings to the experience. Each person in any interaction — sexual or nonsexual — can decide to be intimate or not to be intimate.

TIP

If someone tells you they'd like to have a more intimate relationship with you, don't assume they mean sex. If you're not sure what they mean, you can ask, "What would that look like for you?" or "Can you tell me more?"

Intimacy is experienced on one (or more) of these five levels of connection:

» Intellectual (for example, thoughts, opinions, or values)

» Emotional (shared feelings or emotions)

» Spiritual (including spiritual beliefs, spiritual value system, details about your spiritual practice)

» Physical (how close you get to another person — physical touching, for example)

» Sexual (including sexual conversation and physical/sexual contact)

The first four levels of intimacy — intellectual, emotional, spiritual, physical — can occur in any close relationship with friends or family. The fifth level, sexual intimacy (not just sexual contact), is generally reserved for a more limited number of people.

Understanding two-way intimacy

I wish I could give credit to the brilliant mind that came up with the play-on-words definition of intimacy as "into me you see." This clever and easy-to-remember phrase is an excellent starting point for thinking about intimacy. What's missing is that "into me you see" is a one-way street, rather than the two-way street that most people want to experience in intimate connections with another person or people. Two-way intimacy is best described as "into me you see, and into you I see."

Some relationships, by design, consist of one-way intimacy only. For example, the client-therapist relationship involves deep, intimate sharing by the client, but ideally little or no self-disclosure from the therapist. Most therapists agree that not only is it unprofessional to share intimate details of their private lives with their clients, but it's also harmful to the client-therapist relationship. Not only that, but as a practical matter no client wants to pay their hard-earned money to listen to the latest dramas in their therapist's life! One-way intimacy in these types of relationships is intended to protect and support ethical professional boundaries.

For intimacy to be mutual (a two-way experience), it must include all six of the following characteristics:

>> **You freely share your authentic thoughts and emotions.**

>> **The other person freely shares their authentic thoughts and emotions.**

>> **If the relationship includes physical or sexual intimacy, you freely engage in physical and sexual contact.**

>> **If the relationship includes physical or sexual intimacy, the other person freely engages in physical and sexual contact.**

>> **You listen to and are capable of hearing and taking in (receiving) the thoughts and emotions of the other person.**

You accept what the other person says as their truth or reality, even when you disagree. You're able to and do respond to their invitations for physical or sexual contact (if the relationship includes physical or sexual intimacy).

>> **The other person listens to and is capable of hearing and taking in your thoughts and emotions.**

They accept what you say as your truth or reality, even when they disagree. They're able to and do respond to your invitations for physical or sexual contact (if the relationship includes physical or sexual intimacy).

In your closest relationships, being intimate means there's a healthy mutual flow of sharing thoughts and emotions, along with physical and sexual contact that's mutual and pleasurable (if the relationship includes physical/sexual intimacy).

TIP

If you want to determine how intimate a relationship is, one of the easiest ways to begin is by noticing if one person is consistently more self-disclosing (sharing thoughts and emotions) than the other. When there's an obvious imbalance of sharing between two people, that's a sign that the relationship doesn't have two-way intimacy.

Connecting What You Know with Who You Know

When you're creating boundaries about whom you want to share private information with, you need to understand the link between the levels or degrees of connection you have with others and the levels of your private information.

I created a simple way for you to match your private information with the people it's most appropriate and logical to share it with. The Zones of Intimacy and Zones of Privacy exercise (see "Matching people and information" later in this chapter) gives you a straightforward, easy way to maintain healthy boundaries when you're sharing your private information with others.

Identifying the information you have

Right now, you're storing a vast vault of knowledge and information about yourself. Imagine trying to record all this information starting from the beginning of your life — the date and place you were born, your parents' names, your siblings' names and ages, where you've gone to school, names of family pets, or which sports you've played. And even with all that data, you haven't yet graduated high school!

The bottom line is, you have a lot of information to share about yourself. But it's unlikely you want to share all that information with everyone. For one thing, it's simply too much data to share. But more important, some of your information is more sensitive or private than other information.

Zones of Privacy are a simple framework to help you think about the various levels of your personal information (see Figure 3-1). The Zones of Privacy, when matched with the Zones of Intimacy, which I cover in the following section, help you more quickly match your private information with the types of people you may want to share that information with.

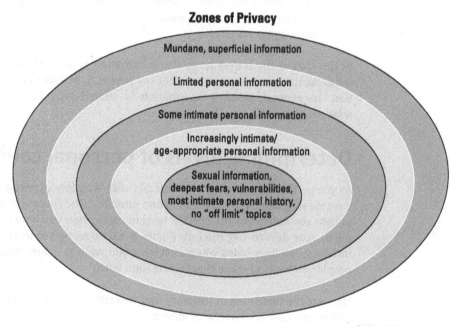

Zones of Privacy

Mundane, superficial information

Limited personal information

Some intimate personal information

Increasingly intimate/ age-appropriate personal information

Sexual information, deepest fears, vulnerabilities, most intimate personal history, no "off limit" topics

FIGURE 3-1: Zones of Privacy describe the five levels of personal, private information you hold about yourself, beginning with the least private (outer circle) to the most private (innermost circle).

© Victoria Priya, LCSW, SEP

TIP

Zones of Privacy apply only to communication between two adults. Deciding what information to share with children must also include determining what's age-appropriate. For example, when a couple decides to divorce and they share this information with their children, what they say to their 3-year-old is much simpler and more general than what they share with their 16-year-old.

Here are the five Zones of Privacy that describe the levels of your personal information:

1. **Mundane, superficial, and primarily neutral facts.** This is basic information such as the state where you live, where you were born, or your age.

2. **Limited personal information.** This includes where you went to school, where you work, and what neighborhood you live in, among other things.

3. **Some intimate personal information.** This level includes details about your family, information that signals your socioeconomic status (such as where you vacation or what kind of car you drive), and information about your health (for example, chronic illness or past accidents).

4. **Increasingly intimate/age-appropriate personal information.** This consists of things like relationship issues, political views, spiritual beliefs, mental health challenges, personal income, or financial net worth.

5. **Most intimate thoughts, emotions, vulnerabilities.** This highest level of private information encompasses your most intimate personal history, including your sexual history.

Notice that at the lowest level, the information is general and only mildly personal. As the levels increase, so does the personal, private nature of the information. In general, Zone 5 information is shared only in long-term intimate relationships.

Determining levels of personal connection

As you go through your day, you interact with a variety of people with whom you have varying degrees of connection and intimacy. The *Zones of Intimacy* are a guide to help you determine the specific level of connection you have with various people in your day-to-day life (see Figure 3-2). Knowing the level of connection or intimacy you have helps you match what you want to share about yourself to the people you want to share that information with.

Here are the five Zones of Intimacy that describe the levels of personal interaction and connection you have with others:

1. **Anonymous contacts.** These are people you don't know, such as cashiers, waiters, or clerks.

2. **Acquaintances.** This zone includes your coworkers, neighbors, people you know through volunteering or civic organizations, or parents at your children's schools.

3. **Casual friends and extended family.** This level includes people you occasionally spend time with or those you see regularly but have limited contact with.

4. **Intimate platonic (nonsexual) friends, close relatives, and your children.** This level includes close, long-term friends, trusted family members, long-time friends of your family, mentors, and your minor or adult children.

5. **Intimate sexual partners.** This zone doesn't include casual, low-, or no-intimacy sexual relationships.

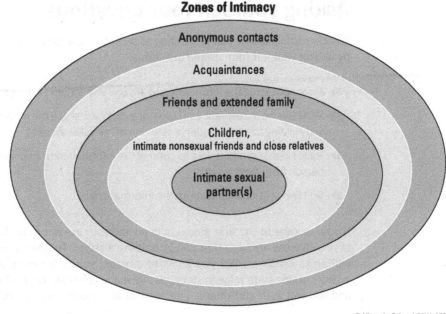

FIGURE 3-2:
Zones of Intimacy describe the five levels of your personal interactions and relationships, beginning with the least intimate (outer circle) to the most intimate (innermost circle).

© Victoria Priya, LCSW, SEP

Just like the Zones of Privacy, the higher-level Zones of Intimacy contain the people with whom you have the most intimacy. Later in this chapter (see "Matching people and information"), I show you how to combine the Zones of Privacy and the Zones of Intimacy so you have an easily identifiable guide for who should know what about you.

**THINK
ABOUT IT**

Matching your Zones of Privacy information (the information you hold about yourself) with your Zones of Intimacy (the people you know), gives you a simple framework to determine who gets to know what about you.

Figuring Out if Information Is Secret or Private

If you've ever wondered whether information you're carrying around is secret or private, you're going to find out now! The difference between privacy and secrecy can be confusing. Knowing whom, when, and what to tell is sometimes baffling, especially if the information is important or may have a significant impact on another person.

Asking yourself four questions

Whether information you're holding is secret or private can be easily determined by asking yourself four simple questions:

>> Have I disclosed the information to anyone else (or am I willing to)?

>> Do I have an agreement with someone that I will share the information, or is withholding the information a violation of my value system?

>> Have I lied or omitted data to conceal the information or to prevent another person from finding out?

>> Do I feel guilt or shame about the information?

If your answer to the first question is no and your answer to each of the last three is yes, chances are high that you're holding a secret. In other words, if you're not willing to disclose what you know to anyone, you're breaking an agreement or acting outside your value system, you've made efforts to conceal the information, and you feel guilt and shame, you're most likely holding a secret.

Understanding your private information belongs to you

If you ask yourself the four questions in the previous section and you answer yes to the first question and no to the last three, the information you have is your private information.

Sharing information (or being willing to), being transparent rather than deceptive, and not feeling guilty means you're not holding a secret. The information is private. It belongs to you, and you're not obligated to share it with anyone.

To make this more concrete, imagine you've been dating someone for a few weeks. You haven't made any commitments to date each other exclusively. In the meantime, a friend introduces you to another person who sounds interesting. You make a plan with the new person to meet for coffee in a few days, and you're feeling uncomfortable, wondering if you should tell the person you're already dating about the coffee date. You may even feel guilty when you think about withholding the information.

However, if you're willing to tell someone else (not necessarily the person you've been dating), you don't have an agreement to tell the person you're dating about other people you date, and you haven't lied or concealed anything, then you can feel confident that the information is private, not secret.

You can choose to tell the person you're already dating about the coffee date, but it may not be the best decision. For example, you may realize that the new person is someone you're not interested in seeing again, and you're enjoying dating the person you already know.

When information you're holding is private, you have a sense of appropriate and healthy ownership of it. Secrets, on the other hand, can feel like they own you. Secrets often involve information that directly impacts another person in a significant, negative way or information they deserve to know.

REMEMBER

The fundamental difference between what is private and what is secret is safety or protection (private) versus concealment or deception (secret).

Admitting something is secret

What if, after you answer the four questions, you realize that you're holding a secret?

Some of the most common secrets are:

>> Breaking an agreement and being unwilling to tell the person with whom the agreement was made

>> Engaging in infidelity, including emotional or sexual affairs

>> Lying about using alcohol or drugs or your sobriety date if you're a person with an addiction

>> Deceiving others about your use of pornography

>> Spending money excessively, breaking agreements about money, not disclosing that you borrowed money, giving/loaning money to family or friends, or gambling

If you're holding a secret, you have two options: You can either disclose the information or continue to hold the secret.

If you decide to keep a secret, you'll be inclined to rationalize or justify your decision. Here are some of the most common rationalizations for keeping secrets:

>> "It would just upset [the person you're deceiving] for no reason."

>> "My partner and I don't agree about this. I said I wouldn't [max out the credit card, have lunch with my ex, drink, and so on] but I did, and I think it's okay."

>> "Nobody tells the truth about [taxes, sex, their income, and so on]."

>> "It's really no big deal anyway. I don't see why I need to share it."

Rationalizations are self-centered, short-sighted, and lack empathy for the person who deserves to know the information. If you keep a secret because you don't want to upset another person, imagine how upset they'll be when they find out that not only did you break an agreement, for example, but you lied when you were asked about it.

If you believe you have a right to a behavior, an activity, or anything else you're concealing, ask yourself what stops you from owning your right to that behavior.

In other words, if you believe you should be able to loan a family member money when you want to, or look at pornography, why not tell the person you're deceiving that's what you want to do? Claiming your right to do what you believe you have a right to do is uncomfortable, but it's healthy for your relationship. Working through differences of opinion or conflicting needs in an honest and direct way builds connection and intimacy.

TIP

Making agreements that you're not fully committed to increases the chances that you'll later have a secret. Your lack of commitment is a predictor that you'll break the agreement, which may lead to lying about breaking the agreement and keeping it a secret. If you're prone to entering into agreements primarily to please or placate others, avoid making agreements you're not 100 percent committed to, or negotiate an agreement that you're confident you can commit to.

REMEMBER

Secrets destroy intimacy. When secrets come out, as they usually do, you not only have to deal with the initial response after the information is disclosed or revealed, but you also have to accept and repair the distrust you created by keeping a secret.

Knowing what to do with a secret

Making the decision to do something about a secret you're keeping — other than continuing to conceal it — is a courageous choice. Anytime you hold secrets, you also carry shame. There are consequences to admitting you've been holding a secret, but the freedom and relief you feel when you're back in alignment with who you want to be far outweigh the negative consequences you experience.

If you know (or think) you're holding a secret that you need to disclose, I recommend you first talk to a neutral third party you trust. This can be a good friend, mentor, sponsor in a 12-step community, counselor, or therapist. The reason I recommend talking to a trusted person first is that if you don't slow down, get your thoughts clear, and make a plan for the best way to share the secret, your disclosure may cause even more damage to an already wounded relationship.

Ideally, the person you talk to first is someone who has no connection to or isn't affected by the information you're concealing. They should be nonjudgmental and have your best interest at heart. If they have a good understanding of the difference between privacy and secrecy, that's a plus because it's possible that what you think is a secret is actually your private information.

The goal of your conversation is to tell them the secret, hear their thoughts, ask for feedback, and create a plan for how to share the information with the person you've been deceiving. If the person you turned to for advice agrees that sharing the secret is the next best step, tell them that you'll follow up with them after you've had the conversation.

Here are some do's and don'ts for sharing information you've been withholding or concealing:

>> *Do* tell the person you need to disclose the secret to that there's something you need to talk to them about. Ask them when is a good time to have a conversation.

>> *Do* take full responsibility for holding the secret by focusing on what you did and avoid mentioning other people. For example, it's better to say, "I broke our agreement about using the credit card. I'm sorry," than to say, "I know you don't approve of me using the credit card without telling you first." The second statement is a perception rather than a fact and fails to take responsibility or to be accountable. The first statement is factual and accountable, and demonstrates remorse by including an apology.

>> *Don't* disclose a secret to someone while they're driving a vehicle, on the phone, at work, or with other people, or without first asking if they're available for a conversation.

>> *Do* apologize for lying, withholding, concealing, or being deceptive by saying, "I apologize" or "I'm sorry."

>> *Do* ask after you've disclosed the information, "Is there anything you'd like to say? Do you have any questions for me?" If the other person doesn't have any questions or doesn't respond, let them know that they can come to you anytime in the future to talk about it or to ask questions.

>> *Don't* defend yourself when the person you disclosed the secret to shares their thoughts and feelings with you. Becoming defensive sends a message that you're minimizing what you did or that you're not sincere or remorseful.

>> *Do* understand and accept that holding secrets damages trust. Lying and deception are usually more harmful to relationships than the facts the lie concealed. Rebuilding trust is your sole responsibility, and it takes time. The time it takes to rebuild trust depends largely on the magnitude of the secret, the length of time the secret was kept, and the strength of your relationship with the person you deceived.

>> *Don't* say, "How long are you going to hold this against me?" You can't rush or force someone to trust again. If you're frustrated by the length of time it's taking someone to trust or forgive you, reach out to friends or other people in your circle of support to process your feelings.

There are no guarantees about how another person will receive the revelation of a secret, but when you share a secret, you become unburdened, as if a weight has been lifted. You'll have the satisfaction that comes from being transparent and *congruent* — meaning that your insides match your outsides and you're living according to your values.

Getting Clear on Who Gets to Know What about You

Now that you know the difference between secret and private information and you've been introduced to the Zones of Intimacy and the Zones of Privacy, it's time to put it all together so you can easily determine who gets to know what about you.

Matching people and information

One of the easiest ways to figure out who gets to know what about you is to match the people you know with your personal information. To do this, you start by identifying where the personal information you want to share fits in the Zones of Privacy. Once you've identified the Zones of Privacy level, go to the corresponding level on the Zones of Intimacy so that the levels of both the Zones of Privacy and the Zones of Intimacy are the same.

For example, say you want to tell your handyman that you're thinking about getting a divorce and you're wondering if this is a good idea. (For the sake of this exercise, assume that your handyman isn't also your psychotherapist, friend, or a family law attorney. It would make more sense for you to tell him if he was also your psychotherapist, friend, and/or a family law attorney, but his multiple competing roles in your life would open up more boundary problems than I can cover in this chapter.)

So, you start by reviewing the Zones of Privacy (levels of your private information) and identifying the zone you believe the "thinking about getting a divorce" information best fits. Because this information is a private thought rather than a reality, Zone 4 is the logical zone for it. Now that you've figured out that the information you want to share belongs in Zone 4 of the Zones of Privacy, review the Zones of Intimacy (levels of connections with people) to identify where your handyman belongs. I would put a handyman in Zone 2, although Zone 1.5 (if it existed) would be a perfect place for a handyman.

You can see that you've got Zone 4 information that you want to share with a Zone 2 person. Uh-oh — that's a problem! If you decide to tell your handyman that you're thinking about getting a divorce, according to the zones exercise, you're sharing information with him that's too personal or private. If you want to stick to the zones method, you need to reserve the "thinking about getting a divorce" information for only Zone 4 or Zone 5 people. These are your intimate platonic (nonsexual) friends or your intimate sexual partner(s).

If your zone numbers for the Zones of Intimacy and the Zones of Privacy match, you're good to go. If they don't, you need to adjust either what you want to share or who you share it with so that the zone levels are the same.

Correcting a people and information mismatch

When you're getting started with boundaries, you may realize that:

>> You've been sharing too much private information with people you need to share less with.

>> You've been sharing too little private information with people you need to share more with.

The reasons for these mismatches of information and people aren't necessarily important. What's important is that you recognize there's a mismatch and begin making adjustments by using the Zones of Intimacy and the Zones of Privacy framework.

Knowing How Much to Share

Even when you're clear about who gets to know what about you, you still have to make many choices and decisions about how much you want to share.

Your choices about what to share are dependent on many factors, and they change over time. For example, as you get to know someone, you become increasingly comfortable sharing more private information with them. On the other hand, if you experience a crisis in your marriage, what you choose to share with your spouse may suddenly and drastically diminish or completely disappear.

Assessing what you want to reveal

REMEMBER

Figuring out what you want to reveal about yourself starts and ends with you. No one has a right to know anything about you that you don't want to share.

Here are some questions to ask when you're wondering how much you want to reveal to another person:

>> What would I like this person to know about me?

>> What is my comfort level for sharing the information I want to share? If your comfort level is low, that may be a sign that you're not ready to share.

>> Is the information I want to share helpful to my connection or intimacy with the other person? If you want to be more connected or intimate, you may want to take more risks and be more vulnerable.

>> Am I considering sharing more than I really want to because the other person is sharing a lot with me or because I feel obligated?

>> What holds me back from sharing what another person is asking me to share? Do I feel like I need to protect myself, and if so, why?

>> Do I want to share this information to impress or diminish the other person? If your answer is yes, be curious about your reasons for wanting to impress or diminish that person. Imagine how you may feel after sharing the information. Are the feelings comfortable or uncomfortable? Will sharing the information serve you? Will it serve the relationship?

TIP

You can also use the Zones of Intimacy and Zones of Privacy exercise (see "Matching people and information" earlier in this chapter) to explore whether what you want to share is a good match for the person you want to share the information with.

REMEMBER

No matter how careful you are about who you share your private information with, some people may betray your trust. Although there's nothing you can do after the fact, you can choose not to share private information with them in the future. If the person is someone you have a long-term relationship with (partner or family member) who has a pattern of disclosing your personal information, you can ask them to stop. If they don't, use the boundary-setting process in this book to determine what to do to take care of or protect yourself.

Knowing when you're oversharing

In an ideal world, everyone would know exactly how much information they want to share about themselves and who they want to share that information with. But in the regular world, where communication is messy and complicated, you find two primary groups of sharers: oversharers and undersharers.

Most people lean toward one side or the other. Take a moment right now to think about whether you tend to be an over- or undersharer. This is good information to have, because then you can make a conscious decision about whether your natural default to over- or undershare is okay with you. If it's not, you can experiment with small shifts to the other side to see how that feels.

When it comes to the consequences of oversharing versus undersharing, oversharing tends to create the most problems and cause the most discomfort for listeners. There are three types of oversharers: those who talk too much, those who share too much personal and private information, and the overachievers who do both!

Talking too much monopolizes conversations and creates an imbalance of listening and talking. Sharing too much personal or private information tends to make people squirm or want to run away. Interacting with an oversharer who talks more than they listen can be exhausting.

A *paradox* (contradiction) of the oversharer is that despite spending excessive amounts of time speaking, or divulging too much private information, their interactions with others are rarely intimate. Oversharing is a mostly one-way communication, which means it's an intimacy blocker.

If you're wondering if you overshare, here are some signs:

>> If you're having a casual conversation with someone for an hour and you've talked for more than 40 minutes, you're probably an oversharer.

>> If you come away from interactions with friends, family, or loved ones and you realize you never asked anyone a question even though you did a fair share of talking, you're probably an oversharer.

>> If you interrupt regularly, you're probably an oversharer.

>> If the private and intimate details of your life are common knowledge to your family and friends, you're probably an oversharer.

>> If you routinely feel a vague but haunting sense of vulnerability after interactions, as if you've shared too much, you're probably an oversharer.

TIP

If you recognize yourself as a *quantity oversharer* (meaning you talk too much), congratulations! Seeing what's true is half the battle, and very courageous. An easy way to begin making a shift away from oversharing is to make a game of balancing listening and talking in your conversations. You can use your smartwatch, or simply pay attention to a nearby clock, to see if you can create more talking/listening balance in conversations. Your friends will love it!

Being mindful of undersharing

If you're often asked, "Can you tell me more?" or encouraged to expand on what you've said, your default setting between under- and oversharing is probably undersharing. There's nothing inherently wrong with being an undersharer, but I want to share a few things to know about undersharing.

Be curious about whether you tend to undershare because you think other people aren't interested in what you have to say or because you believe you're not an interesting person. If either of these beliefs are true for you, ask yourself:

>> Is it really true that people aren't interested in what I have to say?

>> Can I think of one time when I knew that another person was interested in what I had to say? If your answer is yes, this is evidence that people do want to hear from you.

TIP

If you know your undersharing is related to beliefs like these running in the background, consider experimenting with sharing more. I'm a big fan of of using a 5 percent improvement goal anytime you want to make a change. Most people can easily imagine and commit to making a 5 percent improvement. If 5 percent sounds doable to you, run an experiment in which you share 5 percent more and see how it goes.

One of the consequences I've observed when someone doesn't share much or doesn't share as much as other people in the same situation or context is that the people who share more sometimes become uneasy or even distrustful.

Several years ago, as part of a certification program I was completing to facilitate group psychotherapy, all the therapists in the program were required to participate in what's called a *process group*. Process groups, by design, lack structure. They have no identified focus, and essentially require group members to figure out what they want to talk about and how to organize their time together. This particular process group had almost no structure. We would show up for the group and the facilitator would say something like, "Talk amongst yourselves." That was the extent of the structure and the instruction.

Being in a process group is challenging. Because there's no format or rules, the extroverts in the room usually take the lead. After several weeks of timid sharing and a few awkward silences, I started to notice that one woman in the group consistently shared very little or didn't speak at all. This pattern continued for weeks and weeks, and it started to bother people, including me.

Even though I'm usually comfortable sharing in settings like this, I noticed after weeks of low or no participation by this member, I didn't feel comfortable sharing. I had thoughts like "I'm sharing a lot about myself, and she's hardly saying anything. I'm being vulnerable, but she's not being vulnerable at all. I wonder what she's thinking." I experienced what most people do in the absence of information or feedback: My imagination took over, concocting all kinds of scenarios about why she was so quiet.

If you tend to be the quiet person in the room, know that you're never the cause of someone feeling uneasy or uncomfortable. It's clear from the experience I just shared that my discomfort wasn't a result of her silence. My discomfort was rooted in what I was thinking (making up) about her not sharing, which I had no way of knowing was true.

If you explore your reasons for leaning toward undersharing and they're not rooted in feelings of inadequacy or fear, you can freely choose to be a contented undersharer. Just be mindful that your choice may impact others, but that doesn't make it wrong.

By nature, I tend to be an undersharer. One of the best gifts I ever received that encouraged me to share more happened in a three-day couples therapy marathon with Julie Gottman, PhD (clinical psychologist, author, and President of The Gottman Institute). She often asked me to say more about whatever topic we were exploring. Sometimes she would take what I said and then role-play (as me), talking to my husband. She added an incredible level of accurate, heartfelt, and intimate detail to what I had said. If you're an undersharer, ask your life coach or therapist to draw you out more, or role-play so that you can experience in real time what it may look like to share more.

Appreciating that you're the ultimate decider

Every day you have countless opportunities to decide with whom, where, when, and how you want to share information about yourself. Sometimes you will share more than you wish you had shared, and sometimes less. Sometimes your sharing will feel just right.

Telling others who you are and listening to who they are is the way to experience and build intimacy. If you struggle to tell others who you are, appreciate the fact that you have many opportunities to experiment and practice. You are the owner of your private information, and you get to decide if another person has earned the right to hear it. When your intention is to be authentic and known, you can't go wrong.

2

Understanding the Need for Boundaries

Chapter **4**

Appreciating the Ways That Boundaries Improve Your Life

To fully appreciate the countless ways that boundaries improve your life, imagine waking up every morning in a world without boundaries:

>> Walls, fences, and doors don't exist because they create limits and parameters around accessibility to people, land, buildings, and creatures.

>> Arrival and departure times, schedules, or any plans that involve a definitive start or end time no longer dictate how we spend our days. In fact, a world without boundaries would have no need for clocks, timekeeping, or even the concept of time.

>> There are no norms, standards, or laws because they create parameters, limits, and restrictions around what's considered acceptable, appropriate, or legal behavior.

>> No one owns anything because to "own" gives exclusive right of access to one person over another. Ownership naturally creates limits around who gets access to what.

At first glance, an imaginary no-boundaries world may seem freeing or desirable. (In fact, it sounds a lot like the world John Lennon described in "Imagine," the best-selling song of his solo career.)

But when you put them all together, the consequences of a no-boundaries world make the case that boundaries — in the form of limits, parameters, standards, laws, and norms — create the order that protects civil society from descending into *anarchy,* or a complete absence of order or authority. A world with boundaries and limits is the opposite of anarchy: Orderly, calm, structured, lawful, and harmonious.

In this chapter, I show you how personal boundaries improve your day-to-day experience by creating the kind of order that calms your nervous system. The boundary-setting process I explain in this book works for boundaries you want to set with others, as well as boundaries you need to set with yourself. The boundaries you set with yourself (*self-boundaries*) are habits, rituals, or systems that protect you so you can feel calmer and safer.

I also explain in this chapter how you protect others physically, emotionally, and intellectually, and keep them safe through your practice of healthy boundaries. (In Chapter 1, I describe in detail what it looks like when you use personal boundaries to protect other people in the four primary categories of physical, sexual, speaking, and listening boundaries.)

Calming the Nervous System with Order

Just about everyone I've ever known (who had the courage to admit it) has a junk drawer, a junk closet, a junk room, a junk garage, or sometimes even an entire junk house! These spaces are where we put the stuff we don't have any other place for.

The most extreme example of belongings getting out of hand is a home filled from floor to ceiling with the owner's stuff. You see this most often with people who suffer from *hoarding* (an inability to get rid of possessions that have no apparent use). Hoarding is a debilitating disorder that keeps people living in painful isolation and shame.

What's interesting about many homes where hoarders live is that even when their belongings are practically spilling out of doors and windows, there's often a narrow, well-maintained path through the chaos. It usually starts at the front door and leads to the rooms that have the most value to the occupant, like the kitchen or bathroom.

This path in the middle of chaos demonstrates that even in the worst situations of disorder, people find ways to create some order by establishing limits or *self-boundaries* so they can navigate and survive dire, stressful conditions.

To get an idea of how the absence of order impacts you, close your eyes and imagine coming home to a house filled with stuff. You open the door and see a 2-foot-wide path surrounded on all sides with piles of papers, stacks of random items, and trash bags full of stuff reaching almost to the ceiling. What sensations do you notice in your body? What thoughts do you have, and what emotions do you feel?

TIP

Anytime you're feeling anxious, overwhelmed, or powerless, experiment with bringing order to a part of your environment that feels easy and manageable, even if it's just a small, shallow drawer or a small tabletop. Once you've finished, check in with yourself to see if this small act of tidying up has shifted or changed anything for you.

TECHNICAL
STUFF

Disorder, disarray, and chaos naturally cause stress. Stress causes your sympathetic nervous system to go into a fight-or-flight response that elevates your heart rate and blood pressure. That's why creating order is good for your nervous system. Whether you're aware of it or not, you've already created many habits, rituals, and systems that make your life more orderly and calm your nervous system.

Setting your alarm or timer

If you're like most people, you set an alarm or a timer on a regular basis. When I write or do any kind of focused work, I set a timer. Why? Because I've found over the years that when I set a timer and focus 100 percent on writing (or anything else), I get a lot done. I also use timers throughout the day when I make a cup of hot tea, or to remind myself that it's time to transition to another commitment or leave for an appointment.

TIP

Timers are miracle workers when it comes to getting things done. That's because the artificial boundaries they create focus your mind like a laser. Every time you need to do something you must — but don't want to — do, set a timer for 5 minutes and focus only on that task. Most people discover that when they use timers as tools, they routinely work past the timer's alarm.

If you're asked why you set an alarm or a timer, you may say it's because you want to get up on time for work, or you want to make sure you don't miss something important that happens at a certain time. But why do you want to make sure you're on time or you don't miss an event?

Perhaps one of your answers to why you set an alarm is to get to work on time. Here are just a few reasons that may be important to you:

>> You want to keep an agreement you have with your employer to be at work at a certain time.

>> You want to keep your job so you can pay your bills.

>> You think of yourself as a person of your word, and you want to keep your word to your employer.

>> You love your work, and you want to make sure you can dedicate the maximum number of hours each day to getting things done.

>> You're being considered for a promotion (which includes a pay raise) and you want to make sure you're demonstrating commitment and reliability.

If you want to go even deeper, you can ask yourself why you want to keep agreements, why being a person of your word is important to you, or what it would mean for you to get a promotion and make more money. Your answers to these questions point to the significance of having order in your life.

Setting an alarm to get to work on time so you can get the promotion you're hoping for and make more money may mean the difference between living in a small, shabby apartment and buying a beautiful new home in a safe, friendly neighborhood.

When you fail to create order, you experience consequences. Here are a few, using the setting-an-alarm example:

>> Suffering consequences related to breaking agreements, including what you think and how you feel about yourself

>> Putting yourself at risk for not being able to pay your bills because you lost your job, which is a threat to your financial security and safety

>> Seeing yourself as a person who can't keep their word, and experiencing all the negative emotions that go with that self-image

>> Having less time to enjoy work you love

>> Potentially missing out on a promotion and everything that would happen as a result of your promotion

REMEMBER

The simple act of setting your alarm — a boundary you place on yourself — has ripple effects that extend far beyond your present circumstances and may impact your life in ways you hadn't previously imagined.

Sequencing: Putting first things first

If there's one thing you know for sure, it's that you must put your socks on before your shoes. Well, actually you don't have to — it's a choice. However, the problem you run into if you exercise your freedom of choice in this way is that if you put your shoes on before your socks, your socks will get very dirty. They maybe even get holey. But your shoes will stay nice and clean.

This simple shoes-before-socks example illustrates that you follow many sequences in life without any thinking whatsoever. These sequences create order and ultimately make your life run more efficiently and smoothly. (And in the case of socks and shoes, cleaner.)

TIP

Putting on your shoes before your socks shouldn't be confused with this hotly debated question about the correct order: Sock-sock, shoe-shoe or sock-shoe, sock-shoe? It's a highly personal decision, and you may notice that one feels better and more calming (to your nervous system) than the other.

To further explore the impact of sequencing, consider the common expression "Don't put the cart before the horse." If you grew up hearing this expression often, it's likely that your mind bypasses the image of a cart standing in front of a horse and goes straight to some version of the saying "First things first," which is shorthand for the common understanding that a certain sequence or order of things must be followed in many instances.

If you've never thought about what it would be like to put a cart before a horse, or you're hearing this expression for the first time, take a moment to imagine it in your mind's eye.

When I see a cart in front of a horse, my mind immediately sees the horse wandering away to wherever it wants or is led to go. And the cart? Well, the cart just sits there — maybe for a long time.

REMEMBER

You engage in small but powerful rituals of sequencing every day. You may not think about them, but if you fail to follow the proper sequence, the results may be inconvenient, or even catastrophic.

Here are a few common, everyday examples of order created by sequencing:

>> Opening the garage door before backing your car out

>> Putting your clothes in the washing machine before you put them in the dryer

>> Washing your hair with shampoo before applying conditioner

>> Peeling a banana before you eat it

>> Taking the baby's dirty diaper off before putting on a new one

For activities that require sequencing to work properly and smoothly, you must put the steps in the correct order. And when you put them in order, you automatically reduce chaos and increase calm.

TIP

You can invent new sequencing patterns for habits you want to incorporate into your life. Many years ago, I experimented with a new sequence in my morning routine: requiring myself to make the bed before writing in my journal. Because journaling was already a strong established habit, this experiment was highly successful. Today, I can't imagine journaling before making the bed.

Managing your time

If you were one of those kids who often was the last one to be picked up from school, baseball practice, or piano lessons, you know — from a child's perspective — the real-world consequences of not leaving on time to pick up your children.

Or maybe you chronically run behind schedule and arrive late for every lunch, appointment, teacher conference, or party — creating tension, stress, and conflict for you and everyone else.

Managing your time to take care of what's important to you is about you and your boundaries.

The consequences of not creating the order you need to take care of what's most important to you are serious and far-reaching:

>> You send a message to the important people in your life that you're not reliable or dependable.

>> The people in your life who are impacted most by your inability to meet obligations on time (or at all) may come to the conclusion that they're not important to you.

>> If a pattern of being late, missing obligations, or engaging in other forms of negligence persists, not only will you experience painful emotions like guilt and shame, but you may lose your most important relationships because you can't manage your time.

REMEMBER

Creating the order you need to care for the people most important to you not only improves how you feel about yourself but also improves and strengthens your relationships.

Planning ahead to avoid stressful reactions

Imagine waking up one morning, getting dressed for the day, driving to the airport, going to the ticket counter of your favorite airline, and telling the ticket agent, "I'm here for my vacation. I need a ticket to Paris that leaves in the next hour!"

This exuberantly planless scenario reminds me of these wise words from Benjamin Franklin:

> By failing to prepare, you are preparing to fail.

If you're a highly adventuresome type, going to the airport without a ticket, a suitcase, or a hotel reservation may sound like the ultimate in adventure travel. For the rest of us, it sounds like a nightmare or maybe the beginning of a panic attack.

Not knowing how you'll get to Paris, what you're going to wear, where you'll stay once you get there, or how you'll get back home creates a level of uncertainty, concern, and even terror you probably wouldn't ever want to experience. That's why most people, no matter how happy-go-lucky or free-spirited they claim to be, don't show up at the airport without a plane ticket or suitcase.

TIP

If there's anything in your everyday routine that's consistently stressful or anxiety-provoking, review whether you need more planning in that area. Ask yourself what actions you can take to improve your planning so you can experience the order that will create a calmer experience.

Here are a few other examples where planning helps you create order and avoid stress:

>> Mapping out your study schedule at the beginning of the school semester rather than pulling an all-nighter before a big test or a term paper deadline.

>> Deciding the best day of the week to do your laundry or go grocery shopping rather than waiting until you run out of clean clothes or food.

>> Making a list of tasks you need to accomplish for a personal or professional project rather than relying on your memory about what you need to work on next.

Planning — whether it's for a vacation or just a trip to the grocery store with a toddler — is a collection of yes and no decisions based on your needs, wants, and preferences. By tuning in to yourself and identifying the parameters (boundaries) of the experience you want to have, you establish a plan. Your plan creates the order that turns uncertainty, concern, and fear into certainty, confidence, and trust.

Protecting Yourself to Create Safety

One of the most powerful ways personal boundaries improve your life is that they protect you and keep you safe in many situations. In this section, I give you seven examples of ways your boundaries protect you and keep you safe.

The areas of your life where self-protection and safety are important can easily be identified by knowing the four primary categories of boundaries:

>> Physical

>> Sexual

>> Speaking

>> Listening

Wearing a seat belt

In 1985, Texas enacted a law that required everyone to wear a seat belt while driving or riding in a motor vehicle. Because I was born and raised in Texas (I hope you won't hold that against me), I remember the loud complaints punctuated by bursts of moral indignation about the new seat belt law. You would've thought Texans' right to breathe air had been taken away.

Driving or riding in a vehicle without a seat belt causes higher auto insurance costs, serious bodily injury, and sometimes death. Seat belt laws are an example of what happens when individuals make poor choices about their personal boundaries that have a significant financial or safety impact.

REMEMBER

Wearing a seat belt, along with many other forms of self-protection — like practicing safe sex, stopping at red lights, or closing a door for privacy — not only protects you but also protects others.

The National Highway Traffic Safety Administration (NHTSA) estimates that more than 374,000 lives were saved from 1975 to 2017 due to the use of seat belts. The NHTSA also estimates that using lap and shoulder seat belts reduces the risk of injury and front seat occupant deaths by 45 to 65 percent.

Wearing a seat belt is just one example of a physical boundary you set with yourself, and it illustrates how your boundaries protect you, keep you safe, and may even save your life.

Deciding who has keys to your home

I don't know about you, but I'm picky about who has keys to my home. Most people don't hand out keys to their home like candy on Halloween night, and for good reason.

There aren't any right or wrong answers to the question of who should have keys to your home, but your decision should be informed by the level of protection and safety you need. Assuming you make a thoughtful decision about who has a right to have access to your home, giving someone a key signals your high level of comfort, confidence, and trust in that person.

REMEMBER

Your physical safety and your private, personal belongings are important, valuable, and precious to you. Everything that's valuable to you deserves your protection, and when you're protected, you feel safe and at ease.

Eliminating offensive (and offending) people from your life

At the risk of digging up memories you'd prefer to keep buried, I'd like you to take just a moment to remember a few people you've encountered in your life that you categorize as boundaryless or offensive. Ideally, these people are no longer in your life. (But if they are, this book shows you how to take care of that.)

Now, with these unpleasant people in your awareness, imagine that all of them are still part of your day-to-day life. How do you suppose that would feel? When I think about this myself, words like stressful, tense, frustrating, or even frightening come to mind.

TECHNICAL STUFF

The word *offending* refers to illegal or extremely inappropriate behaviors. *Offensive*, on the other hand, describes a wide range of subjective experiences that not everyone may agree on. For example, not everyone defines offensive language or behavior in the same way. Offending and offensive are sometimes used interchangeably, but when someone is engaged in predatory, exploitative, or illegal behavior, offending is the correct term to use.

Your personal boundaries can severely limit or completely eliminate offensive and boundaryless people from your life, so you can feel peaceful, undisturbed, and drama-free.

TIP

When you hear that it's possible to eliminate boundaryless or offensive people from your life, you may wonder, "But what if the person who is boundaryless is my parent (or another relative)?" This is a serious, important question that has a simple, clear answer: You have a right to limit contact or have no contact with anyone, regardless of who they are or how they're related to you. And if their behavior is offending (illegal), you may need to have little or contact to protect yourself and your loved ones.

Practicing safe sex

A retired nurse practitioner who spent her career teaching college students about sex told me that the only thing you need to know about practicing safe sex is this: Use protection all the time.

Her view is that unless you're actively trying to get pregnant, there are no exceptions to this guideline, including for people in long-term monogamous relationships.

When you use your personal boundaries to practice safe sex, you protect yourself from sexually transmitted infections (STIs) or unwanted pregnancy. When you're not worried about STIs and pregnancy, sex is more relaxing, more pleasurable, and more fun.

TIP

You can't make someone wear a condom or use other protection, but you can say *no* to unprotected sex.

Deciding who gets your time

A psychotherapist colleague told me a story years ago about a prospective client who called him to inquire about the possibility of working together. When they got to the subject of fees, the prospective client told my colleague that his former psychotherapist held sessions with him at 7 a.m. for a reduced fee.

My colleague ran another business that he typically worked on in the mornings. He's also a person who doesn't relish having early morning meetings with anyone, for any reason. So he replied to the prospective client, "If I saw you at 7 a.m., I'd have to charge you extra!"

If you're not mindful or selective about who gets access to you or who gets your time, you'll find that most people will take as much of your time as you're willing to give them. It's not because they're self-centered, mean, or clueless. It's because you aren't setting boundaries around when, where, how, and to whom you're available.

TIP

Time is one of your most valuable resources, and you're the ultimate decider of who gets your time. When you set boundaries around your time, you make space to focus on what's most important to you so that what you do is in alignment with who you are and what you want to create.

Steering clear of danger and threats

It may seem obvious, but when you avoid situations that are scary, dangerous, or violent (or just feel that way to you), you're using personal boundaries and you're taking good care of yourself.

You may have been taught that it's a sign of weakness to avoid fights or to want to get away from potentially dangerous situations. But is that true? What if steering clear of threats and hazards is a sign of your strength to do what's natural and logical — to protect yourself?

REMEMBER

If you grew up in a family where you experienced violence on a regular basis, your inner alarm bells may take their time registering dangerous, frightening situations. This doesn't mean there's something wrong with you. You had no choice but to become accustomed to the violence you experienced. The good news is that today you're free to leave unsafe situations, and you can figure out how to recognize signs of danger more quickly by having a solid understanding of boundary violations. (See Chapters 7 and 13 through 18 for more information about boundary violations.)

When you use personal boundaries to keep yourself safe, you're making a courageous choice to take care of you. You may even be saving your life.

Having a place to take shelter

I have to admit that I don't usually give a lot of thought to how much the roof over my head improves my life, but it undoubtedly does. As I write this chapter, the weather forecast says there's an 80 percent chance of rain today, and it's supposed to rain all night.

If I didn't have a roof over my head at this moment, I would need to find a tarp or an exceptionally large cabinet or box to sit in, or go outside and sit in my car so that I could keep working. Otherwise, when the rain started, my laptop would get soaked. It would probably stop working, and then I would need to buy a new one. All because I didn't have a roof over my head.

Imagine what your life would be like if all the physical structures that protect you suddenly disappeared. Your personal boundaries — along with the spaces you create for your protection — keep you safe and improve your quality of life in countless invisible ways.

Using Your Boundaries to Help Others Feel Safe

In addition to protecting yourself, you have the power (and responsibility) to use your personal boundaries to protect others. In this section, I explain the ways in which you can protect other people.

The ways you protect others with your boundaries fall under the four primary categories of boundaries: physical, sexual, speaking, and listening. In this section, I focus on three specific ways you interact with others: physical, emotional, and intellectual. Physical safety includes sexual safety and is created through your use of physical and sexual boundaries. Emotional and intellectual safety are created through your use of both the speaking and listening boundaries.

REMEMBER

Although you have the power to create protection and safety for others, that doesn't mean you're responsible for another person feeling protected or safe. Most people live their lives based on a set of beliefs and ideas (largely unconscious) that act as a filter through which they perceive what happens to them. It's completely possible that someone can believe you failed to protect them or keep them safe when that isn't necessarily the case.

For example, if I believe that a man should walk me to my car after a date (for my safety and protection) but he doesn't, I may perceive his behavior as uncaring or even offensive. However, my thought that he doesn't care about my safety is based on my belief, not his behavior.

TIP

If another person tells you that something you did or said hurt them and you honestly believe that your intent wasn't to hurt or punish them, you can acknowledge (or even apologize) for the impact of your behavior and at the same time know that you didn't do anything wrong. The impact of a person's behavior doesn't imply the intent of their behavior.

If you act in a boundaryless or offensive way, it's your responsibility to be account-able for your behavior. However, you're not responsible for how another person reacts or responds to what you say or do.

Creating physical safety

Protecting others physically means protecting another person's body (which includes both nonsexual and sexual contact) or their physical possessions.

Here are just a few examples of how you create safety for others physically or sexually:

>> You respect physical or sexual boundaries others set with you.

>> You don't drive under the influence of drugs or alcohol, or practice unsafe driving habits.

>> You don't touch other people or their personal belongings without their permission.

>> You practice safe sex.

>> You respect and accept another person's *no*.

Anytime you create physical or sexual safety for another person, you're protecting them from unconscious, boundaryless, or even offending behavior. You're also sending a message that you care about their safety and well-being, which builds trust and intimacy.

See Chapters 8 and 9 for more information about physical and sexual boundaries.

Ensuring emotional safety

Protecting others emotionally means being mindful of the impact of your words and behavior on others.

Here are a few actions you can take to create emotional safety for others:

>> Refrain from name-calling or abusive speech, including yelling and screaming.

>> Be an attentive listener.

>> Refrain from any speech that is blaming or shaming.

>> Don't tell another person what they feel or how they should feel.

>> Avoid making comparisons between two people or sending a message (either explicitly or implicitly) that a person is less-than or deficient.

TIP

One of the best ways to be an attentive listener is to stay curious as you listen, especially if you believe you know everything about the other person because you've known them for years or decades. Listening with an open mind and with curiosity is one of the most valuable gifts you can give another person. See Chapter 11 for more details about the listening boundary.

When you protect someone from emotional harm, you signal to them that they matter to you, which creates more trust and intimacy in your relationships.

Establishing intellectual safety

Using your boundaries to protect other people intellectually means that you accept and honor their right to the thoughts, beliefs, and values they hold.

These are some of the ways you can create intellectual safety with others:

>> Refrain from insulting another person's intelligence or telling them that they see things the wrong way or that they're wrong-headed.

>> Don't make belittling comments about where someone went to school or their level of education.

>> Refrain from calling someone stupid or dumb, or comparing one person's intellect to another's in their presence.

>> Don't tell someone what they do or don't think, or what they should think.

TIP

For more information about using speaking boundaries to create protection and safety for others, see Chapter 10.

When you use your personal boundaries to protect the intellectual safety of others, you contribute to creating a comfortable space for the free flow of ideas between you and others. When you're comfortable and trusting that you can openly share your honest opinions and beliefs, you're also more likely to accept differences or respectfully agree to disagree.

Chapter 5

Setting Boundaries: It's a Learned Skill

D o you remember when you were learning how to drive a car? The driver's ed teacher told you things like "Put your hands on 10 and 2" of the imaginary clockface on the steering wheel, and "Look both ways" before passing through a four-way intersection.

Over time you forgot about these instructions, but they run in the background of your mind and inform you every time you get behind the wheel of a vehicle. That's exactly what it's like learning boundaries.

Just like you weren't born knowing how to drive a car, you weren't born knowing about boundaries. And if your parents didn't understand boundaries or had poor boundaries, it's unlikely that you reached adulthood with good information about how boundaries work. But don't worry. Just like driving, you can master the skills of personal boundaries no matter how old you are.

In this chapter, I explain why it's common for people to get to adulthood without understanding even the basics of healthy, effective boundaries. You see how the poor boundaries (or boundary violations) you observed or experienced in your childhood not only left you in the dark about how boundaries work but also may have put you in danger or harmed you.

I introduce you to six simple steps that are the road map for creating effective boundaries in any situation or relationship, including your relationship with yourself. I cover some of the common mistakes people make when they're learning or leveling up their boundaries, and why it's so important to stick to the basic principles and the six steps. You begin to understand that as you practice the steps and the principles, you'll become clearer, more confident, and less anxious about the boundaries you want to set. Setting boundaries gets easier over time and can even be fun — no kidding!

Realizing That You Didn't Learn Boundaries Growing Up

There's a good chance that one of the reasons you picked up this book is because you didn't learn about boundaries from your parents or caregivers when you were growing up. I can't tell you how many times I've heard someone say after they were introduced to the principles of boundaries, "I didn't even know what boundaries were!"

If this is true for you, I want you to know and embrace two important facts:

>> There's absolutely nothing you could've done as a child to learn better boundaries.

>> There's no time like the present. You're figuring out boundaries now!

One of the most concrete (and alarming) examples that illustrates how people learn boundaries growing up came from a story I heard many years ago about a parent who had what I'll call a clothing-optional lifestyle. While his children were still at home and under his care, his clothing-optional lifestyle meant he routinely walked around the house completely naked.

If you grew up in a family where one or both of your parents walked around the house naked on a regular basis, this may seem normal to you. But for most families, this behavior isn't customary. It's also not healthy or wise to repeatedly expose children to the naked body of a parent or another adult. Adults who were repeatedly exposed to the naked body of an adult when they were children will tell you that they felt fear, disgust, and even repulsion. These feelings strongly suggest that this behavior isn't in the best interest of children and is boundaryless (see Chapter 9).

As shocking as the naked parent scenario may seem, it's worth taking a moment to ask yourself if you would think this behavior was unusual if you didn't know how other families lived. Understanding where and when to wear clothes isn't something you're born knowing. Your parents or caregivers must teach you rules about when to wear clothing, which are largely based on cultural or religious norms. And in the case of the clothing-optional parent, he was teaching his children that it's customary or "normal" for a parent to walk around the house naked.

TIP

Recalling situations or people from your childhood that made you feel disgust or caused an *ick* or *yuck* kind of internal response is often a clue that your family had poor or nonexistent boundaries, or that the adult those feelings are associated with violated boundaries.

A child who grows up in a family where a parent is frequently naked may not understand that this behavior is unusual until they begin spending time at other people's homes and notice that other parents are always dressed. It's not the child's fault that they don't know what's customary or normal. Children simply learn what they're taught.

REMEMBER

You may not have experienced a parent walking around your family home naked, but you probably experienced other examples of a parent modeling weak, poor, or nonexistent boundaries. If you were given very little or no boundaries in childhood or were severely restricted in what you were allowed to do, you aren't responsible for the boundaries you were taught. However, as an adult, you're free to make choices about the boundaries you want to create, keep, or discard.

Accepting that you can't teach what you don't know

Imagine that you're 12 years old again and an adult says to you, "Teach me how to drive a car." You would know immediately (unless you started driving before you were 12) that you couldn't possibly teach them how to drive.

This simple example illustrates that you can't teach another person how to do something you don't know how to do. If your parents didn't know how to teach you to read, drive a car, type, or do anything else they knew you needed to learn, they probably found someone else to teach you. Or they made sure that you learned the skill at school. In the case of personal boundaries, not only are many parents unable to teach what they don't know, in most cases, they don't know there's something their children need to learn!

Many people get to adulthood without any information about boundaries, much less healthy boundaries. The primary reason they didn't get a good education in boundaries is that although boundaries are present in all areas of life, if parents or caregivers don't know what boundaries are, there's no way they can teach them.

Identifying four common boundaries lessons from childhood

If you grew up with parents (or caregivers) who didn't teach you the boundaries skills you need, you probably recognize one or several of the following dynamics that are common in families with poor boundaries:

>> **One (or both) of your parents behaved in a boundaryless way.** They lacked boundaries in one or more of the four primary categories: physical, sexual, speaking, and listening.

>> **One (or both) of your parents was *walled off* (rarely expressed thoughts, opinions, or emotions).** They were often silent in interactions or were like a closed book to their children or others.

>> **One (or both) of your parents failed to protect you emotionally, physically, or sexually.** They either violated your emotional, physical, or sexual boundaries, or they allowed other people to violate your boundaries without speaking up or protecting you.

>> **One (or both) of your parents overprotected or isolated you, or severely restricted your freedom.** For example, they may have prevented you from engaging in age-appropriate activities, playing with friends or visiting their homes, or choosing your clothes or where you went to college.

Before I describe each of these boundary lessons in detail, keep in mind that whatever your parents did or didn't do, you probably thought (at least for the first 5–12 years of your life) that the way they did things was typical of most families.

As a child, you depended on your parents for your survival. Because of the profound dependence they have on adults, children tend to see their caregivers as all-powerful or godlike, at least until they reach an age when they're able to begin taking care of their own basic needs. Until you began to have experiences in the wider world that told you differently, you may have thought of your family's habits or customs as normal.

If you grew up in a family where one (or more) of your parents behaved in a boundaryless way, you learned that boundaries, including generally accepted ways of behaving, norms, or even laws, didn't apply to them. Common feelings you may have experienced living with a boundaryless parent include anxiety, fear, or anger. These are the emotions most people — and especially children — experience when they're in the presence of someone with no boundaries who has lost control of themself.

REMEMBER

Another word for boundaryless behavior is *shameless*. Boundaryless behavior is shameless because the boundaryless person doesn't care about the impact their behavior has on others, and they lack shame.

On the other end of the spectrum, if one of your parents was walled off and rarely expressed their thoughts, views, or emotions:

>> You didn't learn how to share thoughts, views, or emotions because that behavior wasn't modeled for you.

>> You may have felt lonely, sad, or rejected by the parent(s) who was walled off.

REMEMBER

A person can be boundaryless in one of the four primary types of boundaries (physical, sexual, speaking, or listening) and be walled off or have too many boundaries in another area. For example, someone can be boundaryless in their physical behavior yet have too many boundaries around their expression of thoughts, opinions, or emotions (see Chapter 1).

If your parents failed to protect you emotionally, physically, or sexually:

>> You learned that you don't deserve, or don't have a right, to protect yourself.

>> You may have felt afraid or angry.

>> You may have experienced abuse or exploitation.

>> You may be carrying lingering shame related to abuse you experienced.

REMEMBER

When a child is abused by an adult, the child feels shame about what happened to them. The shame someone feels about being abused is referred to as *carried shame* (a term coined by Pia Mellody, author and Senior Fellow of Meadows Behavioral Healthcare). But carried shame doesn't belong to an abused child, or to you if you were abused; it rightfully belongs to the abuser. The section "Giving back the shame of other people's poor boundaries" later in this chapter explains how to work through carried shame.

>> As an adult, you may struggle to protect yourself because you weren't taught that you had a right to be protected, which is how children learn self-protection.

If one or both of your parents overprotected, isolated, or severely restricted your freedom:

>> You may struggle with self-doubt or self-confidence as an adult.

>> You may have had a difficult time leaving home or may still live with your parents as an adult out of fear of independence or a belief that you're abandoning them.

>> You may have strong reactions to or defy people or institutions that attempt to implement limits, standards, or boundaries with you.

REMEMBER

Adults are responsible for their own safety, well-being, and support. No adult is responsible for another adult, unless they have formally agreed to be their caregiver. If you don't have a formal commitment to take care of another adult, you aren't abandoning them if you decide to live apart from them, end the relationship, or choose not to support them financially.

Understanding that boundaries are learned by observation

Like many things you learned growing up, boundaries are rarely learned through conversation, words, or direct teaching. You learned about boundaries primarily from observing your parents, caregivers, teachers, sports coaches, and other adults in your childhood.

You won't have words for boundaries if they aren't given to you, but you'll have experiences that signal whether someone else's boundaries are healthy or unhealthy. For example, when you're in the presence of a person who has good boundaries, their boundaries create feelings like safety, comfort, and trust. When you're with someone who has poor or no boundaries, their lack of boundaries creates feelings like discomfort, fear, suspicion, anger, or even repulsion.

Trusting that an old dog can learn new tricks

No matter what you were (or weren't) taught about boundaries growing up, you can have new and better boundaries today. You're not destined to a life of bad or nonexistent boundaries just because your parents didn't understand how they work. Boundaries are just like driving: Once you know the principles, skills, and simple steps for creating them, your boundaries will get better and better.

It's helpful to have a simple process to identify what you learned (or didn't learn) in the past about boundaries and what you can do about it now. The following prompts provide valuable information and direction for uncovering areas to focus on as you're working on improving your boundaries:

>> Examine the four primary boundaries — physical, sexual, speaking, and listening — to identify and review the boundaries you were (or weren't) taught as a child. (See Chapters 8, 9, 10, and 11 for more information about the four primary boundaries.)

>> Make note of or highlight the boundaries you identified that are healthy and effective. These are boundaries you want to keep and improve, if needed.

>> Make note of or highlight the boundaries you identified that you weren't taught. Pay special attention to poor boundaries, boundaryless behavior, or boundary violations of a parent or caregiver.

>> Based on what you discovered about the boundaries you weren't taught, figure out what healthy, effective boundaries look like for each of those categories and implement them in your life as needed.

REMEMBER

If you've made some truly regretful or even harmful mistakes in your life or violated other people's boundaries in the past, you may believe that because of these mistakes, you've lost your right to set boundaries. This simply isn't true. There's nothing you can do to lose your right to set boundaries, to say *no*, to make a request, or to negotiate with someone who makes a request of you. Failing to set boundaries with others is a disservice to them and may in fact enable their own problematic or even abusive behavior.

Giving back the shame of other people's poor boundaries

If you grew up in a family or were part of a system (school, sports, religion, and so on) where you weren't protected, there's a strong likelihood that you were abused physically, emotionally, or sexually.

Anytime a child is abused, they experience shame or, more specifically, carried shame (see "Identifying four common boundaries lessons from childhood" earlier in this chapter). The basic premise of carried shame is that when an adult acts in a shameless, boundaryless, or abusive way toward a child, the child will absorb and carry the shame.

Children absorb and carry shame from abuse or trauma because:

>> The adult's boundaryless and shameful behavior impacts the child like secondhand smoke. The adult's shame radiates or is transmitted invisibly to the child, and the child absorbs it.

>> Children don't have the boundary skills or tools to prevent the absorption of another person's emotions or feelings, so the child has no means to avoid absorbing the adult's shame and therefore carries it.

If the concept of carried shame is confusing or difficult to understand, think of something that happened to you before the age of 17 that was cruel, mean, or abusive. When you think about the incident, do you feel shame? If you do, this is an example of carried shame. You don't need to carry the shame of something another person did (or does) to you. Their behavior belongs to them, and so does the shame.

TIP

There are specific ways to symbolically give back *unearned shame* — shame that belongs to someone else. The details and processes are beyond the scope of this book, but for now if you identify feelings of shame about anything that happened to you between birth and age 17, a simple way to give back that unearned shame is to say silently to yourself (not to the person who violated your boundaries) every time you recall the incident:

> [So-and-so], you shamed and abused me, and it was wrong. You made me feel shame, and I'm giving it back to you. It's not mine, and it's toxic to me. I won't carry it for you any longer.

Doing an exercise like this cannot hurt the other person. Returning unearned shame is your private work, and the truth is, if they felt, processed, and took responsibility for their shameless behavior, doing so would heal them (and others). That's why when you symbolically *give back* another person's shame it can't hurt them — but it does unburden you from carrying painful feelings that don't belong to you.

Simplifying the Boundary-Setting Process

For too long, setting boundaries has been confusing and overwhelming because of a common misperception that boundaries are categorized by the types of connections you have with others like family members, coworkers, or intimate relationships, for example. This is simply not true.

While it's true that every situation is unique, creating healthy personal boundaries can be accomplished by using the same principles and steps every time. Whether your challenge is with a family member, long-term intimate partner, friend, or coworker, you can use the same six steps to process and create the boundaries you need.

Discovering six simple steps

You can use six simple steps to create any boundary — with other people or with yourself. Once you know and understand how these steps work, your boundary-setting process will be easier, quicker, and more effective.

In Chapters 13 through 18, I explain each of the six steps in detail. For now, here's an overview of the six steps:

1. **Know what isn't working.** To create a boundary, you need to know what's not working for you in a given situation or relationship.

2. **Get clear about your reality.** On a granular level, you must examine what you experienced with your five senses (your *sense data*), what you thought about what you experienced, and the emotions you felt.

3. **Clarify your needs and the outcome you want.** You must identify the needs that aren't being met in the situation to further clarify what's not working. Then you should envision what you would like to experience instead or the outcome you want.

4. **See where you have power before you take action.** This important step helps you identify where your power lies. You can't take action without knowing what you have power over.

5. **Taking action to create a boundary.** Here's where you take all the information you've collected in Steps 1 through 4 and implement the necessary actions to get the results you're hoping for.

6. **Evaluate your results and see what went wrong.** You won't always need to work this step, but it can help you figure out why a boundary wasn't successful and what you can do about it. Chapter 18 shows you how.

Mastering the principles that improve boundary work

For each of the steps, you need to know certain principles that can significantly improve your boundary work. For example, when you work Step 2, if you confuse what you perceived with your five senses with your thoughts and judgments about what happened, your boundary work will be based on faulty data and won't be effective.

Here's a simple example that illustrates how this can happen: You went to the mall, and you happened to see one of your best friends walking by in the opposite direction. She didn't look at or speak to you. (This is the data you perceived with your sense of sight.)

Based on what you saw, you thought, "I can't believe how rude she is. Who does she think she is? I know she saw me; she just ignored me because I'm with my boyfriend and she's jealous because she doesn't have a boyfriend." (These are your thoughts and judgments about what you perceived with your sense of sight.) If you believe your thoughts and judgments are facts, you will identify your friend's actions as being rude, ignoring you, and being jealous. And based on your belief that your thoughts are facts, you may attempt to create a boundary to stop your friend from being rude or ignoring you in the future.

Can you see what may be wrong with this picture? A person not looking at or speaking to you can have many explanations, and only one of them is that they are rude, ignoring you, and jealous.

If you identified this experience as something to create a boundary for, what you would discover after working Step 2 is that there's no boundary to create. The problem, and your challenge, is rooted in what *you* thought or made up about your friend's behavior, not in what she did. The only way your thoughts can be turned into facts is if your friend says, "I was rude, I ignored you, and I'm jealous of you."

TIP

You can significantly improve both your boundaries and your listening skills by making a game out of distinguishing between *sense data* (what you see, hear, taste, smell, or touch) and your thoughts, perceptions, or judgments. When you listen to anyone (or yourself), identify which parts of what they say are thoughts and judgments and which parts are what they experienced with their senses. You'll begin to notice that what people think, perceive, or judge often has little or no association with the facts.

It may be tempting to do a simple review of the six steps and think that's all you need to know about setting boundaries. But if it was that simple and easy, many people wouldn't be struggling with boundaries.

I recommend that you memorize the six steps and study the fundamental principles of each step, which are discussed in Chapters 13 through 18, so you can work through them with more ease and confidence. This will exponentially increase the effectiveness and quality of your boundary work.

Knowing the pitfalls when you're creating boundaries

You face countless pitfalls when it comes to creating boundaries, but here are a few of the most common:

>> You believe your perceptions, thoughts, or judgments about a situation are facts or the truth.

>> You focus on how another person should change so that you can feel better rather than seeing where you have the power to change the situation or your response to it.

>> You don't make requests because you believe that requesting something means you're telling another person what to do.

>> You don't make requests because you think other people should read your mind.

>> In general, you over-focus on what other people do or don't do rather than focusing on your perceptions and emotions and what you can do.

>> When someone breaks a promise or agreement with you, you make demands or tell them what to do rather than discussing how to resolve the issue or letting them know how you plan to take care of yourself in response to what happened.

>> Your requests and agreements are vague and general rather than clear and specific.

Revisiting the basics when you're stuck

I once worked with a therapist who told me, "I want you to go out there and make a lot of mistakes!" What?! She knew I had an unhelpful tendency to try to get things right (every time) and to avoid making mistakes, and this was her way of helping me get over my perfectionism.

We all struggle and make mistakes, especially when we're figuring out something new. Sooner or later, you'll get stuck when you're trying to create a boundary or fix one that wasn't successful. When that happens, the best thing to do is revisit the steps in Chapters 13 through 18, paying special attention to Chapter 18 to discover where the boundary may have gone off the rails.

It's okay. It happens to the best of us.

TIP

Anytime you're in a challenging or difficult situation where you can't easily review the six steps for creating a boundary, you can make a lot of progress by asking yourself two simple questions:

>> What happened that's causing me stress at this moment? Be sure to distinguish the facts (or data) from your thoughts and perceptions.

>> What do I need right now for my own self-protection or self-care?

Creating Boundaries Gets Easier with Time

One of my favorite hobbies is knitting, and knitting is heavy on repetition. One of the most freeing things I've discovered about knitting is that *ripping* — a knitter's term to describe unraveling a project and starting over — is considered a fundamental part of the process. Ripping isn't bad, and it doesn't necessarily mean you made a mistake. It's just something you can count on if you take up knitting as a hobby. You might even say that you haven't knitted until you've ripped.

Boundaries are a lot like knitting. Every day you're presented with many opportunities to exercise your boundaries. From where you choose to sit in a restaurant, to whether you choose to stay in a relationship, you repeat boundary work over and over and over. And sometimes you need to rip, meaning you have to completely undo or rework a boundary you created.

Just like knitting and ripping, you can say that you haven't mastered boundaries until you've completely bombed at least one. The more you knit, the less you rip, and the more you practice boundaries, the less time you spend feeling lost, confused, and unprotected. Your boundary work becomes more effective and easier the longer you do it.

Establishing mastery with repetition

Just like knitting and ripping, boundaries are something you do over and over and over. However, not all boundaries are created equal. Some boundaries are more difficult than others, and these are the boundaries that, once created, boost your confidence and make you feel more masterful.

Here are a few examples of confidence-boosting boundaries:

» Saying *no* to anyone who's difficult to refuse, such as a parent, friend, spouse, or supervisor

» Making what feels like a bold request of another person or an organization (I discuss more about this boundary in the next section.)

» Telling someone you've been dating that you're not interested in having a long-term relationship

» Telling someone you've been dating that you'd like to have an exclusive, monogamous relationship with them

» Returning food in a restaurant that wasn't prepared according to the way you placed your order

» Raising your fees or asking for a raise at work. (All conversations and negotiations about money involve boundaries.)

Some of these scenarios may be easy for you (like returning food in a restaurant), but others may be extremely difficult. The more challenging a boundary is for you, the more confidence you'll build as you create it.

REMEMBER

You'll notice that some of these confidence boosters are difficult conversations or even seemingly negative events. But the truth about confidence is that it grows from courageous action, and courage almost always comes with a dose of fear.

GAINING FREEDOM AND CONFIDENCE

One of the most underappreciated benefits of boundaries is that they create freedom. For example, when someone is intrusive or won't give you the physical or emotional space you need, you can create more space for yourself by setting boundaries with them or blocking their ability to intrude on your space. The same is true for how you spend your time. When you say *no* to invitations or requests, you create time freedom — the ability to spend your time the way you want to. Anytime you create space for yourself physically, emotionally, or around how you spend your time, you create more freedom.

Once you start to notice that you're feeling uncomfortable, pressured, or even bullied, you'll set boundaries that reduce or eliminate these experiences and the difficult, painful feelings that go with them. When you set limits, the confidence you feel motivates you take on even more challenging situations or difficult people you need to set a boundary with.

Dealing with resistance and pushback

Believe it or not, as your boundaries improve, not only will you stop dreading other people's pushback, but you may even look forward to the opportunity to show off your boundaries skills!

For example, a woman once told me that she made a bold request that her husband sell his car and get a new one. She asked him to get a new car because he had been unfaithful to her, and he had driven the other woman around in his car.

When she asked her husband to sell his car and get another one, he replied, "If you're going to ask me to sell my car, then I'm going to ask you to sell your car too!"

For the record, she hadn't had an affair, and her husband had no apparent reason to ask her to sell her car. His response was an embarrassing echo of the toddler defense, "You're not the boss of me!"

In the past, she would've gone down a rabbit hole with him, telling him how unfair and mean he was, or listing all the reasons he should sell his car and all the reasons she shouldn't have to sell her car. Before she became a boundaries ninja, she would've let his silly detour define the rest of the conversation.

But because of her excellent boundaries skills, she replied, "I hear you're going to ask me to sell my car. I might be open to talking to you about that at another time, but right now we're talking about your car. I feel so sad and hurt every time I see your car. It reminds me of the other woman, and I can't ride in it anymore. I want you to sell it and get another one that's a different make, model, and color, and I'd like you to do that within the next month. Would you be willing to do that?"

Here's why her response was so powerful and effective:

>> She acknowledged that she heard what he said.

>> She offered the possibility of discussing his threat to ask her to sell her car at a later time.

>> She immediately returned the topic of conversation to what she wanted to talk about, which was him getting a new car.

>> She told him what it was like for her when she saw his car and stated her unwillingness to ride in it (her limit).

>> She told him what she wanted and was very specific in her description. She even included a time frame/deadline.

>> She ended by making a request, asking him if he was willing to do what she wanted.

TIP

When preparing for a conversation that has any likelihood of becoming difficult or challenging, know your talking points in advance. Your *talking points* are what you intend to talk about or cover in the conversation. When you're clear about your talking points, if the other person tries to confuse, complicate, or otherwise change the subject, all you have to do is return to your talking points. Simple and easy.

The happy ending to this story is that the husband got a new car. The wife didn't get a new car, but here's what she could've done if she'd been secretly hoping for one: When her husband said he was going to ask her to sell her car, she could've replied, "You read my mind! I'm going straight to the dealership right now to trade in my Honda Accord for that Bentley I've been dreaming of!"

When you develop excellent boundaries skills, you're more likely to see pushback and resistance as an interesting challenge. You may even start to see resistance as a game. No kidding! (Chapter 6 has more detailed information on managing resistance and pushback.)

Motivating yourself with results

Almost nothing is more motivating than seeing that your boundaries are working. You may have been living under the false belief that you had to do certain things or behave in certain ways to please people, only to find that when you started setting limits or making requests, that wasn't the case. I regularly hear from people who share their delight — and sometimes shock — about the way their boundaries are received.

Someone told me a while back that they used to believe that when they visited their in-laws, they had to stay at their tiny home and sleep in the spare bedroom with their spouse and four kids, who slept on the floor. The truth was, they wanted to stay in a hotel, where they'd feel comfortable, have more privacy, and get more than a few hours' sleep.

When they finally got the courage to tell their in-laws that they planned to stay at a hotel the next time they came for a visit, not only were the in-laws supportive, but they said it was a great idea because the kids would have more room and a pool to swim in while they were visiting!

When you experience results like this, you begin to question other situations or relationships in your life where you believe you have to do things a certain way to get along with or please others. And even if the other person doesn't like the limits or boundaries you set, you're not doing your relationships any favors by going along with anything you don't sincerely want to do.

Every time you create boundaries that improve the quality of your life — which is one of the main purposes of boundaries — you're inspired and motivated. You see that there are even more possibilities and opportunities to create boundaries that enhance and improve your life.

REMEMBER

When your boundaries start to change and improve, people notice. Their feedback won't always be approving or supportive, but sometimes it will. This is normal and to be expected. What's important about this type of feedback is that it's evidence that you're changing for the better. You're doing something different, and it shows.

Making a "no" freeing instead of frightening

Despite being one of the shortest words in the English language, the word *no* has the power to strike terror in the hearts of many! If you were taught to be kind and to avoid hurting other people's feelings, if you're a recovering people pleaser, or if you grew up in the Deep South of the United States (like I did), you've had your share of struggles with the word *no*.

I don't want to mislead you by telling you that your improved boundaries skills will make saying *no* easy and fun from this point forward. But I'm happy to report that there are ways to make saying it much easier. And when it's easier to say *no*, you feel more relaxed and you spend less time doing things you don't want to do.

TIP

If you want to have some fun experimenting with saying *no*, for the next week say *no* or *I can't* to every request anyone makes that involves you doing something for them. You can even tell them that you're playing the No Game. (Exceptions to the No Game include delegated tasks from your employer or anything related to your family responsibilities, including parenting.)

A great beginning skill for protecting yourself from saying *yes* when you really want to say *no* is to delay giving an answer. For example, say your best friend calls you for the third time this year asking to borrow your pickup truck. You feel irritated and resentful, like you'd rather get a root canal than loan them your truck. The truth is, you wanted to say *no* the last time they asked, but not only did you let them borrow your truck, but you spent half the day helping them clear out a storage unit so they could cancel their rental agreement and save some money. Instead of immediately agreeing or refusing to loan out your truck this time, you can say, "I'll have to check my schedule and let you know."

When someone asks you for a favor, invites you to an event, or makes any other request of you, here are a few options for avoiding saying *yes* when what you really want to say is *no*:

>> I'll need to get back to you about that.

>> Can I get back to you about that tomorrow?

>> I don't think I can make it, but I'll let you know for sure by [the date or time by which you're sure you can reply].

>> Thanks for the invitation. I'll need to check my calendar.

Of course, you need to get back to anyone you promised to follow up with. But once you've given yourself space between the ask and the answer (which you already know is a clear *no*), you've bought yourself some time to figure out how to deliver your answer.

TIP

Here are some tips that can make it easier to say *no*:

>> **Know that "I can't" is a complete sentence.** It's a perfectly legitimate way to say *no*. If you want to soften it a bit, you can say, "I'm sorry; I can't." Just be sure that saying you're sorry is an honest statement for you.

>> **Tell them you've got a commitment.** Your commitment may be to do nothing in particular, which is a real commitment to yourself! You don't need to have a serious commitment, like taking your grandmother to the emergency room, in order to use the word commitment.

>> **Understand that it's okay *not* to give a reason for saying *no*.** For example, it's fine to say, "I can't loan you my pickup truck." You don't need to give a reason. If the other person asks for a reason, you can say, "I just can't." You can repeat this answer as many times as the other person is bold (or persistent) enough to keep asking.

>> **Know that you're not required to deliver a *no* using the same channel through which you received the request.** For example, you don't have to say *no* by phone if you received a request by phone. If you're struggling to say *no,* identify the easiest possible method to deliver your answer. For instance, if

someone asked you to do something by phone but you can't imagine having the courage to deliver a *no* by phone, then send an email. Or if you got a request by email, you can deliver the *no* by text. Whatever gets the job done is the way to go.

» **Avoid giving specific reasons for saying *no*, especially if they're not directly related to facts about yourself or things in your control.** For example, it's better to say, "I can't come to the Tupperware party. I've got another commitment" or "I can't come to the concert. I have the flu," than to say, "I can't come to the Tupperware party. I don't have a babysitter." If the person hosting the Tupperware party has a teenager they're eager to volunteer to babysit your child, you'll be confronted with another potential *no* to deliver. In other words, when you give reasons that have potential answers or solutions, or are easy to debate or argue about, the likelihood of having your *no* challenged increases.

The more comfortable you get with saying *no*, the easier it is and the freer you feel to say it.

IN THIS CHAPTER

» **Seeing how anticipating pushback helps you**

» **Understanding that some people won't like your boundaries**

» **Knowing the strategies to manage pushback**

» **Having go-to phrases for easier responses**

» **Checking in with an accountability partner**

Chapter **6**

Managing Resistance and Pushback: Good Boundaries Won't Make You Popular

When you begin improving and implementing boundaries, people notice.

I don't want to discourage you or be a Negative Nancy, but other people's responses to your boundaries will be less than positive more often than not. It would be wonderful if they grabbed their pom-poms, jumped up and down, and yelled, "Yay, you! Yay, you! Yay, you!" But alas, that's unlikely to happen — unless you have (or can get your hands on) some pom-poms and become your own boundaries cheerleader. Why not?

You may wonder why people aren't more receptive to your new boundaries. After all, boundary setting isn't easy! To help you deal with others' reactions as your boundaries improve, I recommend adopting two crucial mindsets:

» Other people's responses (or reactions) to your boundaries aren't personal, even when they feel personal. Other people's responses belong to them.

» When one person in a relationship, family or organization changes, it impacts the dynamics of those relationships or systems.

REMEMBER

Other people's reactions to your boundaries are 100 percent about them, and 0 percent about you. In fact, their reactions to you mean you're doing something different, which means you're changing and growing.

Change is difficult. People in long-term relationships develop consistent and predictable communication "dances." When you act differently, the changes in your behavior effectively create a change for others. When you change your dance steps by improving or implementing boundaries, your dance partner's old steps won't work anymore.

TIP

As you're getting used to your new boundaries, memorize this phrase and repeat it to yourself often:

Other people's reactions to my boundaries are about them. They're not about me.

In this chapter, I show you what pushback and resistance to your boundaries looks like and why expecting pushback can actually make your boundary work easier, and even fun!

I deliver the bad (yet freeing) news that you're unlikely to win any popularity contests when you start setting boundaries. I discuss how to anticipate and navigate the inevitable pushback. To make navigating resistance easier, I share six go-to phrases you can use when you get resistance or pushback. You also see that some difficult boundaries or crisis situations may require you to work with a boundaries coach, mentor, or therapist.

Defining Pushback and Resistance

Before I show you how to navigate resistance and pushback, you need to know what those terms mean. The following list includes a few examples of statements other people may make when you attempt to set boundaries, along with brief commentary about each example. In the next section, I discuss how to respond to these or similar comments.

>> **"Why are you being so uptight/selfish/self-centered?"** Anyone who has ever made an intentional effort to improve their boundaries has been called some version of uptight, selfish, or self-centered.

>> **"You and your boundaries!"** I've been on the receiving end of this one. Although the words can appear somewhat neutral, the tone in which they're delivered can reasonably be translated as "I'm frustrated with you and your boundaries!"

>> **"You've never said that before. Why do you have to change the way we've always done things?"** The implication of this statement and question is that people either don't or shouldn't change, which of course isn't true.

>> **"You never had a problem with this before. Why now?"** Similar to the prior example, the implication is that people either don't or shouldn't change. Again, that isn't true.

>> **"Your boundaries are hurting our relationship."** This resistance to another person's boundaries can be particularly powerful because of its guilt-inducing quality.

>> **"Why are you punishing me?"** Since healthy boundaries can never be punishment, this pushback question is both a misunderstanding of boundaries, as well as a clear expression that the other person believes they are a victim.

>> **"We're family! This is what families do for each other!"** This resistance to boundaries contains an underlying belief that family members are exempt from boundaries. Family members aren't exempt from boundaries unless you decide they are.

>> **"Whose idea was it for you to say/do this?"** This pushback question implies that you couldn't have possibly come up with the idea to set boundaries or change an agreement on your own.

TIP

Your experience with pushback or resistance from others may not look like any of these examples. Because pushback and resistance are a matter of perception, you get to decide which reactions feel like pushback, even if someone's remarks or observations are completely innocent or not intended to challenge you. You also get to decide how to respond. I recommend that you avoid saying, "You're being a boundary pusher!" It's tempting, and I've done it myself. The problem with telling someone what they're doing is that they may not think they're pushing your boundaries. The other danger of labeling what they're doing as boundary pushing is that it may lead to an unproductive "No I'm not," "Yes you are" debate. That's why I urge you not to tell other people what they're doing but to use the tools in this chapter instead.

Expecting Pushback Makes Boundary Setting Easier

Remember the last time you changed the way you did something? Maybe you changed your eating habits, stopped watching hours of TV every night, or quit drinking or using drugs.

When I was in my mid 20s, I made a life-changing decision to stop using what I came to realize was my drug of choice. After achieving some professional and financial success that was beyond what the average 22-year-old probably expects, I stepped a bit too far over to the dark side (and danced late into the night!). The consequences of my drug use started to frighten me, and I knew I had to stop. Immediately.

When I made this decision, the first thing I noticed in my relationships was that the people I'd been going to bars with, hanging out with, and using drugs with weren't thrilled with my decision, even though (at the time) I was still drinking. Within what seemed to me a relatively short time, the friendships where using drugs was a common denominator simply faded away.

I tell you this story not to suggest that you're going to lose all your friends if you set boundaries, but to illustrate that when you change, the people around you are impacted — even when the changes you make are the best choices for you.

REMEMBER

Improving or getting healthier in any area of your life changes your existing relationships and creates new relationships with people who are on the same path as you.

When you begin implementing and improving your boundaries, you'll get pushback and resistance. You can count on it. In fact, I'd like you to expect it. Because when you understand that it's a natural phenomenon like clouds and thunderstorms, you won't be surprised, and you won't need to waste time being appalled and outraged when someone says, "Oh, there you go again with your boundaries." (Expect an eyeroll too!)

If you want to have some fun with resistance and pushback, you can adopt a kind of "Bring it on" or "Go ahead — make my day" attitude of courageous invincibility. (Just for the record, I don't recommend you say these statements out loud.) When you bring this kind of mindset to negative reactions to your boundary work, it gets easier, feels lighter — and maybe even fun.

RESPONSES MAY BE UNPREDICTABLE

Remember that other people's responses to your boundaries belong to them. To understand what that means, take a moment to notice that not everyone responds to your new limits in the same way. Here are a few ways people may respond to your new and improved boundary-setting skills:

- Some people will become highly offended, reactive, and put off by the changes in you.

- Some people may think your new boundaries skills are interesting or even intriguing. They may tell you, "Something is different about you."

- Some people will absolutely love your new boundaries because they delight in seeing you change and grow. They appreciate that you're taking care of yourself by setting boundaries that help you feel more peaceful and protected.

I wish I could tell you that most people fall in the last category, but the truth is, you get stronger in the gym by experiencing resistance, and the same is true with boundary work.

Keep in mind that more than one of the possibilities I mention here may be a response to the same boundary. For example, I've had the experience of creating a boundary, getting a highly offended response, and then later being told how much my boundary was appreciated. Go figure!

Accepting That Boundaries Cheerleaders Are Unicorns

If you take to heart my recommendation to expect pushback, you'll significantly shorten the turmoil you feel when your partner, family, or friends are less than thrilled about the changes you're making with boundaries. But I do want to acknowledge how frustrating it can be to feel unsupported or even scorned when all you're trying to do is take care of yourself and feel better. You'd think the people you love and the people who love you would want that for you too, right?

It's not that they don't want what's best for you. It's just that they're used to the way things are. They're used to you being a certain way — the way you were before you had a better grasp of personal boundaries. People feel a certain level of grief around change and saying good-bye to the comfortable, reliable way they've always interacted with you.

The people most likely to push back on your boundaries are the people closest to you — the people with whom you have longstanding, long-term committed relationships. These are the kinds of relationships where most boundary issues occur. The more you can accept that pushback is part of improving your boundaries, the less you'll struggle with creating difficult boundaries, and the better you'll feel.

As you go through this transition, it's important to have other people (or this book) to support you when you're feeling misunderstood or wondering if you're doing the right thing. As your boundaries improve, you'll attract people into your life who have better boundaries too. They'll become part of your support system and can encourage you when important people in your life disapprove of what you're doing, when you're simply trying to take care of yourself.

TIP

When you get resistance or pushback from a boundary you set, you'll probably wonder if you're doing it wrong. You may assume that resistance is a sign that you've made a mistake. If you're not sure, check it out with a trusted person who understands how boundaries work. Most of the time you'll see that you're doing fine. You're just dealing with the inevitable pushback.

Anticipating and Navigating the Inevitable Resistance

Now that you understand (and hopefully accept) that pushback and resistance are unavoidable when you start setting boundaries, it's time to explore all the ways you can respond when someone doesn't like your boundaries.

You can handle and manage pushback in many ways. In this section, I give you the following nine options for anticipating and navigating resistance:

>> Sticking to your talking points

>> Parroting a response

>> Acknowledging without agreeing

>> Validating without condoning

>> Empathizing without backtracking

>> Inquiring without caving

>> Entering into silence

>> Taking a relational time-out

>> Assessing the value of the relationship

Throughout this section, you find out how to acknowledge and even validate what someone says without needing to agree with them. And you see how sometimes you must be honest with yourself about how important a certain relationship (or person) is to you.

TIP

When someone persistently pushes back on your limits, they're giving you valuable information about who they are and their ability to show up in relationships. This information may lead you to change how you interact with that person or to end the relationship altogether.

Sticking to your talking points

Politicians and pundits have known for a long time that having a list of talking points (specific statements they want to focus on) is a powerful and indispensable tool. The reason they make lists of talking points and have an annoying habit of not answering questions is that they're fully committed to getting their message out. They're well aware that if they let the interviewer run the show and obediently answer the interviewer's questions, they're wasting the precious time they have to drive their message home.

Anytime you need to have a difficult or high-stakes conversation, make a list of talking points in advance. Your talking points are unique to the situation, what's most important to you, and what you want to accomplish.

Here are some questions to ask yourself to create a list of talking points in any situation:

>> What is the outcome I want from this conversation?

>> What are the most important statements or questions I need to make or ask in this conversation?

>> If the other person tries to distract me from what's most important to me or what I want to accomplish, which talking point(s) can I say or repeat to avoid the conversation being sidetracked from my intended purpose?

To understand how using talking points can help you navigate the challenges of creating boundaries, imagine a scenario that's probably fairly common. You want to talk to your brother about an agreement you made with him 9 months ago. The agreement was that he could live with you for "a couple months" while he got back on his feet after he lost his job. He's now been living in your basement for 8 months. Not only has he failed to get another job, but he also spends most of his time playing video games.

You've reached your limit. You want him to either get a job within the next month or find another place to live. Here are your talking points for your conversation with your brother, followed by how you might present it:

1. **We had an agreement, and this is what happened.** For this talking point you might say, "We had an agreement that you would live here for a couple months until you got back on your feet. It's been 8 months now and you don't have a job."

2. **I need to create a new agreement with you and be accountable for my part in why the original agreement didn't work.** For this talking point you might say, "I need to clean this up because after you lived here for a few months I didn't say anything, and that's on me. Since our agreement was for a couple months, I should have said something earlier. So, I want to create a new agreement with you."

3. **This is the new agreement I want to create and what I'm willing to do.** For this talking point you might say, "If you want to live here, you'll need to have a job. I'm willing to give you a month [or some other specific deadline] to find a job. If you don't have a job by that date, I can't offer you a place to stay any longer."

TIP

When you're preparing to have a difficult conversation that involves boundaries, make a list of your talking points ahead of time. If the other person tries to change the subject or you're tempted to stray from your talking points, all you need to do is look at your list, pick one, and repeat it.

When you tell your brother you want to create a new agreement with him, he may respond by saying something like "Are you kidding me? Do you know what the job market out there is like?" This is a crucial moment for you. You can take the detour he's offering and explain to him why you're not kidding or get into an analysis of the current job market. But remember, neither of these topics is on your list of talking points. You can simply say, "I'm not kidding. I want to create a new agreement with you. I'm willing to give you a month to find a job. If you don't have a job in a month, I can't offer you a place to stay any longer."

If you choose to take the unplanned detour offered by your brother, your attempt to set a boundary will be a waste of time at best, or at worst, a complete failure if the conversation goes off the rails or becomes contentious and volatile.

If your brother doesn't directly respond to your talking points, all you need to do is start at the beginning with your first talking point or pick up at the talking point in your list that fits the conversation. Sticking to talking points means that any attempt to get you to talk about anything else will be futile. If you stick to your talking points, the other person has no choice but to either respond to them or end the conversation.

Parroting a response

When I was in my mid 20s, a friend of mine had a pet parrot named Chico. When she decided to go to massage school, she asked her friends if they'd be willing to let her practice massage on them, so of course I took her up on her offer.

Chico's cage was in the same room as the table where everyone got their massage. Chico didn't have an extensive vocabulary, but he'd completely mastered "Pretty bird!" He'd also mastered whistling. Not whistling a song, but hooting out the kind of catcall whistle every woman dreads.

Getting a massage in the same room as Chico was sometimes, well, interesting. And funny. The repeated exposure to Chico's whistle (and the laughter it created) also seemed to soften the sting of all the past associations with being heckled or harassed on the street.

My point is that parrots have stock phrases no matter what is said to them. You can use the same tactic by simply parroting a response to pushback or resistance by

>> Repeating what someone says

>> Responding with a short, simple phrase like "I hear you" (See the nearby sidebar.)

The advantage of repeating what the other person says, or responding with a short, simple phrase (which you can also find later in this chapter), is that it helps you avoid saying things you don't want to say, reacting, or engaging in off-topic issues when someone is trying to budge you off your boundary.

For example, if someone says that your boundaries are hurting your relationship, you can repeat what they said by stating, "I hear you think my boundaries are hurting our relationship." Or you can simply say, "I hear you."

Repeating what the other person said takes "I hear you" to the next level. When you repeat what they said without any additional comment, it signals to them that you're crystal clear and standing firm. The strength of this technique is that it sends a message that the chances of getting you to backtrack on your boundary are slim to zero.

When someone expresses their opinion or perception (as in, "I think your boundaries are hurting our relationship"), they're not stating a fact. Everyone is entitled to their opinion no matter how outlandish, outrageous, or seemingly delusional it is. That's why it's not advisable, or even useful, to debate or defend yourself when someone expresses their opinion. It's not always easy, but it's often the wisest choice.

If you were taught to be friendly or nice, simply repeating word for word what another person says may seem cold or uncaring. However, the tone and facial expression that go with the words can make a big difference in how the words are received. Also, keep in mind that you're replying with words the other person actually said, so you're giving a neutral, noncombative response. The practice of repeating what you heard is actually a boundary in and of itself. The other person is expressing their view, and you're responding to their view without debate or argument.

"I HEAR YOU"

This simple three-word phrase is one of my all-time favorite tools for, well, keeping my mouth shut.

I've found that saying "I hear you" helps me avoid saying things I don't want to say or getting involved in conversations or arguments that don't serve me, or anyone else. "I hear you" is especially useful when you get resistance and pushback about your boundaries.

Responding with "I hear you" accomplishes two important things:

- It's an acknowledgment to the other person that you heard them so they have no doubt that they were heard.
- It protects you from:
  - Becoming defensive
  - Backtracking on your boundary
  - Saying something you told yourself you wouldn't say
  - Saying something you'll regret

Acknowledging without agreeing

Acknowledging without agreeing is a skill you can use when you're getting resistance to your boundaries. This skill keeps you in the conversation but doesn't sidetrack you from your purpose.

What does it mean to acknowledge without agreeing?

Earlier in this chapter, I present a scenario where you're creating a new agreement with your brother that requires him to get a job in order to continue living with you. Imagine that when you tell your brother he needs to get a job within the next few months to keep living with you, he says, "I'm having a hard time getting out there and applying for jobs or sending out résumés." Acknowledging without agreeing would sound like "Yeah, that can be rough."

Your acknowledgment that finding a job can be rough doesn't mean you're backtracking or implying that it's no big deal if he stays in the basement playing video games. You're simply stating the shared knowledge that looking for a job can be challenging.

TIP

Don't worry that acknowledging what another person says will be perceived as weakness. Acknowledging is a way of communicating that you heard the other person; it isn't a concession or an indication that you agree with what they said.

Validating without condoning

To *validate* means to recognize the worthiness or legitimacy of a situation. When you validate another person, you're confirming that their experience or perspective has value or is legitimate.

Using the example of your jobless brother, here's a response to his statement about applying for jobs and sending résumés that illustrates validating without condoning:

> I know it's hard for you to put yourself out there. I remember what it was like the last time you were job searching.

Notice that you're not saying that his being unemployed for the foreseeable future is acceptable to you, which would be condoning his behavior.

REMEMBER

Where acknowledging sticks to facts, validating is more personal. Validating acknowledges not only that you heard the other person, but also that you can understand where they're coming from.

Empathizing without backtracking

To *empathize* with someone means you understand and you're sensitive to their feelings, thoughts, and experiences. Empathy is a more intimate or deeper response than acknowledgment or validation. Empathy often includes emotion or feeling, and sometimes includes vulnerable self-disclosure by the person who's responding empathically.

Using the same example of your brother who needs to get a job, here's an empathic response:

> I think I have a good idea of exactly how you're feeling. I don't think I ever told you, but when I was laid off a couple years ago, I was depressed for weeks. I lost my confidence, and the longer it went on, the harder it was for me to put myself out there. I get it. Is there something I can do that would make it easier for you to get your job applications and résumés out?

This is a highly empathic response. Not only did you join your brother in understanding his current situation, but you also shared something very personal and vulnerable about yourself. You don't necessarily need to add a question at the end of an empathic response, but the offer to help in this scenario shows your concern, understanding, and support.

TIP

If you struggle to empathize with other people, you can ask yourself a simple question: "What would I be thinking [or feeling or doing] if I was in the same situation as this person?" Your answers to this question give you clues about what the other person may be experiencing. If you want to confirm what you believe they may be feeling you can ask them, "Are you feeling . . .?"

You may worry that if you respond empathically (especially if you offer to help), you'll be perceived as weak or backtracking on your boundary. But if you review the example of an empathic response carefully, you see that it's a simple statement of self-disclosure and an offer to help. There's no hint or suggestion that you don't intend to follow through with your boundary. This is a great example of how boundaries can be both firm and loving.

Inquiring without caving

One of the best-kept secrets about conversation and communication in general is that it's far more powerful to ask good questions than to give good answers. If you're skeptical that this is true, think back to the last time you spent more than 15 minutes in casual conversation with someone who didn't ask you one question.

Questions signal that the questioner is curious, and they're an excellent way to get to know another person. Unless you're in full-on interrogation mode, towering over someone who's sitting in a hard metal chair in a dark room with a bare lightbulb over their head, most people love answering questions — especially about themselves.

When you're on the receiving end of resistance or pushback, asking questions is an excellent way to find out more about what the other person is thinking or why they're behaving the way they are.

In the example of your brother who needs to get a job, you can ask him:

>> What kind of job would you love to have?

>> What do you think is making it hard for you to put yourself out there?

>> What's your favorite job, of all the jobs you've had?

>> What do you imagine you'd do if the roles were reversed, and I was the one living at your house unemployed?

>> How long do you think I should give you to get a job?

When you read the last question, you may think, "I can't ask him that! What if he says he thinks I should give him at least 5 years?!" Here's where the principle of inquiring without caving shines. You can ask any question that comes to mind, but the answers you get don't require you to do anything, including backtracking on the boundary you set.

A question followed by a response is a complete exchange of information — full stop.

TIP

When asking questions of someone who's pushing back on your boundaries, do your best to maintain an attitude of curiosity rather coming from a place of blaming or shaming.

Entering into silence

Silence is a powerful tool, but it must be used wisely. Silence has been called golden, which it is. But silence can also be used as a weapon to dismiss, shame, or shun another person.

The best time to enter into simple silence if someone is resisting a limit you've created is when you've said everything you have to say, and you've listened to everything they have to say (or they're repeating themselves for the second, third, or fourth time).

If you struggle not to defend yourself when someone isn't happy with something you've said or done, or you have a habit of needing to talk things through and come to an understanding every time you have a disagreement with another person, silence will feel uncomfortable. The danger is that the more you discuss or defend your boundary, the greater the chance you'll start doubting yourself, or even decide that your boundary was "wrong."

If you're confident that you've listened, acknowledged, and perhaps even validated or empathized to the best of your ability, silence may be your next best option. If you're feeling relatively calm and know that there's nothing more to do, simply breathe in and out and enjoy the silence.

TIP

If you choose to use silence when getting pushback, don't let it go on too long. If the silence lasts longer than is comfortable for you, you can ask, "Is there anything else you'd like to say?" If the person says *no*, you can end the conversation and go about your day.

Taking a relational time-out

REMEMBER

Throughout this book I use the word *relational* to describe a set of healthy relationship skills that includes being respectful, transparent (open), using healthy personal boundaries, and demonstrating through one's behavior that no person is better than or less than another person.

I've never been a fan of putting toddlers in time-out, but I'm a huge fan of adults taking a time-out when needed, especially in the following situations:

>> You've reached a roadblock or an impasse in a conversation, and one or both of you are simply stating, restating, and re-restating their positions.

>> The conversation has become extremely emotional for one or both of you and is no longer productive.

>> One or both of you have made threatening statements.

>> One or both of you are becoming loud, hostile, aggressive, or emotionally or physically abusive.

>> You're feeling overwhelmed and know that you need to take a break.

Here are the six steps for taking a relational time-out.

1. **Recognize that you're overwhelmed or emotionally flooded.** One or all of the following may occur:

   - You notice physical signs of distress such as increased heart rate (over 100 beats per minute [bpm]), changes in tone of voice, increased body heat, or skin flushing.

   - You shut down and become unresponsive as a strategy to avoid conflict.

   - You raise your voice or begin expressing your anger nonverbally by driving recklessly, slamming doors, or engaging in other threatening behaviors.

2. **Tell the other person that you need to take a time-out.** Tell them, "I'm overwhelmed [or I'm not in a good place to have this conversation] right now, and I need to take a time-out."

3. **Tell the other person the amount of time you need and where you're going or where you plan to be.** Make sure you give yourself plenty of time to process what's happening for you and to get grounded and centered again. For example, if you think you need an hour, say you need two hours.

4. **Take additional time, if needed.** If you realize while taking a time-out that you need more time, let the other person know as soon as possible.

5. **Be accountable about your commitment.** Return at the time you said you would.

6. **Reengage about the hot-button topic.** When you return, either ask the other person if they want to reengage about the issue or schedule a mutually agreeable time in the future to talk about it.

TIP

If your heart rate goes above 100 bpm during a conversation, bring your awareness to your breathing and begin paying attention to your thoughts and emotions. If bringing attention to your breathing, thoughts, and emotions doesn't get your heart rate under 100 bpm within 2 to 3 minutes, consider taking a time-out. (You can measure your heart rate manually, with a pulse oximeter, or using any wearable device that tracks heart rate.)

The following are time-out do's and don'ts:

>> *Do* take ownership of your need for a time-out. In other words, don't rely on the other person to call for a time-out when you know you need one.

>> *Do* reengage about the hot-button topic after the time-out is over.

>> *Don't* use time-outs as a strategy for avoiding or delaying talking about a topic that's difficult or painful for you.

- >> *Don't* say, "You're upset, and I think you need a time-out." Refrain from making the other person the reason a time-out is needed. Use *I* statements and take ownership of your need for a time-out and for your own emotions.

- >> *Don't* refuse to accept the other person's request for a time-out by physically following them, continuing to talk to them after they requested a time-out, or refusing to let them leave the room or building.

WARNING

If someone refuses to let you leave when you ask for a time-out, you're being held hostage. If you feel that you're in danger and that the other person has become irrational or dangerous, call 911.

Assessing the value of the relationship

If you've had frequent unpleasant encounters with someone who pushes back and challenges most or all of your boundaries, you may want to consider how important the relationship is to you.

Only you can evaluate the balance sheet of what you're getting versus what you're receiving in the relationship. You may determine that the pushback and complaining you're getting from the person are a small price to pay for their many positive qualities. But if the balance sheet comes up short in the positive qualities column, it may be time to phase out or end the relationship.

Collecting Go-To Responses for Your Tool Kit

In this section, I share more phrases or responses you can use to manage resistance. But before I do, I want to revisit the list of examples of pushback from the previous section "Defining Pushback and Resistance," and give you some potential responses:

- >> **Why are you being so uptight/selfish/self-centered?** You'll be tempted to be defensive when you receive this pushback, but I recommend, "That's interesting. You think I'm being uptight/selfish/self-centered?" If they say, "Yes," you can reply, "That's interesting," or "I hear you."

- >> **You and your boundaries!** No response is needed, except maybe a smile (but only if it feels genuine for you).

>> **You've never said that before. Why do you have to change the way we've always done things?** There are many potential responses to this pushback, but you can try this one: "That's true. I've never said this before." You can stop there, or you can add something like "You can keep things the way you want to, but I'm changing this."

>> **You never had a problem with this before. Why now?** You can say, "You know — you're right; I didn't have a problem with it before, but I do now." If the other person continues to pressure you to explain yourself, simply repeat what you said, word for word. You can repeat what you said as many times as it takes the other person to realize that their efforts to make you explain yourself aren't yielding the result they want.

>> **Your boundaries are hurting our relationship.** One potential response is "I hear you. I see it differently." Or "That's interesting. I feel like they're helping me a lot."

>> **Why are you punishing me?** If you feel 100 percent confident that there's no punishment in your boundary, you can respond to this one with a question: "Am I punishing you?" If the other person says you are, you can ask them to explain how you're punishing them. They're likely to say something like "You won't go to the office Christmas party. You know how important that is to me." To which you can reply, "I do know how important it is to you. I don't want to go to the party, and if I go when I don't want to, it will be a punishment to myself. Thanks for understanding."

>> **We're family! This is what families do for each other!** One potential response is "We're family; that's true. We just have different ideas about how boundaries work, and that's okay."

>> **Whose idea was it for you to say/do this?** One light-hearted response is to answer the question with this one: "Mine?" Or if you'd like another option, you can blame me and this book.

You could be right!

I must give credit to a client for this brilliant response to boundary pushing. She adopted this simple four-word response and used it when she was talking to a certain family member who had a particularly bad case of believing that their way was the right way.

Here's what this response sounds like in practice:

Boundaries Resister: "I can't believe you said no to your sister when she asked you to babysit her six children for two weeks while she goes to Hawaii. That was selfish of you."

You: "You could be right!"

Boundaries Resister: "Ever since you started setting boundaries, you've been really hard to get along with. I think all these boundaries are hurting our relationship."

You: "You could be right."

REMEMBER

When you say, "You could be right," you're not saying that the other person is right and you're wrong. You're also not agreeing with them. You're simply expressing the possibility that they may be right, and you're preserving your right to have another opinion.

I'll need to get back to you about that

Telling another person that you need to get back to them is a highly effective strategy — for pushback and resistance, and in many other situations as well.

Here are some circumstances where buying some extra time is particularly helpful:

» When someone is pressuring you and you're not sure how to respond

» When someone tries to override a boundary you set

» When someone attempts to negotiate or renegotiate a boundary with you when you're not interested and you're struggling to respond with a definitive *no*

» When you're feeling emotionally or physically exhausted or not well

» Anytime you're feeling weak or wobbly about your boundaries

TIP

The acronym HALT (Hungry, Angry, Lonely, Tired) is a great tool to assess your level of preparedness for dealing with difficult conversations or navigating pushback to your boundaries.

Go to the Oh! zone

The Oh! zone is a tool I picked up about 20 years ago in a 12-step group. A woman in the group shared that anytime her husband said something she found extremely triggering, provocative, or ridiculous, she would pull this highly effective two-letter response out of her communication toolbox.

Responding with a simple "Oh!" is an excellent strategy to protect you from saying something you'd rather not say. It's also nice to have when you can't think of any meaningful response to what you just heard.

"Oh!" is deliciously vague, essentially meaningless, and undeniably neutral. It tends to fly under the radar and rarely evokes a negative or challenging response.

Consider the Oh! zone a multipurpose response tool, effective in a variety of situations.

Practice boundaries aikido

The Japanese martial art of aikido (aye-*key*-doe) has always fascinated me. What makes aikido different from other martial arts is that it teaches the practitioner how to use the energy or force of the attacker to deflect or defeat them, rather than relying on the force of the person under attack. In other words, it's based on principles of nonresistance or going with the flow.

The Aikido Association of America describes aikido this way:

> In Aikido we strive to work in cooperation with a partner, still employing effective technique against an energetic and realistic attack, yet doing so by blending with the attack and redirecting its energy back to the attacker.

A simple example of how aikido can work: An attacker runs straight toward you. You lean forward just before they reach you, using the energy of their speed to essentially "guide" them over your back so that they fall behind you.

The spiritual teacher Eckhart Tolle expresses another version of boundaries aikido in his book *A New Earth: Awakening to Your Life's Purpose* (Penguin):

> When enthusiasm encounters obstacles . . . it never attacks but . . . by yielding or embracing turns the opposing energy into a helpful one.

Boundaries aikido is a great option anytime you're in a situation where the natural consequence of another person's behavior is as effective or even more effective than a boundary. Using boundaries aikido not only saves you time and energy but may be a more powerful consequence for the other person.

One of the most effective uses of boundaries aikido is when someone is criticizing or even verbally attacking you in the presence of other people or in public. If you have no need to protect yourself (meaning you're not in physical danger), you can choose to say nothing, letting the other person's words or actions speak for themselves. I've used this skill many times, and it's powerful — provided you're clear, centered, and grounded.

Don't use boundaries aikido with a physically aggressive or abusive person. This tool should be used only when you're confident that you're not in danger.

CONNECT WITH AN ACCOUNTABILITY PARTNER

If you struggle to manage resistance or pushback and find yourself regularly caving to other people's objections, detours, or pity parties, it's time to get help from a boundaries coach, mentor, or therapist. (Chapter 20 has information to help you find a life coach or mental health professional.)

Remember: Asking for help is courageous and vulnerable. Some people feel embarrassed about needing help or working with a life coach or therapist. But the truth is, most highly successful people are constantly receiving coaching and asking for feedback or advice. Their desire to improve and their awareness that they can't see what they can't see motivates them to get information, help, or support when needed.

Don't hesitate to get help — ever.

IN THIS CHAPTER

» Knowing whom you need to set a boundary with

» Seeing the connection between emotions and boundaries

» Understanding resentment

» Identifying boundary pushers and boundary offenders

» Defining boundary ruptures and boundary violations

» Acknowledging trauma from boundary violations

Chapter **7**

Knowing When You Need to Create a Boundary

When you're getting started with setting boundaries or improving the boundaries skills you already have, you may wonder how to figure out when it's time to set a boundary. It's a good question!

One of the most effective shortcuts for knowing when you need to set a boundary is paying attention to your emotions, especially feelings of anger and resentment. These are the emotions most people experience when a limit or boundary is challenged, disregarded, or violated.

In this chapter, I show you that boundary setting isn't just about setting boundaries with others. There are some boundaries you must set with yourself. I also explain the connection between your emotions and the boundaries you may need to create, along with how resentment sabotages the boundary-setting process and what to do about it.

I give you six common characteristics of people who are chronic boundary pushers and boundary violators. You begin to understand the difference between boundary violations and boundary ruptures, and see how some boundary violations create traumatic responses and how you can address them.

Recognizing Whom You're Setting a Boundary With

You set boundaries with two categories of people: yourself and everyone else. See the nearby sidebar "Creating boundaries with yourself" and Chapter 4 for more information on self-boundaries. For boundaries you want to set with other people, it's important to consider who the other person is to you and the role they play in your life.

To better understand what that means, think about a concept I cover in Chapter 3 called Zones of Privacy and Zones of Intimacy. *Zones of Privacy* apply to your personal information, and *Zones of Intimacy* describe the levels of connection you have with other people.

Here are the levels of connection you have with others in the Zones of Intimacy:

1. **Anonymous contacts.** These are people you don't know, such as cashiers, waiters, or clerks.

2. **Acquaintances.** This zone includes coworkers, neighbors, people you know through volunteering or civic organizations, or parents at your children's schools.

3. **Casual friends and extended family.** This level includes people you occasionally spend time with or those you see regularly but have limited contact with.

4. **Intimate platonic (nonsexual) friends, close relatives, and your children.** This level includes close, long-term friends, trusted family members, long-time friends of your family, mentors, and your minor or adult children.

5. **Intimate sexual partners.** This zone doesn't include casual, low- or no-intimacy sexual relationships.

When you're considering creating a boundary that involves another person, it's wise to consider who the person is to you. Zones of Intimacy will help you determine the level of connection you have with the person.

TIP

It's important to determine how close (or not) someone is to you before thinking about setting a boundary. Some people have such an inconsequential role in your life that, practically speaking, you have no need to set a boundary with them.

For example, if the cashier at Walmart stares at you without saying a word as you're checking out and paying for your 39 items and 7 bags of groceries and supplies, you probably won't want to create a boundary with them.

But just for fun, think about your options for setting a boundary with the Walmart cashier:

>> You can move all your stuff to the next checkout lane that appears to have a friendlier cashier.

>> You can decide that you've had enough of Walmart and their staring cashiers and leave, never to return.

>> You can make a request of the staring cashier that they be kinder or more friendly to you. Making a request to create an agreement with the cashier is the only option if you want them to change their behavior.

Notice that the first two examples are within your power to do. The third option requires the participation of the staring cashier.

While it's highly unlikely you'll want to set a boundary with a cashier at Walmart, if you came home from a 2-week business trip and your spouse of 23 years stared at you and didn't speak to you for days, you wouldn't want to ignore their behavior. You'd want to directly address this uncomfortable and disconnecting situation by either making a request that your spouse engage with you or letting them know what you intend to do to take care of yourself if something doesn't change.

Paying Attention to Your Emotions

If it wasn't for your emotions, you'd probably never know that you need to set a boundary. Powerful "negative" emotions like fear, anger, sadness, hurt, guilt, and shame are the most common emotions associated with the need to set boundaries.

There are no negative, bad, or wrong emotions. Your emotions are constantly giving you important information about you and your present experience. Anytime you experience a painful emotion, ask yourself, "Is there a boundary I need to set in this situation?" There may not be, but you can use your emotions to help you figure it out.

REMEMBER

The emotions of guilt and shame often signal a need to set a boundary with yourself. For example, if you feel guilty because you called your partner a "complete and total idiot" to their face for the fifth time this week, you may want to consider creating a boundary with yourself that you'll refrain from this problematic (and unattractive) habit.

Recognizing the signs of anger

Anger is one of the most common emotions you may feel when you need to set a boundary. That's because most people naturally feel angry when another person tries to overstep their boundaries or outright violates a boundary.

Here are some examples of situations where anger — as it relates to boundary setting — is a natural response:

>> Your ex is more than an hour late picking up your son for visitation for the third time this month.

>> When you have a disagreement with your friend, they yell at you and call you names nearly every time.

>> Your supervisor regularly texts you on the weekends despite you letting them know that you're not available outside regular business hours.

>> Your neighbor frequently parks their car in your driveway without telling you or asking permission.

Some people are afraid of anger because of past experiences when expressed anger — their own or others' — felt frightening or dangerous. Or, they may have been taught that anger is bad or undesirable.

You may struggle with anger if:

>> You grew up in a family where one or both of your parents didn't express anger appropriately.

>> You've been criticized for being angry.

>> You've been told that anger is bad by your family, culture, or spiritual/religious community.

If you bristle when you hear the word *anger*, here are some additional words you can use to describe this powerful emotion:

>> Irritation

>> Frustration

>> Indignation

>> Resentment (anger rooted in a belief that you're a victim; see the section "Uncovering Resentment," later in this chapter)

>> Rage

Except for rage, all these words describe ordinary, everyday anger. Rage, on the other hand, is violent, out-of-control anger.

Frequent outbursts of rage can have several root causes, but the most common are:

>> Not having the skills to examine, explore, and question your thoughts

>> Extreme entitlement or grandiosity (self-importance)

>> A history of witnessing another person raging (usually in childhood)

>> A severe mental health disorder

REMEMBER

Anger — like all other emotions — is neither good nor bad. Problems with anger don't happen because someone feels angry, but rather because of how they express it.

Expressing anger in indirect or unskillful ways can cause discomfort or fear in others. On the other hand, when anger is expressed cleanly and directly, it's healthy and relational (respectful and transparent). If you're afraid of your anger and you suppress it, your anger is likely to become more frequent and intense. As medical studies have shown, suppressed anger can lead to health problems like high blood pressure or a heart condition.

TIP

Many women struggle to own their anger because they've been taught or conditioned to believe that expressing anger isn't ladylike or is unattractive. This disempowering belief stops women from asserting and standing up for themselves, even when their boundaries are being violated. *Owning* your anger means recognizing, acknowledging, and expressing it cleanly and directly.

To illustrate that not all anger is negative or bad, here are some of the gifts of anger:

>> Anger can be a sign that something in your life isn't working well or isn't working the way you want it to. Anger gives you valuable clues about what needs to change so you can feel more peaceful or calm.

>> Anger is a common sign that a limit or boundary has been crossed, which helps you more quickly identify what you need to do to protect or take care of yourself.

>> Anger can be a sign that you need to practice more self-care, speak up for yourself, or stand up for yourself in some way.

>> You're more likely to get your needs met and avoid creating resentment and grievances when you acknowledge and cleanly express anger.

>> When you express your anger cleanly and appropriately to another person, you're being intimate with that person because you're telling them who you are in that moment.

Identifying the anger underlying repetitive stories

A telltale sign that you haven't faced, processed, or owned your anger is when you either tell the same story or replay a past incident in your mind over, and over, and over, and over. If you can't see the anger (or other painful emotions) buried in the repetitive story, you won't recognize the opportunity to set a boundary or take care of yourself.

Repeating stories about how you've been victimized or how the world or other people are out to get you causes you to get stuck in a victim mindset. Engaging in self-inquiry through the boundary-setting process helps you:

>> Identify your anger or other painful emotions which I explain in Chapter 14.

>> Discover the truth about the incident or situation, rather than focusing only on your thoughts and perceptions (see Chapter 14).

>> Find options for addressing the problematic situation, which I discuss in Chapters 15, 16, and 17.

Feeling overwhelmed and stressed

Two strong indicators that you need to set a limit are that you feel overwhelmed or stressed.

As I was writing this chapter, I became curious about the dictionary definition of the word *overwhelm*. English speakers immediately understand the meaning of the word *over*, but *whelm* isn't a commonly used word in the English language.

Merriam-Webster's definition of *whelm* is:

> To turn (something, such as a dish or vessel) upside down usually to cover something: cover or engulf completely with usually disastrous effect

Disastrous effect sounds bad enough, but when you put the word *over* in front of *whelm*, you get overly disastrous effects. Yikes! This is exactly how you may feel when you're overwhelmed — that you're facing an intensely disastrous present or future.

When you're overwhelmed, it can mean you have too much to do, too many feelings, too many responsibilities, too many people wanting your time/money/energy, too much on your plate, and so on. It's like a flashing red neon sign screaming, "Reduce! Eliminate! Limit! Cut back! Back off! Boundaries!"

TIP

The next time you're feeling overwhelmed and stressed ask yourself, "Where's the 'too much' here? How can I make this easier? What thoughts or emotions do I need to process? What can I delegate or how can I lighten my load?"

Understanding the reasons behind complaints

It may sound hard to believe, but if you're honest, you may (reluctantly) agree with me that complaining is kind of fun. If it wasn't fun, people wouldn't spend so much time doing it! But along with telling repetitive stories, complaining is a way to nurture a sense of being a victim or establish a feeling of superiority over others.

For example, if I complain about the outrageous, self-centered email I got from a friend, I'm not-so-subtly implying that I know better than they do, or that I would never send the email they sent, or that I would never act the way they did.

Complaining rarely includes even a hint of an intention, desire, or plan to take meaningful action to resolve the problem. Of course, everyone complains from time to time — that's normal. But if complaining has become a part-time hobby for you, you're participating in your own disempowerment.

If you want to shift from complaining to a more productive and empowered approach to life, anytime you catch yourself complaining, ask yourself:

>> What's the intention or purpose behind my complaining?

>> Do I need to do something to take care of myself in this situation?

>> Do I need to set a boundary with someone, or even myself?

You may find that underneath your complaining is fear or a lack of courage to do what you know you need to do.

TIP

Turning complaints into requests is one of my favorite relationship skills from the work of Terry Real, couples therapist and author. Turning a complaint into a request requires you to objectively examine what you're complaining about and come up with a request that may transform the complaint into a solution. I highly recommend putting this tool in your relationship communication toolbox.

The good news is, you're in the driver's seat when it comes to complaining. You can decide to curb your complaining and start focusing on what you can do instead, which may mean setting a boundary.

Uncovering and Facing Resentment

Resentment is a highly problematic emotion (related to anger) that must be uncovered and faced if you want your boundaries work to be effective.

Here are a few signs that you may be resentful:

>> You're frequently irritable or angry, often for reasons you're not aware of.

>> You have a long-standing pattern of seeing yourself as a victim of other people, circumstances, or life in general.

>> You regularly ask other people to explain their behavior with questions like "Why did you . . .?" or "Why are you . . .?"

>> You frequently complain and tell repetitive grievance stories.

Uncovering resentment can be difficult and painful, especially when another person has hurt or betrayed you. Past wounds may cause you to feel entitled to your resentment, and this entitlement will keep you stuck in the past and disempower you.

Facing your resentments is courageous because it propels you out of the passivity of feeling like a victim and into action. You're always free to stay exactly where you are, but if you want to live a peaceful, harmonious, and joyful life, you must uncover resentment and replace it with ownership of your life and your happiness.

Defining resentment

Merriam-Webster defines *resentment* as "a feeling of indignant displeasure or persistent ill will at something regarded as a wrong, insult, or injury." The words *indignant* and *persistent* are key to understanding the negative power of resentment, because resentment is anger that has become a habit.

My all-time favorite definition of resentment comes from Pia Mellody, author and Senior Fellow of Meadows Behavioral Healthcare. She defines resentment as "victim anger." Think of resentment as a combination of the emotion of anger coupled with a belief that you're a victim.

Every person at one time or another will be a victim or will be victimized. However, once the incident or situation of being victimized ends, remaining a victim is a choice. Taking on, clinging to, or nurturing a victim identity is disempowering. When you latch on to the idea of yourself as a victim, you become a victim of your choice to identify as one.

Identifying as a victim is not only disempowering for you but also harmful to your relationships. Having a habit of creating or nurturing resentments makes developing and maintaining relationships extremely difficult.

Seeing how resentment prevents solutions

Similar to complaining, holding on to a resentment can feel preferable to the alternative of doing the hard work of seeing the truth of a situation or setting a boundary.

THINK ABOUT IT

People sometimes choose not to get help for a long-standing resentment or fail to work on improving their boundaries because they know they'll have to make difficult, life-changing decisions they've been putting off. What they can't see is that the work they're avoiding has the power to change their life permanently for the better.

Holding on to resentments and feeling like a victim naturally prevents you from solving the problem that created the resentment. That's because you believe your problem is someone else's fault, meaning the only way for you to feel better is if the other person fixes the problem.

When you see yourself as the starting point for creating what you want to experience, you develop a healthy dislike of resentment. You recognize how dangerous resentment is to you and to your relationships.

Discovering the boundaries underneath resentments

To discover the boundary underneath a resentment, you must first get clear about the resentment. A clear description of the resentment points you to the potential boundary you may want to set.

Here are some examples of common resentments and potential boundaries:

>> You resent that your spouse (or roommate) doesn't participate in housework at the level you think they should. Possible boundaries you can create or actions to take include:

- Stop doing any housework that creates resentment for you. This is a boundary (stop doing housework), which you have the power to create.

- Hire a housekeeper to do the housework you don't want to do. If you have the ability and means to hire a housekeeper, you can resolve the issue yourself.

- Talk to your spouse (or roommate), make a request, and create an agreement about who is responsible for specific tasks or chores. You have the power to create a boundary by making a request and entering into an agreement (provided an agreement is reached).

>> You resent that when you spend time with your best friend, they talk 80 percent of the time. Possible boundaries you can create or actions to take include:

- Make an effort to speak up more often when you're spending time with your friend.

- Tell your friend that your conversations feel unbalanced, and you'd like them to feel more balanced. That means you'll be speaking up more and taking responsibility for getting what you want.

- Request that your friend be more mindful about balancing your conversations. You can create an agreement that the two of you will do your best to have more balanced conversations and that both of you will speak up if the conversation feels unbalanced.

>> You resent that one of the team members you supervise at work is always late to meetings. Possible boundaries you can create or actions to take include:

- Have a conversation with your team member. Create an agreement with the team member to be on time to meetings by making a request and receiving a *yes* from them.

- If you have an agreement with the team member to be on time and they're violating the agreement, you can impose a consequence for arriving late to meetings.

- Fire the team member for repeatedly violating the agreement.

» You resent that your spouse spends too much money. Possible boundaries you can create or actions to take include:

- Make a request of your spouse to limit spending to a specific amount and create an agreement with your spouse.

- Cancel credit cards that are in both of your names. (Because your name is on the account, you don't need their approval or permission, but I do recommend that you communicate your intention before taking action.)

- Separate your money from your spouse's.

If you want to eliminate resentments, take time to identify and describe them in detail. Resentments typically fall into one of three categories. Below is a list of those categories, followed by the action to take for each:

» **Resentments you eliminate by changing your behavior.** For example, if you don't like having lunch with your friend who spends 80 percent of the lunch date talking nonstop, you can decide to balance the conversation and follow through by speaking more when you're together.

» **Resentments you eliminate (or make progress on) by making a request to create an agreement.** If you resent your partner because they don't tell you when they go to the grocery store, for example, and you think they should, you can ask them to let you know when they go to the store so that you can tell them if you need them to pick something up. (See Chapters 2 and 17 for more information about expectations and creating agreements.)

» **Resentments you eliminate by accepting the truth or reality of a situation.** When you see the faulty logic in your resentments, the power they hold over you lessens or disappears. For example, if you resent your sister for having a house on the lake when you don't have one, what you're really thinking is that you're a victim of your sister because she has something you don't have. Believing that you're a victim because someone has something you want is flawed thinking.

Recognizing Boundary Pushers and Offenders

Being able to spot people who push and resist boundaries is a skill that not only saves you time and frustration but also makes your life saner and safer.

In this section, I discuss the following signs that you're dealing with a boundary pusher or boundary offender:

>> Not taking *no* for an answer

>> Talking at you, not with you

>> Ignoring rules, limits, or norms

>> Ridiculing your attempts to set limits

>> Breaking agreements or commitments repeatedly

>> Noticing your own body sensations and intuitions

You may not be put off or offended by some of these behaviors, and that's okay. However, these are behaviors that many people find annoying, upsetting, or disturbing. Some are abusive and offending.

Not taking "no" for an answer

When someone refuses to take *no* for an answer, they're violating a boundary. *No* is a nonnegotiable boundary, which means it's not open to discussion or negotiation. (See Chapter 12 for more information about nonnegotiable boundaries.)

TIP

People who regularly don't take *no* for an answer are giving you important information about themselves: They don't have the ability to honor and respect other people's boundaries. Until they demonstrate through a change of behavior that they can accept your *no* the first time, it's foolish to expect them to show up any other way.

Since you occasionally encounter people who don't accept *no* for an answer, here are a few ways you can respond to them to reinforce your answer:

>> My answer is still *no*.

>> I'm not sure you heard me. I said *no*.

>> We've already discussed this, and my answer is *no*.

>> You can ignore their attempts to get you to change your mind and either end the conversation, change the subject, or leave.

Talking at you, not with you

At its most basic level, the purpose of interpersonal communication is to know others and to be known by them.

People who talk at you and not with you have another idea about communication. Their definition of interpersonal communication is that they talk, and you listen. When they speak, it's an endless monologue that leaves you feeling like a prop. They're a wall of words. They're difficult to listen to, and they're even more difficult to have a conversation with because they only care about one thing: hearing the sound of their own voice.

In the world of personal boundaries, people who have a habit of talking at you rather than with you have poor speaking boundaries. They don't appreciate or consider the negative impact of their boundaryless talking. See Chapter 10 for more information about speaking boundaries.

TIP

If there's someone in your life who simply talks too much, figure out how to respectfully interrupt them. Brainstorm ideas with someone who has good conversation-steering skills. Identify three options for skillful interrupting, experiment with putting them into practice, and find at least one that works for you.

Ignoring rules, limits, or norms

Some boundary pushers and boundary offenders believe that rules, limits, or norms don't apply to them. They prioritize their wants and needs over others and feel entitled to expect their preferences to take precedence.

Here are a few examples of how someone may ignore rules, limits, or norms:

>> They come into your home and change the TV channel, open your curtains, or get into your refrigerator — all without asking or receiving your permission.

>> They routinely ignore traffic lights, stop signs, or other rules of the road.

>> They don't pay their bills on time or take care of financial commitments by the agreed upon time frame.

>> They expect and demand special treatment in a variety of contexts. For example, they cut in line, demand a service that isn't customary, or express indignation when a business policy doesn't align with how they want to do business or be treated.

>> They're always late and become offended when anyone brings their chronic lateness to their attention.

WARNING

People who regularly ignore rules, limits, or norms often have legal problems, including excessive traffic tickets or violations, lawsuits, or even arrests for criminal behavior. If you excuse or overlook a partner or family member's habit of ignoring rules or limits, you may unknowingly put yourself in harm's way.

Ridiculing your attempts to set limits

Being ridiculed or made fun of for the limits you attempt to set is a common experience when you start implementing and improving your boundaries. Change is difficult. It's difficult for you as you're developing new skills, and it's difficult for others who are used to, and comfortable with, the former you.

People, even those closest to you, may say things like:

>> Here we go again. You and your boundaries!

>> Who told you to do this?

>> What's gotten into you? You used to be so easy to get along with.

>> This used to be okay with you. What happened?

>> Oh, I guess you're going to set another boundary. Great.

TIP

If someone in your life repeatedly makes fun of your attempts to set boundaries, collect a few go-to phrases and responses you can use when needed. Refer to Chapter 6 to help you create a list of go-to responses.

The following list includes a few options for responding to the statements in the previous list. Notice that there's a fair amount of humor in most of these responses. Admittedly, humor can sometimes come across as sarcasm. However, humor is one of the most effective (and disarming) ways to respond to someone when they make fun of you for trying to set a boundary. It's challenging at first, but when boundary work becomes easier, responding with lightheartedness and humor becomes second nature to you.

>> **Here we go again. You and your boundaries!**

- What can I tell you? I'm always learning and growing!

- I know! Isn't it a beautiful thing?

>> **Who told you to do this?**

- Me!

- Don't blame me — it's that book on boundaries I'm reading!

>> **What's gotten into you? You used to be so easy to get along with.**

- I don't know . . . boundaries?

- I know — I was a total pushover. I'm loving the new me.

>> **This used to be okay with you. What happened?**

- That's true; it did used to be okay with me. But not anymore.

- People change! I guess it's evolution.

>> **Oh, I guess you're going to set another boundary. Great.**

- That's exactly right. I'm glad it works for you.

- Yeah, I think I'm finally getting the hang of this.

Breaking agreements or commitments repeatedly

Breaking agreements or commitments for no reason is a boundary violation. When someone repeatedly breaks agreements and commitments, they are a *chronic boundary violator*.

If you choose to continue a relationship with someone who repeatedly breaks agreements, you'll experience unnecessary disappointment and stress. You may even face significant financial or health consequences. If someone in your life repeatedly violates agreements and boundaries, see Chapter 20 for details about how to take a boundary to the next level.

TIP

Making a conscious decision to end an agreement or commitment is different from breaking an agreement for no reason. There are many good reasons to end an agreement. Getting new information you didn't have when you made the agreement or changes in you or your situation can cause an agreement you previously made to no longer be workable for you. Ending or renegotiating an agreement requires communicating with the person or organization with whom you have the agreement. (See Chapter 19 for more information about renegotiating agreements.)

Noticing your own body sensations and intuition

When you're with people who feel safe, your body and your nervous system relax. That's why your body and your *intuition* — seemingly out-of-nowhere hunches — are both excellent sources of information for recognizing boundary pushers or boundary violators.

Even if your thoughts or emotions don't seem to register that someone is trying to overstep your limits, your body likely will — provided you know how to listen to it.

Physical sensations like the following may be telling you to pay attention:

>> Increased heat in your body

>> The skin of your neck or face becoming red or flushed

>> Feeling unable to get your words out, or losing your voice as you try to speak or speak up for yourself

>> Increased heart rate, especially if it goes above 100 beats per minute

>> Sweaty palms

Intuition is like a sixth sense and can provide information that may not be accessible through your five senses — sight, sound, smell, taste, and touch. Intuitive hunches often come in the form of surprising thoughts or internal images.

TIP

People sometimes ask if intuition can be considered data or facts. The simple answer is yes, provided you maintain a healthy attitude of provisional certainty about your intuition. *Provisional certainty* means you acknowledge your intuitive hunch while being open to the possibility that it may be partially or completely inaccurate.

You may feel uncertain or reluctant to rely entirely on your body sensations or intuition when you're assessing a situation or another person. However, if the sensation or intuition is strong or powerful, don't ignore it. You can use the experience to gather more information about the person or situation, or delay making a big decision or deepening a connection or relationship with someone.

Understanding Boundary Violations and Ruptures

Understanding the difference between boundary ruptures and boundary violations is crucial for knowing when and how to set a boundary.

In general, boundary ruptures rarely require setting a boundary because they're caused by natural (including human-caused) events that are typically unexpected, unintentional, and completely impersonal. On the other hand, boundary violations often require setting a boundary. They may be intentional, and they usually feel extremely personal.

REMEMBER

Before I describe the difference between boundary violations and boundary ruptures and how they occur, here's a reminder of the four primary categories of boundaries:

>> Physical

>> Sexual

>> Speaking

>> Listening

Classifying boundary violations

A *boundary violation* occurs when a limit or boundary has been crossed, breached, or broken.

Boundaries are violated in two ways:

>> When an agreement or commitment is broken for no reason or without notice or communication

>> When a physical, sexual, speaking, or listening boundary is violated

Examples of broken agreements include:

>> You make an agreement with a friend to meet at a certain time for lunch, and your friend doesn't show up or let you know they can't make it.

>> You enter into an informal agreement or a legal contract, and the terms of the contract or agreement aren't fulfilled.

>> You're in a long-term monogamous relationship, and one person in the relationship has sexual contact with someone outside the relationship.

The importance of the broken agreement or the severity of the breach determines how you respond. For example, the way you respond to a friend who doesn't show up for lunch would be very different from the way you respond to an unfaithful partner. (See Chapters 18 and 19 for more information about how to manage broken agreements.)

TIP

Anytime you feel confused about how to respond or what steps to take after a commitment or boundary is broken or violated, rate your level of distress or upset on a scale of 1 to 10, with 10 being the highest level of distress or upset. This rating helps you decide what action, if any, you want to take. Ideally, incidents you rate as a 10 will receive a high-level response, while incidents you rate as a 2 will get a lower-level — or maybe even no — response.

Here are some examples of boundary violations involving the four primary categories of physical, sexual, speaking, and listening boundaries:

>> Physical boundary violations:

- Touching someone without their permission

- Touching someone's personal belongings without their permission

- Knowingly exposing another person to a contagious illness

>> Sexual boundary violations:

- Touching someone sexually without their permission

- Touching another person sexually (including a long-term committed partner) when they can't consent to sex because they're asleep, incapacitated, unconscious, or under the influence of drugs or alcohol

- Exposing other people to sexual experiences or material, including nudity, sexual acts, and pornography, without their permission

>> Speaking boundary violations:

- Intentionally implying that another person has less value than you because of their appearance, education, sexual orientation, financial status, and so on

- Yelling, cursing, name-calling, and other expressions of contempt

- Lying or deceiving another person

>> Listening boundary violations:

- Refusing to listen to someone when they're speaking respectfully to you

- Being intentionally distracted while someone is speaking to you
- Using nonverbal communication like eye-rolling, body posture, or facial expressions to signal disapproval, disagreement, or even contempt

Defining boundary ruptures

Boundary ruptures are different from boundary violations because they're completely unintended and unplanned. Boundary ruptures can happen because of another person's actions, or due to natural causes such as weather-related events.

Thanks to a dog named Cecil from Pittsburgh, I have a real-life example of a boundary rupture to share with you.

Cecil's humans went to the bank one day and withdrew $4,000 in cash. When they got home, they put the $4,000 on their dining room table. Because of his keen sense of smell, Cecil apparently came to the conclusion that whatever was on the dining table was pretty special (or had, at one time, been in the cash register of a fast-food restaurant). Whatever the reason, Cecil decided to make an afternoon snack of his humans' $4,000.

After recovering from the horror of having their money consumed by Cecil, the couple's hopes rose when they recalled this simple digestive truth: What goes in must come out. They got creative (and somewhat dirty) and managed to salvage a large portion of their chewed and digested cash through diligent attention and meticulous washing of the money (not to be confused with *money laundering*) they collected from Cecil's poop.

If someone had come into the home of Cecil's humans and taken the $4,000 off their dining table, we would all agree that their boundaries had been violated on multiple levels. But the case of Cecil and the $4,000 was a boundary rupture (which fortunately didn't cause Cecil any harm).

Examples of boundary ruptures include:

» The natural consequences of weather-related events, such as tornadoes, fires, tsunamis, earthquakes, or hurricanes, causing water to enter your home or complete destruction of your personal property

» Another person unintentionally intruding on your privacy in a public restroom, dressing room, or at home

» A car accident caused by someone who has a health emergency while driving or is otherwise unable to avoid the accident

BOUNDARY VIOLATIONS IN CHILDHOOD

Your unique personal history impacts how you size up situations (or people) for the purpose of creating a boundary. If you grew up in a family where boundaries were poor or practically nonexistent, you may have a lot of questions or be confused about when to set a boundary.

If your boundaries were repeatedly violated as a child, that means you were abused. One of the consequences of childhood boundary violations is that you struggle to identify boundary problems as an adult. That's because you had no choice but to adjust and adapt to your situation because you depended on your parents or caregivers for your very survival. (See Chapter 5 for more information about how your childhood experience impacts your personal boundaries as an adult.)

The good news is that by understanding personal boundaries — specifically, boundary violations — you know how to recognize and take care of boundary problems more quickly and with more ease.

Remember: If you struggle to know when your boundaries are being challenged or violated because your boundaries were repeatedly violated when you were growing up, know that your current struggles aren't your fault. Creating personal boundaries is a learned skill, and you can do it!

REMEMBER

Even though boundary ruptures are unintentional and completely impersonal, that doesn't mean they don't cause harm or trauma.

Recognizing Trauma Created from Boundary Violations or Ruptures

Knowing that you've experienced a boundary rupture or boundary violation is important, but it's just as important to recognize that you may have been traumatized as well.

Some boundary violations and ruptures are more likely than others to create trauma. They include:

>> Experiencing physical or sexual assault, especially if the abuse is persistent or ongoing

>> Experiencing physical, sexual, or emotional abuse in childhood

>> Suffering physical or mental injuries during military deployment

>> Being a member of a family, organization, or institution that has a rigid set of rules you must follow to avoid consequences or punishment

>> Enduring ongoing harassment, stalking, or surveillance (being watched)

TIP

If you experienced significant trauma as a child, you're more vulnerable to boundary violations as an adult. Chronic boundary violations in childhood impact your ability to perceive danger and threats. Knowing how your boundaries were violated as a child helps you identify specific boundary work to focus on as an adult. See Chapter 5 for more details about the boundary lessons you learned in childhood.

Defining trauma

Trauma is a psychological-emotional response to a negative event. My approach to how trauma develops and how to treat it comes from my training as a Somatic Experiencing® Practitioner and the work of Peter Levine. Levine is the developer of Somatic Experiencing®, a gentle form of treating trauma that focuses primarily on tracking the sensations of the body while recalling a past traumatic event.

According to Levine, *trauma* is highly likely to develop when you experience an event where both of the following elements are present:

>> You perceive an incident or event as overwhelming or as a threat to you or someone else.

>> In that situation, you're unable to prevent the threat or escape it. In other words, you can't complete a fight or flight response.

This definition of trauma is extremely effective for understanding both adult and childhood trauma. If the incident is severe enough or is sustained over a long period of time (for example, war or a hostage situation), you are likely to develop post-traumatic stress disorder (commonly abbreviated PTSD).

THINK ABOUT IT

Understanding trauma as a combination of how an event is perceived and being powerless to change it explains why children are more vulnerable to being traumatized than adults are.

Children are more vulnerable to being traumatized because:

>> They feel overwhelmed or threatened by many experiences that have little or no impact on adults. A child's relative lack of life experience, still developing

brain, and inability to self-protect cause them to be more vulnerable to distress, threats, or *overwhelm* (see the previous section "Feeling overwhelmed and stressed").

>> Children have little or no ability to stop or escape an overwhelming, threatening experience, especially when their parents or caregivers are the cause.

Experiencing traumatic responses due to boundary violations and ruptures

When someone becomes traumatized by a boundary violation or rupture, they may have one or several of the following responses:

>> Engaging in avoidance behaviors, especially related to the traumatic event (For example, if you were recently in a car accident, you may not want to drive for a while.)

>> Having negative intrusive (unwanted) thoughts

>> Being fearful or startled by loud noises

>> Feeling *hypervigilant* (alert to danger everywhere)

>> Experiencing flashbacks about the event

>> Feeling highly sensitive to anything that reminds you of the event

>> Having trouble sleeping or eating

>> Finding it difficult to focus on tasks or being unable to concentrate (when reading a book, for example)

Getting help for unresolved trauma

If you've experienced a past trauma and you're having ongoing symptoms that negatively impact your quality of life, find a mental health treatment provider who specializes in trauma to work with as soon as possible.

Look for someone who has specific training to treat trauma. Terms like *trauma-informed treatment* don't guarantee that the provider has specific training to treat trauma. Interview the provider and ask them for information about what kind of trauma training they have and if they have a certification in a particular method of treating trauma. If the provider can't answer your questions or appears put off by them, find someone else to work with.

3

Exploring the Types of Boundaries and How They Work

Understand physical boundaries so you can protect yourself, other people, and your personal belongings.

Discover sexual boundaries so you can feel safe and protected while being intimate and vulnerable.

Recognize boundaries for speaking so you can create safety, understanding, and connection in your relationships.

Improve your listening boundaries so you become not only a better listener, but also a more effective speaker.

Explore the four nonnegotiable boundaries.

Chapter 8

Physical Boundaries: Who Can Get Close to You and Your Physical Possessions

Have you ever wanted to tell someone to back off? If you have, you're already one step ahead when it comes to understanding physical boundaries.

Because you survived the drama of preschool brawls over who got to build a tower with those coveted brightly colored plastic blocks, you already know that sooner or later, someone is going to overstep your physical boundaries or act as though they have a claim to your personal possessions. If you don't know you have a right to decide who touches you or who has access to your personal belongings, you won't be able to set a boundary.

And if you want to play fair (unlike those preschoolers who took your blocks), you also need to have the courage to realize when you may be violating another person's boundaries. When it comes to personal boundaries, what's good for the goose is good for the gander. That means not only do you protect yourself with your physical boundaries, you're also responsible for protecting others with your physical boundaries.

In this chapter, I walk you through an introduction to physical boundaries, which are one of the four primary boundaries. (The other three are sexual boundaries, boundaries for speaking, and boundaries for listening, which I cover in Chapters 9, 10, and 11.) Knowing what physical boundaries are is the first step in understanding how they work. Having the right words to talk about them helps you feel more confident as you navigate the sometimes messy world of boundary setting.

This chapter describes physical boundary violations and explains why physical boundaries are nonnegotiable. Translation: *No* means *no*. You're also introduced to an occasionally overlooked subcategory of physical boundaries I call *energetic boundaries*. You can't always see energetic boundaries, but you can definitely feel them, especially if you're very *empathic*, or a highly sensitive person. When you're aware of other people's energy and how it impacts you — especially when it feels terrible — you can figure out how to protect and take care of yourself.

Defining Physical Boundaries

You may have never thought of it this way, but your body is your personal territory. If you're intrigued by the idea of your body as territory and you want to get fancy about it, you can name your body Charlene's Chateau or Michael's Manor. Your body is your domain. And like all domains, it has an outer limit. The outer limit of a parcel of land is often a wall or a fence. The outer limit of your body is your skin — holding everything together and protecting you.

In the same way governments and courts establish laws about land and property, you get to set the parameters for your territory in the form of physical boundaries.

>> When you protect yourself with physical boundaries:

- You're aware of how close you want to be to others physically. Your preferences are based on your chosen standards rather than on others' standards or any other external factor that doesn't align with your preferences or values.

- You're able to maintain the physical closeness or distance you want. This means you're able to stop someone when they get too close to you.

- You're aware of how much access to your personal belongings you want to give to others.

- You're able to maintain the access to your personal belongings that feels comfortable for you. You stop others when they take or use your personal belongings without your permission.

>> When you protect others with your physical boundaries:

- You respect their nonnegotiable right to decide how close they want to be to you or if they want to be touched.

- You respect the physical closeness or distance another person wants from you. You stop yourself when someone tells you that you're getting too close to them.

- You respect their right to choose how much access they give you to their personal belongings, and you abide by the limits they set.

REMEMBER

Not all cultures (or even all families within a culture) agree on what's appropriate when it comes to physical closeness and touching.

The bad news is, you may have to learn other people's boundaries or limits by experimentation, which can be messy. The good news is, you're the ultimate decider about how close others get to you, and who gets to touch you.

Deciding how close others get to you

You already have an idea about how close you like to get to other people. You acquired these preferences through a variety of experiences. Your childhood relationships, cultural norms, and simple trial and error all play a part in learning how to navigate personal interactions, relationships, and boundaries.

Sizing up distance

Your preferences for physical closeness with someone are largely determined by the nature of the relationship. For example, being physically close to your family, your spouse, or your children should feel more comfortable than having the same closeness with a stranger sitting next to you on an airplane.

REMEMBER

There are no universally agreed upon parameters for how close other people can get to you. And even if there were, you get to decide the distance that feels comfortable for you. No one gets to make that decision for you.

Most people are comfortable interacting with strangers (or people they don't know very well) at a distance of about three feet or more. This is approximately one arm's length. You can try it right now. Hold out your arm and imagine someone you don't know standing less than an arm's distance in front of you. What do you notice? If you feel any discomfort at all or find yourself wanting to back away, you need more distance from the imaginary stranger in front of you.

Keep in mind that an arm's length is a general guideline for determining how close others get to you. If you've got unusually short arms, you may want two arm's lengths. Or if you're a person who prefers more physical closeness, your perfect length may be half an arm! Regardless of your arm length or what your mind tells you about how close is too close, let your body and your senses be your guide. Your body will always tell you when someone is too close or too far away.

Accepting touch (or not!)

You also get to decide who touches you, and when, where, and how it happens. (Chapter 9 explains more about touch and sexual boundaries. This chapter focuses on nonsexual contact.)

You may never have given it much thought, but you already have agreements about nonsexual touch with some people in your life. These agreements may be unspoken, but you (and the other person) have created a physical connection where nonsexual touch is mutual and enjoyable. For example, you and a friend who regularly meets you for meals out or for special events may give each other a big hug and perhaps even a kiss when you greet each other, and then sit close together as you enjoy a fun conversation.

You've probably given your consent to being touched by a stranger in certain — often scripted — situations. For example, if you're in a group of people who have been asked to join hands, when you extend your hand, you're nonverbally signaling that you agree to be touched. If shaking hands when meeting another person is a norm in your everyday life, when someone extends their hand to you and you respond by extending your hand to them, you're agreeing to be touched.

As you may have discovered, more than a few people have no clue about how physical boundaries work. And they are the people who get too close or touch you without thinking much about it or who won't ask if they can touch you before they do. In these situations, you may not be able to stop them before it happens (because you didn't see it coming), but you can stop it from happening again. In Part 4, "Creating Personal Boundaries," I show you how to create a boundary. Armed with a few simple steps, you'll know what to do when you encounter a boundaryless person who gets too close or touches you without your permission.

Choosing how close you get to others

Knowing how close to get to other people doubles the complexity of physical boundaries. That's because not only are you figuring out how close you want to be to the other person, but you're also paying attention to how close they want to get to you. You can't go wrong by asking another person's permission before you touch them — especially if you don't know them very well.

TIP

How do you ask someone for permission to touch them? Questions like "May I hug you?" or "May I hold your hand?" are clear, thoughtful, and respectful ways to ask for consent.

When you ask another person for permission to touch them, you're letting them know that you understand how boundaries work, and you respect their right to say *yes* or *no*. Implied in this interaction is that you will respect their answer if it's *no*. Because most people don't understand the principles of healthy boundaries, your courage to ask these simple questions and your willingness to risk receiving a *no* gives you a chance to show your advanced-level boundaries skills!

The amount of distance between two people should be determined by the person who needs the most distance. That means if you're in a heated conversation and the other person moves from sitting next to you on the sofa to a chair a few feet away, they've established a new, greater distance between the two of you. If you challenge them or complain about the distance they've created, you're not respecting their physical boundary.

TIP

If you're in doubt about how close to get to another person, it's a safe bet to give them the same distance you prefer, unless you're someone who prefers a less-than-arm's-length distance between you and other people. In that case, you may want to give them a little more room than feels comfortable to you.

This level of detail about physical closeness and touch may seem over the top. You may feel as though your freedom to be yourself is being unduly restricted by these guidelines. Of course, you can exercise your freedom to touch people without regard to their preferences or their boundaries. But that doesn't mean you should! The consequences may not be worth the freedom.

If you don't understand how physical boundaries work and how quickly they can be misunderstood or overstepped, digging a little deeper into the nuances behind physical closeness and touch will help you avoid regrettable, embarrassing, or problematic incidents.

Determining who can touch your belongings

Physical boundaries apply to your body and personal space, but they also apply to your personal belongings. Your physical belongings are part of your domain, and you have a right to decide who gets access to and touches your stuff.

If your neighbor wandered into your garage last year without being detected by anyone (other than your security camera) and "borrowed" the chain saw you haven't seen since, you know how frustrating it can be when people don't respect your right to your personal belongings. The good news is, you've got a digital recording of your neighbor's boundary violation. The bad news is, you'll need to have a conversation with your neighbor if you want your chain saw back. I can practically hear the temptation you're feeling to sneak into their garage to reclaim your property, but their garage is their territory.

So what can you do? Your domain includes deciding who gets access to your property, and when, where, and how their access occurs. Unfortunately, family members, friends, or neighbors sometimes create "exception rules" that these kinds of limits don't apply to them. These rules are generally unspoken and exist only in the rule creator's mind. It's not your job — or your obligation — to be a mind reader or let them have whatever they want!

I once lived with two sisters who routinely went into each other's closets to borrow handbags and other personal belongings. In their case, it didn't seem to cause much stress. However, if you don't want your best friend to go shopping in your closet or slip a few bracelets into their tote bag when they visit, you have a right to put a stop to it. Someone else's rules aren't your rules unless you agree that they are.

Naming Physical Boundary Violations

Overstepping other people's physical boundaries is serious business, so we need to get specific and spend some time naming physical boundary violations.

Because you first learned about physical boundaries from your family of origin (see Chapter 5 for more details), if your family didn't maintain healthy physical boundaries, you may not have the right information to know when you're overstepping a physical boundary or when someone is violating your physical boundaries. This is especially true if you experienced physical boundary violations (also known as *physical abuse* or *trauma*) in childhood.

That's why it's important to identify and define physical boundary violations. You need to know that some physical boundaries are so important that crossing them must be considered big no-nos — or boundary violations.

Touching a person without permission

In general, you should refrain from touching another person you don't know (or don't know very well) without their permission. Some people balk when I recommend this, especially highly expressive and physical types who love to hug and plant big kisses on the cheeks of their friends and family.

When I suggest they ask the other person, "Can I give you a hug?" you'd think I just told them they need to have the question engraved on high-quality stationery and sent by special delivery. What's the worst that can happen if you ask? They may say *no*. But wouldn't you rather know that someone prefers not to be hugged than hug them and find out later they didn't like it? Or better yet, put yourself in their shoes. Would you rather be asked, or not?

A few years ago, I was having breakfast at a hotel restaurant in Santa Monica, California. I noticed that one of the servers had a habit of touching the customers, including me, on the shoulder when he came to the table to take orders or to make sure everything was going okay with the meal. He touched me on the shoulder several times. I found it irritating and presumptuous — not because he was the server and I was the customer, but because other than where he worked, I didn't know him at all!

If you asked me before this incident to define my physical boundaries for interacting with servers, I may have said I'd prefer they not sit down at my table and tell me all their problems. But I can't imagine saying that I didn't want servers to touch me on the shoulder. Not because it was okay with me if they did, but because it wouldn't have occurred to me that a server at a restaurant would touch me. You discover a lot about your own physical boundaries from the annoying — and sometimes frightening — ways people approach you and your body.

Engaging in abusive or dangerous physical contact

REMEMBER

Being physically abusive or threatening is a violation of other people's physical boundaries.

Physical abuse includes slapping, hitting, shoving, or not allowing a person to leave a room, a vehicle, or their apartment. When someone stands close to another person and yells and screams in their face (more on speaking boundaries in Chapter 10), that's threatening behavior!

People who have the unattractive habit of acting up in this way will say things like "I didn't touch you!" True, unless the spit that flew out of their mouth while they were raging at you hit you in the face. Gross. Threatening behavior by its very nature creates fear of physical harm, and that's why it's a physical boundary violation.

Stalking (harassing someone with unwanted and obsessive attention) is also threatening, abusive behavior. It's not only a serious boundary violation — it's illegal.

Exposing others to contagious illness without disclosure

In March 2020 most of the world's population became enrolled in a planetary master class on contagious illness and physical boundaries in the form of COVID-19. For reasons beyond the scope of this book, there were many strong opinions and disagreements about how to protect people from this tiny virus.

Exposing another person to a contagious illness without disclosing that you're contagious is a physical boundary violation. This is why children are asked to stay home from school if they've had a fever in the past 24 hours. And it's why there are laws protecting people from some contagious diseases. According to the Centers for Disease Control and Prevention, 10 states in the United States have laws requiring a person with HIV to disclose their status to sex partners.

REMEMBER

Be kind. Protect others from contagious illness in the same way airlines protect you from secondhand smoke. Isolating (if needed), maintaining a safe distance, and disclosing if you believe you're contagious are best practices for doing your part to protect others and practicing healthy physical boundaries.

Eavesdropping, spying, or refusing to give someone privacy

This category of physical boundary violations has a high creep factor, but bear with me — it's too serious to overlook.

Eavesdropping is when someone secretly listens to the conversations of another person. *Spying* is when someone watches or observes another person in a stealthy manner that's completely unknown to the person who's being secretly observed.

In the digital age, the definition of eavesdropping and spying has been expanded to looking at another person's phone, text messages, email, social media, or other online accounts without their permission and without their knowledge. These intrusive behaviors are physical boundary violations, and some are illegal in certain situations.

Refusing to give another person privacy is a more direct and obvious way of spying on them. Examples of not giving another person privacy include not allowing them to close a door or removing a door or barrier (including clothing) that would allow them to have privacy. Not only are these actions physical boundary violations, but they're also physical and emotional abuse.

Accessing personal belongings without permission

A few years ago when my husband and I were selling the condo we'd lived in for 15 years, the Realtor told us that we should expect prospective buyers who toured our home to open our drawers and closets and look at all our stuff. Yikes!

If you shudder at the thought of someone (especially a stranger) digging through the contents of your bedside table, rifling through boxes of your personal papers, or peeking into your medicine cabinet to gawk at your current cocktail of pharmaceuticals, then you have a physical boundary of protecting your stuff from other people. Just like your body, your personal property is under your jurisdiction and management. You have a right to decide who gets to access your stuff, when, and for how long.

REMEMBER

Before you get too far along with your plans to install an invisible, electrified force field around your most treasured possessions, remember that like all physical boundaries, this one is reciprocal. The Golden Rule says that if you don't want someone peeking inside your medicine cabinet, you need to stay out of theirs.

Knowing that Physical Boundaries Are Nonnegotiable

You may already be completely satisfied knowing that you're the decider when it comes to who gets to touch you and your stuff. But it gets better!

What if you knew that from this day forward you don't need to waste your time defending yourself or arguing for your position when someone tries to talk you out of a physical limit you set or says you don't have a right to make certain decisions involving your body or your personal possessions? Well, now you know! That's the beauty of understanding that physical boundaries are nonnegotiable. When you say *no*, you get to make it your final answer. Period. End of story.

For example, imagine that you have a friend who has a habit of drinking a bit too much alcohol when the two of you go out, and you're (rightfully) uncomfortable about riding in the same car with her. She calls and asks if you want her to pick you up for the fun night out the two of you planned the previous week. Remembering that you don't like to ride in the car with her when she's been drinking, you tell her that you'd prefer to take your own car. If she's like a lot of people, she'll get offended and ask why you won't ride with her. She may even say, "What's wrong with you? You always ride with me!"

Your decision to take your own car is a boundary you created related to your physical body, which means it's nonnegotiable. Like many people, your friend may pressure you, attempting to get you to change your mind. She doesn't understand (or accept) that a physical boundary is nonnegotiable. She doesn't know how to take *no* for an answer. (For more information on nonnegotiable boundaries, see Chapter 12.)

REMEMBER

The simple truth is that your physical boundaries are nonnegotiable. *Merriam-Webster* defines *nonnegotiable* as "not open to discussion or reconsideration." Case closed!

If you can count on one thing when you're improving your personal boundaries, it's that some people won't like your new boundary-setting skills. Not a bit. Rest assured that this is normal, and there's nothing wrong with you. In fact, their pushback may be evidence that you're doing something different (and right) for you. And the good news is, setting boundaries gets easier the more you do it.

TIP

You're likely to feel at least a little uncomfortable about your friend's pushback and you'll want to have some strategies for dealing with it. Chapter 6 shows you how.

Exploring Energetic Boundaries

If you're perplexed and wondering what energetic boundaries are, you're in luck! I explain them in this section.

Before I get to a formal definition, I'd like you to ask yourself if you've ever been in a situation where you could tell, without any obvious visual or auditory clues, that someone was feeling angry, sad, suspicious, or any other emotion. In other words, have you ever been able to tell how someone was feeling even when they weren't saying anything?

I'm guessing that you said *yes*. That's because when people feel sad or shameful, they often appear smaller or almost imperceptibly sink down into their chair. On the other hand, when people are angry, they often appear larger, and their movements may become more forceful and exaggerated.

But sometimes it's more subtle than that. And if you're a highly sensitive person or very *empathic*, you know what I mean. Some people are so perceptive and intuitive about what's going on with other people that they employ certain tactics to protect themselves from "picking up" other people's negative energy.

You may have heard people toss around the word *energy* in various contexts or refer to *auras* or *chakras* (two types of spiritual energy), but energy can mean many different things to many different people. For this discussion, I use a definition of *human energy field* from a November 2016 article in the *Journal of Holistic Nursing* titled "Human Energy Field: A Concept Analysis":

> A luminous field of energy that comprises a person, extends beyond the physical body, and is in a continuous mutual process with the environmental energy field.

You could debate the luminous part, but what I want you to get is that human energy extends beyond the physical body and is connected with the environment. Another way to think about the human energy field is to imagine that it's like a scent or perfume humans emit or radiate that can be seen, felt, and sensed.

Here are some ways in which you may be aware of a person's energy in your environment:

>> **You feel uncomfortable, anxious, or fearful for no apparent reason.** Sensing someone's energy may mean you also feel their emotions.

>> **You sense danger for no apparent reason.** Based on your perception you have an urge to distance yourself physically from another person or to leave.

>> **You notice when a person's energy seems to fill up a room.** One of the ways you can immediately notice a person's energy is when they take up a lot of space, but not necessarily with their physical body. This experience is often more *felt* than seen. However, you may see dramatic gestures, movement, or body language or someone who is extremely still or quiet.

>> **You feel that your attention is being demanded.** Some people have a knack for demanding that you pay attention. Sometimes the way they do it is obvious (like staring intensely at you while they're talking). Sometimes it's not.

> I remember one Christmas I was at my father's house when a relative unexpectedly arrived right before the meal with a bag full of oysters that needed to be shucked. Since the idea was to eat them, of course it had to be done right then!

Situations involving other people's energy aren't always directly or overtly physical, but they're experienced on the physical level. They can be managed by creating a physical boundary of distance or protection and through using other techniques like visualizing a wall of protection, for example. I give you several out-of-the-box tips for using visualization to create a feeling of protection in Chapter 21.

Chapter **9**

Sexual Boundaries: Yes and No Are Complete Sentences

Sexual boundaries are an important, serious, and sometimes thorny topic. You've probably heard phrases like "No means no" or "No is a complete sentence." These phrases express one aspect of sexual boundaries: They are nonnegotiable. Although they're concise and helpful, these phrases don't fully describe or define what sexual boundaries are. They don't provide any information about how to implement your own sexual boundaries or help you understand how (and why) to honor and respect other people's sexual boundaries.

In this chapter, I define sexual boundaries and stress that ultimately, you're the only person who gets to decide what your sexual boundaries are. I share a list of common sexual boundary violations and show you that just like physical boundaries, sexual boundaries are nonnegotiable — meaning that an established sexual boundary isn't open to discussion.

I explain the important topic of consent and introduce you to a concept of rejection that may be new for you. Reimagining rejection and knowing how to think about it can change the way you perceive everyday interactions, including how you navigate receiving a *no* in sexual encounters and other situations.

Defining Sexual Boundaries

We'll start with getting clear about what sexual boundaries are.

Your sexual boundaries consist of the following:

>> Your physical body as you engage in sexual activity with yourself or another person.

>> The specific parts of your body that you identify as sexual, which is solely up to you.

>> Any activities with another person that you define as sexual. Your definition of sexual or nonsexual activities is personal to you. What you define as a sexual activity may not be what another person (or your sexual partner) defines as a sexual activity.

>> Your preferences about with whom, when, where, and how you're sexual, which are all defined by you.

In Chapter 1, I discuss one of the primary purposes of boundaries: to protect yourself and to protect others. Your sexual boundaries are operating well when you protect yourself from a sexual experience that is unwanted and when you protect others by not engaging sexually with them when it's unwanted, inappropriate, or offensive.

>> When you protect yourself with sexual boundaries:

- You're aware of how close you want to be to others sexually. Your preferences around closeness are based on your chosen standards rather than on others' standards or any other external factor that doesn't align with your preferences or values.

- You're able to maintain the sexual closeness or distance you want. This means you're able to stop someone when they get too close to you sexually or when they touch you sexually in a way you don't want to be touched.

>> When you protect others with your sexual boundaries:

- You respect their nonnegotiable right to decide how close they want to be to you sexually or if they want to be touched.

- You accept *no* as a complete sentence and a final answer. After receiving a *no*, you don't attempt to negotiate, persuade, manipulate, or pressure the other person to engage sexually with you.

- You respect the sexual closeness or distance the other person wants. You stop yourself when the other person tells you that you're too close to them sexually or when they tell you they don't want a certain type of sexual touch or contact.

REMEMBER

When your sexual boundaries are weak or nonexistent, you'll struggle to protect yourself, protect others, or both. In other words, you'll have difficulty protecting yourself from others' unwanted sexual contact, or you won't reliably protect others from your boundaryless sexual behavior.

Realizing that you are the chief decider

Nowhere else in the boundary-setting department is it more important (and liberating) to know that you're the ultimate decider when it comes to your sexual boundaries.

It's vital that you understand this because there are many people — including people near and dear to you — who will try to take on the role of chief decider for you. And this is especially true for women.

For example, if you're a woman and someone thinks you're having too much sex, you may be called promiscuous, loose, or worse. If your sexual boundaries are less flexible than another person thinks they ought to be, then you're a prude or frigid or too uptight. But you get to decide what your sexual boundaries are. You can have no boundaries at all (I don't recommend this, but it's still a choice), or you can choose to have no sexual contact with anyone — ever.

Ultimately, it doesn't matter what anyone — your church, your mother, your friends, and even your long-term intimate partner — thinks about your sexual boundaries. They're entitled to their opinion about your sexual boundaries, and you're entitled to yours. And even better: Your sexual boundaries are no one's business but yours!

REMEMBER

If you have agreements about sexual boundaries with another person (to be monogamous or to use birth control, for example), those boundaries are the other person's business. An agreement means that both of you have a right to know if the agreement is broken. Agreements made with partners around sexual boundaries are different from sexual boundaries created solely by and for yourself.

Understanding your value system

As the chief decider of all things sexual in your life, you're free to make decisions that feel right for you. Decisions about with whom, when, where, and how you have sex are influenced not only by your own preferences but also by your need to ensure safety for yourself and others, as well as your *value system* — the principles, norms, and values you live by.

For example, if you're in a monogamous relationship, your value system doesn't include being sexual with a person outside your relationship. If you were taught as a child that self-stimulation or solo sex was wrong or a sin and you hold this view today, you would be acting outside your value system if you engaged in this activity.

Expressing your sexuality through sexual contact with yourself or others is optional, not a requirement. You can choose not to be sexual with anyone. You can decide to be *celibate* (abstain from sexual activity) for a temporary period or choose celibacy as a lifestyle. Decisions to be sexual or not be sexual are neither good or bad, right or wrong — provided that everyone involved is safe, and sexual encounters are mutual and not coercive.

When it comes to sexual expression, getting clear about your value system and honoring it helps you feel safe — emotionally and physically. Acting outside your value system creates stress, and stress (for most people) is an arousal-killer and a turnoff.

Deciding with whom, when, where, and how

You're the ultimate decider about with whom, when, where, and how to have sex. When you make the *with whom* decision, here are some common questions you may ask yourself:

>> What are your thoughts, perceptions, or opinions about a potential sexual partner? Do your thoughts about the person make them a more (or less) desirable potential partner?

>> How do you feel about this person? Do your feelings (or emotions) about them match the kind of feelings you want to have about a sexual partner? (Attraction plays a significant part in the *with whom* criteria.)

>> Does this person feel safe to you? When you're in their presence, do you feel at ease and trusting?

If someone you're not attracted to (or someone you don't feel safe with) sends you signals that they'd like to be sexual or have a sexual relationship with you, that person wouldn't pass the *with whom* test.

The *when* question involves awareness of how you're feeling in that moment. For example, if you just got home after a particularly grueling 14-hour day at work and your partner wants to be sexual with you, their *when* would probably not align with yours at that moment.

REMEMBER

Differing views or desires about the ideal frequency of sex are often a source of conflict in intimate relationships. This common issue falls under the *when* category. Differences in the desired frequency of sex should be expected and not considered to be a sign that your relationship is flawed or doomed.

Right now if you asked any two people what their preferred or actual frequency of sex is, their answers would likely not match. To expect that two people will agree on when they should have sex the majority of the time is simply unreasonable and sets couples up for unnecessary conflict.

Talking about and working through an impasse over timing is a topic beyond the scope of this book, but for now rest assured that you're not required to say *yes* to a sexual partner every time they want sex. Aligning with your partner on the frequency or timing of sex is something you should explore, discuss, and stay curious about together. Ideally your conversations will result in an agreement between the two of you that feels collaborative, mutual, and maybe even fun!

When you're in a physical place that feels safe and you're experiencing pleasure, then your *where* is an optimal setting for sex. If you're feeling at all uncomfortable about where you are, you may need to either change something in your surroundings that helps you feel safer (by closing a curtain, for example) or go somewhere else that feels more comfortable to you.

Deciding *how* to be sexual is the most challenging and complex part of the with whom, when, where, and how equation. The *how* of sex includes decisions such as where you like (or don't like) to be touched, which sexual activities you like (and don't like), or whether you like (or don't like) to incorporate toys into your sex play. These decisions are unique, personal, and solely yours to make. As long as these choices aren't emotionally or physically harmful to you or others, anything goes!

REMEMBER

If you're in the middle of a sexual encounter and your partner starts touching you in a way that doesn't feel safe or pleasurable, your response in that situation can be a request for something different or you can simply say *no*. On the other hand, if the touch feels both safe and pleasurable, you're a *yes!*

TIP

One of the most helpful things you can do to discover your *how* is to identify the contexts, the environments, the places on your body, and the ways you like to be touched as well as any sexual positions, toys, and activities you enjoy. Gather information like you're a detective. This will help you better communicate your *how* to your partner.

Discussions about with whom, when, where, and how wouldn't be complete without mentioning that sexual partners may not agree with you or have the same responses to those questions.

For example, you may not like giving oral sex to a partner, but your partner may want oral sex. Does that mean you have to give your partner what they want? Absolutely not. If your partner respects your boundaries, why would they want you to do something that makes you feel uncomfortable?

Or maybe your partner wants to bring porn into your sex life, and you don't want to. You have a right to choose not to include porn in your sex life or in your life at all.

You get to make decisions that are best for you. Other people have a right to their opinions and preferences. But their opinions and preferences shouldn't cause you to alter or abandon your boundaries.

REMEMBER

A *nonnegotiable boundary* is a boundary that isn't open to discussion, debate, or negotiation. Nonnegotiable boundaries are like stop signs. Both sexual and physical boundaries are nonnegotiable, and that means a verbal *no* to physical or sexual touch is a firm and resounding *no*.

Naming Sexual Boundary Violations

Because sex is a topic that's uncomfortable for many people to talk about, you may not have good information about what makes a certain behavior a sexual boundary violation.

Knowing what sexual boundary violations are helps you make sense of times in the past when you felt that something wasn't right or felt "off." With this information, you can begin to talk about boundary violations more confidently — whether they occurred in the past or when they're happening in the present. Naming sexual boundary violations helps you not only identify them in the future but also avoid or put a stop to anything that feels uncomfortable or unsafe.

TIP

Because it's impossible to name every sexual boundary violation, keep in mind that sexual boundary violations often have a kind of *ick factor* about them — meaning they may provoke feelings of disgust or repulsion.

The ick factor of sexual boundary violations is different from the disgust you may feel when you have a strong negative judgment about another person's sexual preferences or practices that don't necessarily impact or affect you.

The disgust or repulsion you feel about another person violating your sexual boundaries arises because of the shameless quality of the offending sexual behavior that's intentional and maybe even premeditated. In other words, when your mind registers *ick*, you're picking up on the shamelessness of the behavior you're experiencing. Your feelings are there to help guide and protect you.

Demanding sex or unsafe sexual practices

In Chapter 2, I cover the topic of demands and explain that as tempting as making demands can be, they have no place in healthy adult relationships. An adult doesn't have the right to demand anything from another adult, and this is especially true for sex.

You, and everyone else, have a right to say *yes* or *no* to sexual touch or sexual contact. No one has a right to your body, and you don't have a right to anyone else's body. No person has a right to demand sex from you or to demand that you engage in sexual acts or behaviors that feel uncomfortable or unsafe to you.

Here are a few examples of unsafe sexual practices:

>> Not using protection or birth control

>> Participating in any sexual act that exposes you to unwanted pregnancy, disease, or emotional, physical, or sexual harm

>> Having sex in a public place where you may be seen or arrested for indecent exposure

>> Giving another person access to or possession of sexual photos or videos of you

>> Engaging in anonymous sex online when your identity can easily be discovered by the appearance of unique physical features, tattoos, or other easily identifiable characteristics

If anyone pressures you for sex, demands sex, or tries to get you to engage in unsafe sexual practices, they're attempting to or are violating your boundaries. You have a right to say *no* to any sexual activity that feels uncomfortable or unsafe — no matter who the other person is or what their relationship to you is.

Ignoring a "no"

You can signal in many ways that you're not interested in sex or in a specific type of sexual touch. For example, you can put your hand up to signal *stop* or gently (or not so gently) push someone away. However, I highly recommend that when you're being sexual with another person, you avoid using nonverbal communication to convey a *no*, and instead speak the word *no* out loud. Using this short yet powerful word keeps communication between you and your sexual partner clear and unambiguous.

No doesn't have to be a full-stop sentence, but it's fine if it is. Depending on the context and your preferences, you can add what you'd like to experience instead. For example, you can say to your partner, "Would you touch me here instead?" or "I'd prefer a softer touch. Would you do that?"

Even though it's ideal to use your words and say *no* to something you don't like, that doesn't mean powerful nonverbal cues can rightfully be ignored. For example, if your partner touches you in a way that you've asked them not to, or in a way that's uncomfortable, and you get up and start getting dressed, that's a strong nonverbal cue that you don't intend to continue the sexual interaction. Just because you didn't use the word *no*, that doesn't give the other person a right to continue to pursue or pressure you for sex.

REMEMBER

You can't rely on nonverbal cues to communicate about sex, but your unambiguous cues have a right to be respected. If you state a clear, vocal *no* and the other person persists in attempting to be sexual with you, they're violating your sexual boundaries.

Engaging in inappropriate sexual conversation

Inappropriate sexual conversation involves talking about sex to a person in a context or setting where the topic of sex wouldn't typically be discussed.

Here are some examples of engaging in inappropriate sexual conversation:

>> Bringing up sex or sexual matters in workplace conversations with coworkers or between a supervisor and direct report.

>> Talking to your adult (or minor) children about your sexual relationship with your spouse or anyone else.

>> Making sexual comments, bringing up sexual topics, or asking sexual questions in the context of a customer or client relationship. Examples include clerk-customer, homeowner-contractor, or landlord-tenant relationships.

>> Initiating any sexual conversation with a minor child that's not for the purpose of education or the safety of the minor.

- Having any sexual conversation with someone where the balance of power in the relationship is unequal — specifically, when the person with more power initiates sexual conversation. Relationships where power imbalances exist include teacher-student, employee-employer, and clergy-parishioner interactions, among others.

- Bringing up sexual topics or asking questions about sexual matters in a doctor-patient or therapist-client relationship when the topic wasn't raised by the patient/client or isn't directly related to their care — especially when the patient/client feels uncomfortable or unsafe.

Exposing a person to unwanted sexual experiences or contact

Being exposed to intentional, unwanted, and nonconsensual sexual experiences or contact is a boundary violation. In some cases, exposing someone to nonconsensual sexual experiences is illegal.

Examples of unwanted sexual experiences or contact include:

- Engaging in exhibitionism. *Sexual exhibitionism* is intentional, unwanted, and nonconsensual exposure of sexual body parts (or full body nudity) for the purpose of sexual arousal. The behavior can occur anywhere — for example, in a vehicle, through a door or window, or online. Exhibitionism may include unwanted exposure to solo or partnered sexual activity, in addition to nudity. When exhibitionism occurs in person, it's not only a boundary violation but may also be considered indecent exposure or public lewdness, which is illegal.

- Experiencing unwanted sexual contact or physical touching (covered in more detail in the next section).

- Exposing a minor to age-inappropriate sexual material, behavior, language, conversation, or print/digital pornography. Exposing a minor to age-inappropriate sexual material or behavior is a form of sexual abuse, regardless of the minor's response to the exposure. For example, if an adult exposes a minor to pornography and the minor responds "positively" (meaning they're interested in what they see or they become aroused), the adult has still sexually abused the minor.

- Subjecting someone to print or digital pornography against their will, especially in a public setting such as the workplace, on an airplane, or at school.

Touching a person without permission

For our purposes, touching a person without permission refers specifically to sexual touch or touching sexual body parts. The touch can occur either through clothing or skin-to-skin. Touching another person sexually without their permission is unwanted, nonconsensual, and offending behavior.

The technical term for touching others without permission, specifically in public places, is *frotteurism*. Frotteurism is defined as the "practice of achieving sexual stimulation or orgasm by touching and rubbing against a person without the person's consent and usually in a public place." This behavior is classified as a form of sexual battery, which is not only a boundary violation but is also illegal in many states in the United States.

Shaming a person about their sexual preferences/choices

In this context, sexual preferences refers to with whom, when, where, and how you prefer to be sexual, not to your sexual orientation.

Your sexual preferences and choices are uniquely yours — and rightly so. Provided that they're safe, mutual, and pleasurable, your sexual preferences are perfect for you.

There are lots of strong feelings about what people should or shouldn't do in bed. But ultimately, you're the decider about what works for you — assuming it's safe and consensual. It's unlikely that you'll become intimately involved with someone who strongly disapproves of your preferences. But you may find yourself in a situation where someone you care about or even love pressures you to stray from your stated preferences, or even your boundaries. They may pressure you by shaming or embarrassing you, or trying to guilt you into changing your mind or choosing to engage in a sexual activity that you don't want or like.

REMEMBER

You have the right to make autonomous (independent) decisions about with whom, when, where, or how you want to be sexual. No one, including a long-term intimate partner or spouse, has a right to make these decisions for you. Ever.

If someone you're in a sexual relationship with pressures you to stray from your preferences, standards, or value system, ask yourself, "Is it loving, caring, or respectful for someone to try to persuade me to abandon my standards or my boundaries?" The answer is *no*.

WARNING

If you experience repeated pressure to violate your preferences, your value system, or your standards for safe, healthy, pleasurable sex, the person who's pressuring you isn't a safe sexual partner.

Talking about another person's body

I suspect that every woman reading this book knows what it feels like to hear another person comment on her body. Parents and relatives do it, and strangers do too. Most women experience this kind of unwanted attention as irritating at best and dangerous at worst.

Talking about another person's body for the purpose of evaluation or comparison is a form of objectification. *Objectification* is a not-so-subtle form of dehumanizing another person — making them into an object.

Your body is no one else's business. No person should comment on another person's body unless the intention is care or kindness. For example, several years ago when I was at a professional conference, my friend and colleague Anna quietly told me I had broccoli between my teeth. Thank you, Anna!

Talking about other people's bodies can be a form of emotional and sexual abuse when it's done in the presence of a minor. I can't tell you how many stories I've heard about people who grew up in families where one or both parents routinely commented on other people's looks or made fun of their appearance. This kind of emotionally abusive behavior teaches children that people are objects, and others have a right to comment on their appearance and look down on them for being less-than. When a child is routinely exposed to this kind of objectifying behavior, they learn to *self-objectify* — to objectify themselves. They become self-conscious, regularly compare themselves to others, and feel inadequate.

Refusing to give someone privacy

Being denied privacy or opportunities to have private space is stressful, embarrassing, and abusive.

The following are a few examples of denying another person privacy, specifically as it relates to sexual boundaries:

>> Not allowing someone to close or lock a bathroom or bedroom door

>> Removing the door to a bedroom (or other room)

>> Not knocking on a door before opening it

>> Sharing explicit photos or videos of a sexual partner who asked that the material not be shared

>> Entering the bathroom while someone is showering or bathing without asking permission

Other ways to refuse to give someone privacy include asking intrusive questions or demanding to know about their sex life. Some people believe they have a right to know all the details about their partner's solo sexual activities, or their thoughts and fantasies, for example. You can create an agreement with your partner to share information about your solo sexual activity, but no one has the right to details about your sex life or your sexual thoughts.

Claiming a right to another person's body

Every person's body belongs to them, and to no one else. Certain religious traditions hold the view that a woman's body belongs to her husband. You may choose to share that belief, but when viewed through the lens of healthy functional boundaries, giving someone a claim to another person's body is emotional, physical, and sexual abuse.

Not only is claiming a right to another person's body a form of abuse, but marital rape is a crime in all 50 states in the United States

The Indiana Coalition to End Sexual Assault & Human Trafficking, Inc. (ICESAHT), formerly Indiana Coalition Against Sexual Assault (INCASA), published the following statistics on marital rape in 2000:

>> The incidence of reported marital rape is 14 percent. This percentage doesn't include unreported assaults, and therefore underestimates the prevalence of marital rape.

>> Half of all women who are physically abused or battered are also survivors of marital rape.

>> A survey in the United States found that husbands or ex-husbands were identified as the attacker in 10 percent of all sexual assault reports filed by women.

>> Rape and sexual assault were reported as the only form of abuse by 23 percent of married female respondents.

Engaging sexually with another person is one of the most personal, intimate, and sacred acts people can experience. Granting someone the right to demand this level of intimacy from another person is dehumanizing to both people.

Examples of sexual trauma include:

>> Sexual harassment, which includes being stared or jeered at, mocked, or followed in public by someone

REMEMBER

Sexually harassing another person is a form of physical or sexual threat.

>> Repeated unwanted exposure to sexual comments, conversation about sex, sexual jokes, sexually explicit material (print or digital), or pornography

>> Sexual assault that may or may not include penetration

>> Rape

If you've been the victim of sexual trauma, your sexual boundaries were violated by the trauma you experienced. Because your sexual boundaries were violated, you may have a much higher need to create strong sexual boundaries than someone who hasn't experienced sexual trauma. You may understandably be more cautious and less flexible about what you consent to than someone who hasn't experienced the same trauma.

TIP

If you're a sexual trauma survivor, be kind and gentle to yourself. If you haven't already, work with a trained trauma therapist who can help you process what happened so you can heal. You can restore and reclaim your sense of sexual autonomy and sovereignty.

When you're identifying and creating sexual boundaries, you need to know what helps you feel safe. Here are some questions to help you discover what you need to feel safe when you're having sexual contact:

>> **What helps you feel safe when you're being sexual?** Your answer may include specifics about timing, environment, protection, monogamy, or verbal reassurance from your partner.

>> **Thinking back to the last highly pleasurable sexual experience you had, what contributed to your feelings of safety and relaxation?** Make a list of everything you remember from this experience and identify those things that were particularly helpful for creating safety.

>> **What do you need from your partner to feel safe when you're being sexual?** Your answer may include more conversation, commitment to monogamy, use of protection, certain kinds of touch, or agreements made before having sexual contact.

>> **Are you comfortable asking your partner for what you need to feel safe sexually?** If your answer is *no,* you need to determine what would make it

easier for you to share this information. Or if possible, you can create this level of safety yourself.

>> **Are there any safety needs you're neglecting or ignoring?** If your answer is *yes,* you should examine what must happen for you to meet these needs yourself, or ask your partner if you need their participation to meet your needs.

You're in charge of when and with whom you share your sexual trauma history. When you're ready, talk to your sexual partner about what you need. If your partner appears disinterested or doesn't honor the limits you need for safety, then they're not the best partner for you.

REMEMBER

Because of the prevalence of physical and sexual violence, especially toward women, if you're in a sexual relationship with a woman, it's more likely than not that she has experienced sexual trauma.

Here's a brief list of what you can do to be supportive of a sexual partner who is a trauma survivor:

>> Be interested in but follow their lead on how much they want to share about their trauma history.

>> Accept that when it comes to healing from trauma, there's no set timeline. Avoid putting pressure on your partner to "get over" what happened to them, or to be ready for sex or a particular sexual activity.

>> Never underestimate the healing power of going slow and asking permission during both sexual and nonsexual interactions. Simple questions like "Can I hold your hand?" can be powerfully healing for sexual trauma survivors.

>> When you sense that your partner is struggling with traumatic memories or the impact of their trauma, ask them, "How are you feeling? Is there anything I can do to support you?"

>> Find out how other people have supported a partner who experienced sexual assault or trauma.

Rejecting the Idea of Rejection

Nobody likes rejection. If I asked you what the worst kind of rejection is, I imagine you'd say it's either sexual or relationship rejection. Defining *sexual rejection* is simple: The person you want to have sex with doesn't want to have sex with you or doesn't want to engage in a certain sexual activity with you. *Relationship rejection* is what you feel when another person either doesn't want to have a relationship with you or just doesn't want the kind of relationship you were hoping for.

Before you despair as you watch the video playing in your mind of all the past rejections in your life, I have some good news for you: You can reject rejection before you let it reject you!

Humans have a fascinating automatic ability to turn a *no* into a rejection. But when it comes to navigating sexual relationships and boundaries, you'll be much better off if you assemble an indestructible mental barricade between the words *no* and *rejection.*

A dictionary isn't much help when it comes to exploring what rejection really means, because *rejection* is defined as the act (or action) of rejecting. You have to dig deeper to get to the bottom of the meaning of this word that holds so much power over so many.

Merriam-Webster defines *reject* as "to refuse to accept, consider, submit to, take for some purpose, or use." The first, and ultimately the most important, thing I want you to notice about this definition is that it describes what the rejector is doing, rather than who (or what) is being rejected. If the act of rejecting had anything to do with who or what is rejected, the definition would instead read something like this: "refuse to accept, consider, submit to, take for some purpose, or use, thereby rendering the rejectee (yes, that's a real word!) a loser and a worthless human being."

Reread the previous paragraph at least once. On second thought, read it as many times as you need to fully grasp the idea that rejection is solely about the rejector, and not about the rejectee.

If you're like most people, you've believed for so long that rejection is a reflection on the rejectee that it's going to take a conscious effort to undo this thought distortion and complete the deprogramming. That's what I aim to do. Stay with me. It will be so worth it.

Knowing that rejection is perception

When someone rejects anything (including a sexual advance or encounter), their choice is 100 percent about them. Think about it — who else could their choice be about?

This simple but elusive fact is why I don't believe in rejection, and why I'm inviting you to abandon your belief in rejection too. At one time, you probably believed in Santa Claus. I did. But I'm guessing you don't believe in St. Nick today. It may be harder to stop believing in rejection than it was to stop believing in Santa Claus, but the gift of feeling more at ease and confident in relationships (and life in general) is a gift that keeps on giving. And that's even better than Santa Claus!

It's instructive to look at and explore a classic childhood rejection story: You're at the eighth-grade dance and you see Suzy, the prettiest girl in school, standing on the other side of the gym. You finally get up your nerve to walk across the room to ask her to dance. You open your mouth and manage to get all the words out. Mostly in the right order and without too much stuttering or stammering. Suzy smiles, but then she looks down at the floor, shakes her head, and says *no*. Your brain screams, *REJECTION!*

But slow down, get curious, and ask: Is it true that you were rejected? Most people will say, "Duh, really? Of course, I was. She said no." But you're saying that because you've attached a very personal, painful meaning to receiving another person's *no*. In this situation, the prettiest girl in school says she doesn't want to dance. If you create a story that you're unwanted, inadequate, a horrible dancer, too short, too tall, smelly, too rich, too poor, or a complete and total loser, all from her two-letter, one-word response, not only are you engaged in baseless flights of fantasy, but you're also harming yourself. That's right, you are harming yourself. You're telling yourself that you're unwanted, inadequate, a horrible dancer, too short, too tall, smelly, too rich, too poor, or a complete and total loser. Ouch!

But is it true? Is it true that Suzy at the eighth-grade dance thinks all those awful things about you? Maybe, but probably not. Is it possible that she's painfully shy? Or that she thinks she's a terrible dancer and doesn't want to embarrass herself? Or maybe she's having a vicious and noxious bout of gas and she's terrified an unwanted eruption will occur as you twirl her around the dance floor! Who knows!?

Can you see the possibility that rejection is nothing more than your perception of what someone thinks or feels about you?

You may say, "Yeah, but my spouse left me after 32 years of marriage. You can't tell me that their decision wasn't about me!" I don't like to argue with my readers, but I can definitively say that your spouse's choice to leave you wasn't about you. How can it be about anyone except them?

Have you ever heard one of those stories about someone who got dumped by their spouse only to find out the next week that the dumpee is already engaged to someone else? When you hear a story like that, does it mean the person who got dumped is a different person than the person who got engaged? Did they undergo a magical transformation that converted them from a completely unacceptable partner to a deliciously desirable soulmate in one week?

When you believe that rejection is a reflection on you, what you're saying is, you're an awesome person when someone says *yes* or wants to be with you, and you're a loser when someone says *no* or chooses not to be in a relationship with you.

Rejection is pure perception, and never a reflection on you.

Misunderstanding the meaning behind another person's *no* or seeing rejection as a reflection on you can hurt. When someone you're in a long-term relationship with says *no* to sex (or anything else), it may feel particularly painful. Later in this chapter I give you tips for how to stay curious and connected after receiving a *no*. In the meantime, see if you can simply be open to the idea that another person's *no* isn't a reflection on you.

Misinterpreting another's *no* also has a serious and potentially dark side. When someone is more vulnerable to perceiving rejection than the average person, they're more reactive and triggered when someone says *no* to them. They may even become enraged or dangerous.

A person who is hypersensitive to receiving limits of any kind or being told *no* is more likely to ignore or override boundaries. In situations like this, use your physical boundaries (more on those in Chapter 8) to create distance and space between you and that person in case they're inclined to become aggressive, dangerous, or even violent.

Understanding that another's "no" is impersonal

To paint a picture of what it's like to understand on a deep level that another person's *no* is impersonal (meaning it's not about you), I want to tell you about Olivia. Olivia was an adorable Cavalier King Charles Spaniel (CKCS) who was part of my family for 12 years until, like many Cavaliers, she succumbed to heart failure.

Olivia's destiny was to be a pet dog, but she could have been a show dog. In fact, she appeared in two CKCS calendars! I think of her as an ambassador of beauty and love. Those were the qualities she radiated everywhere she went.

If Olivia had been able to speak, rejection wouldn't have been in her vocabulary. I imagine if I had tried to explain rejection to her, she would have stared at me with her big, beautiful brown eyes and cocked her head as if to say, "Huh? I don't get it." Based on her approach to interacting with other creatures — human and otherwise — it was clear she couldn't possibly believe she would ever be rejected.

Her attitude toward every creature she encountered (except an occasional Saint Bernard, bossy Chihuahua, or stern, suspicious-looking person) was, "Oh wow, this is going to be great! Let's get to know each other!"

When she didn't get the response she was instinctively primed for based on her obliviousness to (so-called) rejection, she didn't miss a beat. She never looked dejected or disappointed. She didn't throw her cute little 17-pound canine body on the ground and have a temper tantrum. She just kept on going — wagging her beautiful wispy black-and-white tail back and forth. By the time she moved on to the next person or the next animal friend, it was as if she couldn't remember what just happened. Olivia couldn't perceive rejection. And her inability to perceive rejection didn't hurt her one bit. In fact, it served her very well.

REMEMBER

Everything other people say and do is about them. Everything you say and do is about you. When you understand that another person's *no* isn't personal and can't be about you, you can't feel rejected.

Becoming curious after receiving a "no"

So, what can you do after a sexual partner says *no*, other than feel hurt, dejected, or angry?

I recommend you become curious instead. Having an attitude of curiosity is especially helpful when it comes to sexual interactions, which are often confusing, messy, and fraught with difficult emotions.

Your partner's *no* isn't a reflection on you. The more you can think of their *no* as a simple matter of fact rather than an indictment on your desirability, the better off you'll be. You'll also increase the likelihood of staying connected, even during difficult moments.

TIP

If you're prone to feeling rejected or angry when your partner says *no*, experiment with taking a break — even for just a few minutes — when you notice painful emotions boiling up. (In Chapter 6, I show you how to take a relational time-out.) During your break, remind yourself that your partner's *no* isn't personal. When you're ready, you can reengage by thanking your partner for understanding you needed to take a time-out, and asking one of the questions in the following list:

>> Is there something else you would like to do?

>> Is there something on your mind you'd like to talk about?

>> Would you like to snuggle or talk?

When you stay curious after your partner says *no*, you're demonstrating that you accept their limits, you want to stay connected, and you're open to what that can look like.

Chapter **10**

Boundaries for Speaking: Filtering Your Thoughts before Sharing Them

I f you've ever shuddered at the notion of other people being able to see your thoughts displayed on your forehead like a stock ticker running at the bottom of a TV screen, you're already one step ahead with speaking boundaries.

Speaking boundaries are the essential filter between what you think and what you say. When you have no filter between your thoughts and your words, anything and everything you think travels straight from your mind and out of your mouth. It's frightening, isn't it?

Having healthy, effective speaking boundaries makes you an excellent communicator. Great speaking boundaries also:

» Keep you out of trouble by helping you refrain from uttering words you know shouldn't be spoken

» Help you avoid regret by reducing the number of unconscious or downright mean things humans say from time to time

>> Help you avoid the need to make apologies for one too many foot-in-the-mouth incidents

>> Have a huge impact on how easy — or hard — it is for others to listen to you and take in your words

In this chapter, I explain the three vital components for having an important or difficult conversation, along with how to increase the likelihood that what you say will be heard by the other person. I introduce you to a tool that exponentially improves how you respond to someone when they're upset or complaining (especially when they're complaining about you), and I describe the most common speaking boundary violations.

Articulating Data, Thoughts, and Emotions

Before you talk to anyone about a topic that's important to you or has been a source of conflict in the past, I highly recommend that you take time to get clear about the situation by answering the following questions:

>> What did I experience with my five senses of sight, sound, smell, taste, or touch when the incident occurred?

>> What are my thoughts about the facts I identified with my senses?

>> What emotions do I have about what happened or about my thoughts about the facts?

TIP

Another powerful way to identify what you experience with your senses is to ask, "What could I have recorded with a video camera when the incident occurred?" If there's anything you experienced that can't be recorded with a video camera (other than a taste or smell) don't include it as a fact or data.

Chapter 14 provides more detailed information to help you use your answers to these questions in the boundary-setting process. In the meantime, you can simplify the three questions as chronological steps in the process of getting clear about a situation:

1. **Identify the data.**

2. **Pinpoint your thoughts about the data.**

3. **Recognize your emotions.**

TIP

Anytime you feel uncomfortable, disturbed, or distressed about an interaction or incident, these questions help you get clear about the root of your negative emotions. Often, you find that your negative emotions aren't due to the facts of a situation, but rather to your thoughts about the situation.

Slowing down and taking time to think about what you experienced is not only a vital part of the boundary-setting process, but also an excellent way to prepare for important or challenging conversations.

When you don't take time to look at the facts of the situation, your thoughts, and your emotions, your conversations are less constructive, and you may say something you regret or need to walk back or clean up later.

To make this point more concrete, here's an example using a home-improvement project to illustrate how identifying data, thoughts, and emotions works.

You and your partner have been working on a kitchen renovation project with a contractor named Bob. Your partner made a request (and you agreed) to be included on any emails or text message communications with Bob while the project was in process.

Yesterday your partner called you at work and said:

> Did you tell Bob he could come to the house this morning to look at the kitchen? He showed up at 10:30, and I was in the middle of a phone call with a client.
>
> Why didn't you check with me first? I thought I told you to include me on all your communications with him. If you'd done that, I could have told you both that I'm not available! You were supposed to include me on all your communications with him.

You don't need a high level of emotional intelligence to know that your partner was surprised and angry about Bob showing up unannounced.

If you're like most people in this situation, you'll get defensive and respond by saying something like "I was doing you a favor! You told me you didn't want Bob coming to the house in the afternoons, so I told him to get there before noon. From now on why don't you talk to Bob?!"

TIP

When you find yourself becoming defensive and reactive, that's a sign that your listening boundary is either unsteady or offline. See Chapter 11 for more information about how to develop highly effective listening boundaries.

This imaginary, yet very relatable, conversation demonstrates how easy it is for everyday communications to go sideways or completely off the rails.

If you, as the listener in this situation, take the time to slow down and process the incident by exploring the data (or facts), as well as your thoughts and emotions about the incident, here's what you can acknowledge, starting with the data:

>> Bob called me the day before and asked if he could come over to our house at 10:30 a.m. the next day. I told him that was fine, but I forgot to tell my partner.

>> My partner called me at work to tell me Bob showed up unexpectedly.

Some possible thoughts you may have about what happened include:

>> Oh no, here we go again.

>> Ugh, I forgot to tell my partner Bob was coming over.

>> I can't believe my partner's so upset. I was trying to help out.

>> I can see why my partner's upset. I agreed communications with Bob would go to both of us.

>> My partner's going to make me pay for this.

The potential emotions you may have, based on the facts and your thoughts, include:

>> Fear

>> Frustration

>> Compassion

>> Embarrassment

By identifying the data, as well as your thoughts and emotions about what happened, not only do you get clarity about what you experienced, but you also have all the information you need to begin thinking about how to respond.

TIP

Some challenging or difficult conversations are naturally improved by adding a request. For example, in the Bob the contractor story if you hadn't created an agreement with your partner about communicating with Bob, one or both of you can make a request to create an agreement about how you want to handle future communications. See Chapter 17 for more information about how to craft an effective request.

Speaking to Be Heard

Once you've identified the data, thoughts, and emotions of the situation, you can begin considering exactly how you want to respond.

It may seem glaringly obvious to say that when you speak, you want people to listen. But the truth is, many people routinely speak in ways that make it challenging to listen to them.

Here are a few examples of things people say that make listening difficult:

>> **Are you really going to . . . ?**

This question indirectly suggests that you have a negative judgment or opinion about what the other person is going to do or what you think they're going to do.

>> **Why did you . . . ?**

Why questions imply that you believe what the other person did was wrong, bad, inappropriate, and so on. *Why* questions are often an unconscious substitute for making a clear and direct statement about what you really think and how you feel about an incident or situation.

>> **I can't believe you . . . !**

This statement conveys disapproval, disappointment, and blame. It shows a lack of courage to make an honest, vulnerable statement about what you think and feel about what happened.

>> **You always . . . .**

This statement conveys blame and disapproval but also implies (through the word *always*) that what happened was the result of an unalterable character flaw rather than a human mistake.

Other speaking habits that make listening difficult include talking for long periods without stopping, not being curious or asking the other person questions, or routinely telling people what they think, what they feel, or why they do what they do.

REMEMBER

In the following sections, I give you five guidelines for increasing the likelihood that your words will be heard and received. But before I get to the specifics, here's a review of what I tell you in Chapter 1 about how to use speaking boundaries to protect yourself and others:

>> When you protect yourself with speaking boundaries:

- You understand that in personal (rather than casual or professional) conversations, the primary role of speaking or talking is to be known by the other person.

- You know how to determine who gets to know what about you. You match your private information with the level of connection or intimacy you have with the other person. (See Chapter 3 for more information about matching your private information with the people you want to share it with.)

- You understand that speaking clearly, respectfully, and coherently not only protects others, but also protects you from unnecessary conflict, disconnection, or future regret.

>> When you protect others with your speaking boundaries:

- You understand that in personal (rather than casual or professional) conversations, the primary role of speaking or talking is to be known by the other person.

- You think about what you're getting ready to say before you speak so that your words are as clear, respectful, and coherent (understandable) as possible.

- You have a filter between your thoughts and the words you speak because you know that not everything you think or feel needs to (or should) be spoken. You think about how to say what you need to say in a way that can be received or taken in by the other person. You understand that to be truly heard you must speak in a way that makes your words easier to receive or hear.

- You speak clearly, respectfully, and coherently and avoid using words or a tone of voice that's disrespectful, blaming, shaming, or abusive.

TIP

There's a lot to know about speaking boundaries. Be patient with yourself. Approach your use of these skills as a process that improves over time as you experiment with them.

Human communication is complex, difficult, and messy. You constantly face new situations that create new questions about how to respond or how to speak in the most effective way. Speaking well, in a way that others can hear, is a lifelong pursuit. You'll enjoy the journey more when you view it as an adventure in becoming an excellent communicator.

Thinking ahead about your purpose or intention

Anytime you're preparing to have an important or challenging conversation, take time to think about your intention or the purpose of the conversation from your viewpoint.

Getting clear on your intention keeps the focus on what's most important to you. Sticking with your purpose helps you avoid getting sidetracked by another person's defensiveness or attempts to change the subject.

To understand how that works, consider the earlier example about the surprise visit from Bob the contractor from the speaker's perspective. Think about your intention before telling your partner how upset you were that Bob showed up unannounced.

In the example, you made a request (and your partner agreed) to be included on any email or text message communications with the contractor while the project was in process. Unfortunately, when Bob came to your house, you had no idea he was coming because your partner didn't tell you.

To maximize the effectiveness of your communication, before talking to your partner, ask yourself, "What is my purpose or intention?"

TIP

I recommend that you be brutally honest with yourself when you answer this question. You may have some intentions that aren't, shall we say, very kind or nice — and that's okay. It's best to give free rein to your thoughts, because suppressed thoughts have a sneaky way of popping up and having their say later.

Here are some possible answers to the question about the purpose or intention of talking to your partner about Bob showing up unannounced:

>> You want to tell your partner off. After all, they broke an agreement!

>> You want to remind your partner of the agreement the two of you made.

>> You want to tell your partner that the next time Bob comes to the house and you don't get advance notice, you're not going to let him in!

>> You want to create a plan so you don't have this experience in the future.

Once you consider all your possible intentions, choose the one that's the most relational (respectful and transparent) and solution-focused (rather than blaming or shaming) and has the highest likelihood of creating the outcome you want.

REMEMBER

Keeping your eyes on the prize is the goal here. Your inner teenager may be chomping at the bit to give your partner a piece of your mind or to complain about the broken agreement. But if your true intention is to avoid similar experiences in the future, that won't be your best option.

Reviewing the answers in the list, which one do you think fits the situation best? If you identified the last one as the most effective, solution-focused intention, you're correct!

The second answer, *You want to remind your partner of the agreement the two of you made*, isn't the best fit in this situation because at best, it simply states a fact — the two of you had an agreement. At worst, this option points out your partner's mistake. Neither of these messages will get you what you want unless your *only* intention is to point out your partner's mistake.

Getting an agreement to have a conversation

When you need to have a conversation with someone about an issue that's even mildly important to you, I recommend you ask them if they're open to talking to you before launching into the conversation. You can't know a person's state of mind, availability, or willingness to have a meaningful conversation unless you ask them.

Here are five steps for getting an agreement to have a conversation:

1. **Tell the person you'd like to have a conversation with them.**

2. **Tell them what you'd like to talk about by giving them a brief description.**

   For example, in the Bob the contractor scenario, you can say, "I'd like to talk to you about Bob coming to the house today."

3. **Ask the other person if they're open to having a conversation with you about the stated topic.**

4. **Wait for their answer.**

   At this point, the person may say *yes*, or they may say they're not available now but will be later. If they say they'll be available later, ask them when they'd like to talk. If they say they don't know, or they won't give an answer, let them know when you'll follow up with them.

5. **If the other person says *yes* to Step 3, ask them when is a good time to talk.**

   They may say they're ready now, and you can proceed with the conversation. If they say they want to talk later, ask when — and agree on a specific time. If they don't know or they won't give an answer, let them know when you'll follow up with them.

REMEMBER

When you ask someone a yes or no question, they have the right to say *yes* or *no*, or to propose an alternative solution or agreement. If someone says *no* to a request to have a conversation, you can use the boundary-setting process presented in Chapters 13 through 18 to decide what to do next.

Sharing your emotions first

At the beginning of this chapter, I provide three questions to help you process an incident or situation before having a conversation. The questions prompt you to identify the data first, and then your thoughts and emotions.

As you're deciding what you want to talk about with another person, you'll rely on the same information. However, I recommend that you make one minor change in the order you share the information. I suggest you start by sharing your emotion(s), then saying what happened (or providing data), and concluding with what you thought about what happened.

Processing an incident or situation is an internal, private exercise that has a different purpose than talking to someone about that incident. Stating your emotions first (rather than the data and your thoughts) creates more connection because emotions are self-revealing and vulnerable, and may immediately give the listener important — and previously unknown — information about you that impacts their experience of the conversation.

TIP

Your emotions are your personal experience and aren't debatable. Talking about facts or data, on the other hand, sometimes leads to disagreements or disputes about what actually happened.

Here's the order I recommend for talking to another person about an important issue:

1. **Share your emotion(s).**

2. **Share what happened, sticking to the facts.**

3. **Share your thoughts.**

Returning to the Bob the contractor example, here's what the conversation would sound like when you address your emotions before the data and your thoughts, starting with getting an agreement to have a conversation:

> I need to talk to you about what happened this morning at the house. Is this a good time for you to talk?

Assuming your partner says *yes*, you proceed:

> I'm so frustrated. Bob showed up at the house this morning at 10:30, and I had no idea he was coming. I was so embarrassed because I was on the phone with a client, and I had to ask them to hang on a minute while I answered the door and talked to Bob.
>
> When I realized you hadn't told me that Bob was coming even though you knew, I thought you didn't care about the agreement we made or think about the fact that I was working from home.
>
> I don't want to experience this again. Would you be willing to come up with a plan so this can be avoided in the future?

Notice that you begin by sharing your emotions (frustration and embarrassment), and then what happened, or the data. Next, you tell your partner what you thought — that they didn't care about your agreement or think about you working from home. Finally, you share what you want and make a request to have a conversation about how to avoid similar incidents in the future.

This is an excellent example of highly effective speaking boundaries for the following reasons:

>> You express your anger without blaming your partner.

>> When you tell your partner what you think, you express it as a perception rather than a statement of fact about what they did or their intention.

>> You state what you want and ask your partner to help create a mutually agreeable plan for the future.

Formulating "I" statements

I once had the good fortune of spending three days in a marathon couples therapy session with my husband, facilitated by Julie Gottman, PhD (clinical psychologist, author, and president of The Gottman Institute). At one point during the marathon, I did what almost everyone does at some point in couples therapy. I left my circle of control (what I have power over) and wandered over to my husband's. I don't recall my exact words, but I imagine I said something like "You don't . . ." or "You think. . . ." Swiftly and deftly, Dr. Gottman looked at me and said, "Describe yourself, not your partner." Describe yourself, not your partner, is the equivalent of using "I" statements.

Using "I" statements is a widely recognized communication skill, but in case you're new to using "I" statements, here's why they're so useful:

>> Using "I" statements or talking about your own internal experience is self-revealing, vulnerable, and intimate.

>> When you use "I" statements, you take ownership of your thoughts, your emotions, and your perceptions.

>> "I" statements are easier to listen to than "You" statements and may minimize a listener's potential defensiveness.

>> When you use "I" statements, you're talking about yourself, and whenever you're talking about yourself and your own experience, no one can (effectively) argue with you about it.

TIP

Beginning a statement or conversation with "You" rather than "I" tends to come across as blaming and can make it far more difficult for the other person to hear you. Sentences starting with "You" are often followed by blame statements like "You left the toilet seat up — again!" Try this instead: "I'm so irritated! When I went to the bathroom just now, I sat down on the toilet and the seat was up. Since you're the only other person in the house, I'm asking you to please put the toilet seat down after you use the toilet. Would you be willing do that?"

Considering the listener's capacity to hear

When I say that before having a conversation with someone you need to consider their capacity to hear you, I'm not suggesting they need hearing aids. In this case, a listener's capacity to hear describes their relative ability to truly listen to, receive, and take in your words.

Listening can sometimes be difficult or even impossible for many reasons, including:

>> You're highly irritated or triggered.

>> You're not feeling well physically.

>> You're distracted or engrossed in a project or other activity that requires intense focus.

>> You just got some bad news, and you can't focus on anything else at the moment.

>> You're already upset or angry with the person speaking to you, and your motivation to listen to them is extremely low or nonexistent.

Before you decide to approach someone for a conversation, consider their ability to listen. If you don't think the listener can hear what you have to say and thoughtfully consider it, postpone the conversation to a time when their listening capacity is better.

On the other hand, if you think they can hear you, proceed!

TIP

People often ignore their intuition (or plain facts) about another person's ability to listen. If you perceive that another person isn't capable of listening to you even when they say they are, you'll do yourself, the other person, and the relationship a favor by delaying the conversation.

Leading with Agreement

Leading with agreement is one of my favorite communication and speaking skills. It comes from the work of Terry Real, a couples therapist and author.

Leading with agreement is an indispensable tool for having difficult or contentious conversations because you intentionally listen for what you agree with and begin your response by stating the area(s) of agreement. Leading with agreement has the potential to turn an angry, defensive response into a surprising and disarming meeting of the minds.

Although leading with agreement can be a challenge at first, you only need to follow two steps:

>> As you listen to another person (particularly in a difficult conversation), you make a mental note of anything and everything they say that you can agree with.

>> When you respond, the first words out of your mouth are something to the effect of "I agree . . ." or "That's true. . . ."

With practice, leading with agreement makes you a better communicator and speaker and significantly improves your listening skills.

TIP

Although leading with agreement is an ideal skill for difficult conversations, I encourage you to try it in casual and professional interactions. Most people love it when you agree with them, so why not?!

Identifying what you can agree with

The vital first step for leading with agreement requires you to identify something the other person said that you can agree with. Another way to think about it is, you need to find something in their statement about which you have the same perception — no matter how insignificant it may be.

Leading with agreement requires at least a beginning level of proficiency with listening boundaries. If you tune someone out when they're talking to you or you're busy formulating your response while they're talking, you won't be able to use this skill. (See Chapter 11 for more information about listening boundaries.)

Using the example from earlier in this chapter about the untimely arrival of Bob the contractor, here are a couple of statements your partner made that you may agree with:

>> You didn't tell your partner that Bob was coming to the house at 10:30 a.m.

>> Your partner did ask to be included on all communications with Bob, and you said that would happen.

Once you identify what you agree with — even if it's only one tiny data point from a 10-minute tirade — you've completed the first step.

Ignoring what triggers you

When you're in a heated, contentious conversation with someone and they're telling you everything that's wrong with you, what you did, and how you did it, it can be extremely challenging to sort through all their words to find something you agree with.

Knowing how to filter someone's words and find agreement is one of the reasons leading with agreement makes you a better listener. It requires a higher level of consciousness that enables you to avoid becoming consumed by your own stressful thoughts or painful emotions to find something — anything — you can agree with.

WARNING

Leading with agreement is optional, always. If someone is harassing or verbally abusing you, you're not required to agree with anything they say. In fact, I recommend that you protect yourself with the tools you've picked up from this book (especially the information about the four primary boundaries in Part 3). However, if you want to build, heal, or repair your relationship with another person, leading with agreement is the way to go.

Typically, when you feel as though you're being verbally attacked, you're inclined to respond by defending or counterattacking. Going back to the Bob the contractor example, your responses may sound like the following comebacks:

>> What did you expect me to do?! Bob called me.

>> I guess I forgot. Okay, I'm human.

>> I didn't say I would include you on phone calls, just texts and emails! (This statement is factually correct; however, it's unhelpful and unnecessarily provocative.)

>> Whatever.

>> I was just trying to move this project along. Why are you so worked up about this?

Instead of responding from the viewpoint of feeling triggered or verbally attacked, focus on at least one thing you can agree with.

THINK ABOUT IT

People with fragile or big egos find leading with agreement nearly impossible. Big egos love to be right and prove others wrong, which makes leading with agreement excruciatingly painful for them. Fragile egos (sometimes masquerading as big egos) crumble or disintegrate in the face of anything they perceive as criticism. Either way, they ultimately make the whole interaction about them.

Beginning with "I agree . . ."

When you're ready to experiment with this tool, I strongly recommend that you form your response by starting with the words "I agree." After all, people love it when you agree with them! Plus, when you tell someone you agree with what they said, you signal that:

>> You heard them, and everyone wants to know they're heard.

>> You're open-minded and open-hearted. Otherwise, you wouldn't be able to find something you agree with, much less tell them.

>> You're not defensive, which is an especially unattractive — yet very common — human characteristic.

>> You're willing to be vulnerable. After all, they just said a lot of unpleasant things about you, and here you are agreeing with them.

In the Bob the contractor example, here's how the listener can reply using leading with agreement:

>> You're right. I should have told you. I apologize. I'm committed to doing a better job of keeping you informed in the future. Would you prefer that Bob calls you?

>> I agree with you. It was wrong of me not to let you know that Bob was coming over. Is there anything you need from me going forward?

>> That's true — I was supposed to include you in our communications. I'm going to do my best not to let it happen again.

Notice that the replies include "You're right" and "That's true." Telling someone that they're right or that what they said is true may be more difficult for you than saying "I agree." These alternative openers for leading with agreement are effective options, but when you're getting started with this tool, I recommend sticking with "I agree."

TIP

An apology and a willingness to repair the situation or make amends are also included in some of the responses. These additional statements aren't required when you lead with agreement. Consider them bonus phrases that take your communication and speaking skills to the next level, and use them to experiment with how you articulate your agreement.

Naming Speaking Boundary Violations

Speaking boundary violations occur anytime you speak disrespectfully to another person, or when you directly (or indirectly) suggest that the person you're talking to has less value than you.

You can violate someone's speaking boundaries in many ways, I describe six of the most common examples of speaking boundary violations in this section.

THINK ABOUT IT

Many people wrongly assume that when they're upset about the way someone talked to them, their boundaries have been violated. When a person says something to you that you don't like or agree with, your dislike or disagreement doesn't make what they said a boundary violation. What you have experienced is an unnecessary negative emotion based on a belief that your boundaries were violated.

Yelling, screaming, and ridiculing

You probably have an idea of what it sounds like when someone is yelling or screaming at you, but I've discovered over the years that people have a wide range of definitions about what constitutes yelling.

I was in a couples therapy session many years ago when one spouse said to the other, "Stop yelling at me." I was caught by surprise because although their conversation was intense, I wouldn't have labeled it yelling.

I imagine there must be a certain decibel level at which almost no one would disagree that someone is screaming, unless they were deaf or needed hearing aids. But since no one knows the exact decibel level that defines yelling and screaming, let's just say that if someone can hear your voice outside your home (and you don't live in a yurt, straw hut, or tent), you're probably yelling. Yelling and screaming are forms of verbal and emotional violence, and should be avoided at all costs.

Ridiculing another person means making fun of, laughing at, or mocking them in a mean-spirited or cruel manner. Ridicule can be expressed directly with words or through a tone of voice that sounds sarcastic or condescending.

Ridicule is different from *playful teasing*, which is a lighthearted, humorous exchange that everyone thinks is funny — including the person being teased.

Once when I was on vacation and having dinner with my husband and son, I glanced down at my salad and said, "Look, there's bacon on the salad!" My son, who was about 10 years old at the time, said, "Mom, those are craisins." For years after that incident, anytime one of them spotted a craisin they reminded me of this incident, and everyone (including me) laughed and thought it was funny.

When you're on the receiving end of ridicule and your listening boundaries are weak, you feel hurt, angry, and often embarrassed. (See Chapter 11 for more information about listening boundaries.)

Examples of ridicule include:

>> What would you know about raising kids?

>> What's wrong with you? (Including references to any aspect of another person's body, thinking, or behavior.)

>> You always think you're right. Or other statements including *always* or *never*.

>> Are you really going to eat/wear/do that?

Interrupting persistently

Because of the fluid and spontaneous nature of human conversation, it's impossible to entirely avoid interrupting other people. But if you make interrupting a habit and you don't do anything to change it, it's a boundary violation.

Continuously interrupting implies that you don't want to hear what the other person is saying or that you think what you have to say is more important. Not allowing others to speak or to finish their sentences is disrespectful and dismissive.

TIP

Impulse control (difficulty controlling your actions or reactions) is one of the dominant symptoms of some mental health disorders. Impulse control can cause someone to have difficulty waiting their turn to speak. If impulse control is causing negative consequences in your life, find a mental health treatment provider to work with who can do a professional assessment and help you find an effective solution.

Speaking contemptuously

Contempt is another word for strong dislike, or even hatred. Being *contemptuous* of another person implies that you believe you're better than them and, by extension, they're less than you. The expression *looking down your nose* at someone is another way of describing contempt.

You can't necessarily identify contempt by certain words that are spoken or by tone of voice. The negative impact on the listener caused by speaking contemptuously originates from the speaker's feeling of disdain or hatred.

You can be contemptuous of someone in a conversation without saying anything that can be interpreted as disrespectful or abusive. An observer of the conversation may not perceive the contempt, but the listener or target will almost always feel it. For example, you tell your sister that a friend of yours owes you money and she asks, "Do they have a gambling problem?" Most people wouldn't think her question was contemptuous. However, your sister knows that you've struggled with a serious gambling addiction and repeatedly tries to shame you for it. Based on this background, her question can easily be perceived as contemptuous.

TIP

If you believe someone is speaking to you contemptuously and you want to say something about it, it's better to say, "I'm uncomfortable with the way you're talking to me," than to say, "You're being contemptuous." The second statement appears to be a fact but is actually a perception. Because facts can be proved or disproved, the listener can disprove your statement by saying, "No, I'm not," which will likely start a debate about who's right and who's wrong.

Blaming or shaming another person

Blaming or shaming is a way of telling someone that they're wrong, they're bad, or they made a mistake. People make mistakes every day, but blame and shame aren't the most effective or respectful means of responding to human imperfection.

Here are some examples of blaming or shaming:

>> Why did you leave the door unlocked last night? (*Why* questions tend to imply that the speaker disapproves of something the listener did or that the listener did something wrong.)

>> It's your fault we never get to go on vacation.

>> If you would just tell me how you feel our relationship would be better.

>> Why do you always have to ruin special occasions?

TIP

Blaming and shaming are forms of punishment and send a message that the other person is worth less or defective. If you're upset about something another person said or did, use the boundary-setting process described in Chapter 13 to create a respectful and constructive solution.

Attempting to control, coerce, or manipulate

Anytime someone tries to control, coerce, or manipulate you they're attempting to deny you your freedom. You're entitled to behave as you behave, think what you think, and feel what you feel. If you're not violating someone's boundaries, they don't have a right to try to change you or your behavior.

Examples of attempting to control, coerce, or manipulate include:

>> Telling another person how they should behave or what they should think or feel

>> Telling another person that their beliefs or values are wrong and attempting to change their beliefs or values

>> Ridiculing someone for their beliefs or values

>> Attempting to limit a person's freedom of movement or their access to other people

>> Withholding information another person deserves to have or deceiving them

TIP

If you have a habit of using indirect strategies to get your needs met, figure out how to make effective requests and create agreements. See Chapter 17 for more information about how to create an agreement.

Refusing to speak

There are two primary ways people withhold communication or refuse to speak that may be considered boundary violations:

>> Refusing to speak to someone you have frequent physical contact with, such as a person you live with or a coworker

>> Consistently refusing to answer questions or acknowledge that someone is speaking to you

When you refuse to speak to someone you're in close physical contact with or respond to someone who's speaking to you, you're using your silence as an indirect and passive-aggressive way to punish them, make a point, or get a need met.

Refusing to speak is often a learned behavior people pick up in their childhood home through observing their parents or caregivers engage in it. Not speaking to a person you have regular contact with is cruel and invalidating because you treat them as if they doesn't exist. See Chapter 5 for more information about how your childhood impacts your boundaries as an adult.

Chapter **11**

Boundaries for Listening: The Mother of All Boundaries

Being a skillful listener, especially during difficult conversations, is hard work. Even in ordinary daily interactions, listening can become a herculean chore when other people go on, and on, and on, and on about a whole lot of nothing or serve up a vague and hard-to-decipher word salad. If you do manage to follow what you believe another person is trying to say, what your mind creates from the words you hear with your ears can be nothing short of astonishing. That's because listening requires understanding and implementing effective boundaries.

Listening is a valuable skill. That's why so many people hire coaches, psychotherapists, and other professional listeners. People long to be heard, and to be understood. High-quality listening is a form of emotional labor, and good listeners are exceedingly rare. But the tools and information in this chapter can help you become one of those special people.

The primary purpose of listening is to discover, know, and understand who the speaker is.

In this chapter, I show you what it really means to listen well and how to use basic tools and strategies to become a better listener. I explain how scanning what you heard for agreement makes you not only a better listener, but also a better communicator. I show you why it's important to stay true to your own reality while listening, rather than abandoning what you know to be true in favor of what the other person said. I help you avoid miscommunication and recognize behaviors that are highly undesirable when it comes to listening, also known as *listening boundary violations*.

Understanding the Deeper Meaning of Having Two Ears

Have you ever wondered why humans have two ears and only one mouth? The first explanation I ever heard for this anatomical asymmetry is that we should listen twice as much as we speak. Except for the *should* in that sentence, I like this explanation.

But I think there's an even deeper meaning to the two ears design: Listening is at least twice as difficult as speaking.

Every time you receive incoming information in the form of the spoken word, an email, a text, or some other form of communication, a complex and mysterious process occurs by which you receive and filter what you've heard. The internal filters through which you hear other people's words consist of your personal history, your beliefs, value systems and so on.

Your internal filters contain beliefs such as "People don't like me," or "This person is always a jerk," or "I never get what I want." They get in the way of you receiving clean, clear communication even when the other person has superb speaking boundaries.

Here's an example that makes the preset filter problem more concrete: You come home from an extra-long day at the office and your spouse says, "I really missed having dinner with you tonight." Your filter for this situation is a thought that you should've managed your time at the office better so you'd be home for dinner. Your filter creates massive guilt and shame inside you. So, based on what you're believing about yourself and how that makes you feel, you reply to your spouse,

"Why are you giving me such a hard time for being late!? You know I'm working my butt off for this family!"

Do you see what just happened? Your response was based on all your guilty and shameful feelings, which were directly related to your own thoughts, but not to what your spouse actually said. You completely missed the sweet sentiment your spouse shared with you — that they missed you.

Scenarios like this one occur in various ways every day, all day long. You probably know this to be true from your own experience. The good news is, the information and tools in this chapter can help you change the quality of your listening forever. No kidding.

Using Basic Listening Tools

For most jobs, having the right tool is essential. In some situations, the right tool can make the difference between getting a task done in one minute and spending all day watching YouTube tutorials, getting nowhere, and then having to call for professional reinforcements.

When you don't have the right listening tools and need help, the professional reinforcements are psychotherapists or other mental health professionals. Most don't charge as much as a plumber on a holiday weekend, but it's still worth the time, heartache, and money you'll save if you can master the tools for effective listening without having to call for reinforcements.

Don't beat yourself up for not having these tools already. Many people need remedial education in how to listen well because they didn't have good role models growing up. Or maybe you've rarely, or never, been in the presence of someone who knows how to listen. Unless you're a trained mediation facilitator (mediation training is a master class on developing expert listening skills), you probably learned to listen by observation and trial and error. You can change that beginning now.

>> When you protect yourself with listening boundaries:

- You understand that the primary role of listening is to discover or understand who the other person is.

- You actively assess what you're hearing to avoid taking on blame or shame, or agreeing with another person's perceptions that don't match what you believe to be accurate or true.

- You understand that what other people say is a description of their reality — their thoughts, beliefs, opinions, judgments, and so on. What they say isn't a description of you unless you agree that it is. For example, if someone tells you that you're rude, that's their opinion about you. It's not a fact or the truth. You get to decide whether you share their perception that you're rude.

» When you protect others with your listening boundaries:

- You listen to discover or understand who the other person is rather than to judge, blame, or shame.

- You strive to maintain an attitude of curiosity while listening.

- You actively monitor your thoughts, body sensations such as heart racing or sweating, and emotions as you listen to avoid reacting or becoming defensive.

In this section I give you four basic listening tools that you can begin using right away. Pick one, or more, to add to your listening boundaries toolbox and experiment with putting them into practice.

Putting on your reporter hat

When I was an intern in graduate school, I worked with a seasoned therapist who shared with me that when she listened to clients, she would imagine that she was a news reporter researching a story. She would picture a fedora perched on top of her head and a pencil stuck behind her left ear. She used this image to remind herself that her job was — at least in the beginning — to simply record the facts.

TIP

Anytime you're listening to another person, especially when you're in a challenging or high-stakes situation, you can dramatically improve the quality of your listening skills by imagining that you're a reporter and you're interested only in the data or the facts.

Of course, there's always more to know, understand, and process from the interaction, but getting the facts down first is a great start.

Recording the speaker's actual words

One of the most important things you can do when you're listening is to pay attention to the words being spoken. I know this sounds obvious, but you'd be surprised how hard it is! The more you pay attention to and recall the words that were spoken — or record them in your head — the easier it is to understand what the other person said, what they meant, and how to respond when it's your turn to speak. Otherwise, you run the risk of creating a bad translation of what they said by substituting your words for theirs.

When your listening boundary is strong, you can remember most of what someone said — or at least have a general idea of what they said. For example, if your friend Jane says to you, "I'm so angry that Joe didn't get home until 2:00 a.m. last night," recalling what she said as "Jane's upset that Joe got home late" is a fair and reasonable paraphrase of what she shared with you.

However, sometimes people substitute words or even ideas that were never spoken instead of paraphrasing the speaker's words. In the preceding example, a mistaken substitution may sound like "Jane was out of control last night because she thought Joe was at a bar drinking with a woman." Jane said she was angry; she didn't say anything about a woman.

Here are other examples of word substitutions you may make while listening:

>> You "heard" the person say they were outraged when they actually said they were irritated.

>> You "heard" the person say, "Your cooking is terrible," when they actually said, "I don't like bison burgers."

>> You "heard" the person say they don't like spending time with you when they actually said they need at least 2 hours of alone time every day.

The danger in not paying close attention to a speaker's words — recording them, so to speak — is that your mind fills in the mental blanks with your *interpretation* of what they said, which is often very different from what they actually said or intended. Unfortunately, your interpretations frequently suggest something negative about you — your unlikability, incompetence, poor character, or some other undesirable characteristic. And that feels awful.

In the end, recalling the speaker's actual words is faster and easier than rummaging around inside your mind trying to figure out what they said or what they meant. Staying close to what people say will save your brain a lot of effort you can use on something more productive and fun, and may spare you from unhappiness, misunderstandings, and even conflict.

TIP

If it's hard for you to stay on track or remember what people say in difficult (or everyday) conversations, ask them if it's okay to take notes while they're speaking. Most people won't mind, and many will appreciate the sincerity you bring to listening. Just be sure to look up occasionally so they know you haven't gotten lost in your note-taking.

Staying curious

Curiosity is one of your best tools when it comes to good listening. If you're curious, you can also be open-minded. Listening with curiosity is about not having preconceived ideas or believing that you know what another person will say next or how a situation will turn out.

Staying curious while listening is extremely difficult because of the internal filters through which you hear others' words. It's also difficult to stay curious when you're listening to someone you've known for years, decades, or your whole life. Unknowingly, your mental image of your spouse of 36 years may look more like an ancient, calcified fossil than a living, breathing human who's still a work in progress — just like you. Make a conscious effort to blow the dust off that image and breathe some life into it. Where there's life, there's hope!

When your mind is crammed full of preconceived or fixed ideas about the speaker or the situation, it's hard to stay curious. Humans also have a habit of formulating a response in their head while the other person is still speaking, which makes it hard to stay in the moment and maintain curiosity. One of the simplest ways to stay curious while listening is to focus first on the speaker's words, and then on your thoughts and emotions.

TIP

If you want to take it up a notch and have fun with curious listening, you can experiment with keeping one (or all) of these phrases in mind as you listen:

>> Wow, this is fascinating!

>> I wonder what they'll say next?

>> It's so interesting that they think that. I wonder how they came to that conclusion?

TIP

One of my mentors, Pia Mellody, author and Senior Fellow of Meadows Behavioral Healthcare, often shared her trick for staying curious while listening. She would lean forward as if listening intently, widen her eyes, and say to herself, "So that's who you are!" (Of course, you have to remember to say this silently to yourself, not out loud.)

These tools may seem silly, odd, or even ridiculous. But they're perfect *pattern interrupters* (tools for intervening on ingrained habits) for a busy mind that believes it has a crystal ball that sees into the future and already knows what's going to happen next.

Receiving words impersonally

I hope you won't disagree when I tell you that you're the center of the universe. No, this cosmic statement isn't a joke. Although humans have beautiful, awe-inspiring capacity for compassion and empathy, it doesn't change the fact that we're all the center of the universe. But of course, only *our* universe.

And even if you strongly disagree with this idea because you consider yourself a selfless giver, you can still get more mileage than you bargained for if you develop the skill of not taking anything personally.

THINK ABOUT IT

In fact, this skill is so important that it's one of the four agreements presented in Don Miguel Ruiz's book *The Four Agreements*. Ruiz describes these agreements as codes of conduct "that can rapidly transform our lives to a new experience of freedom, true happiness, and love." I don't know about you, but I'm for anything that gives me more freedom, happiness, and love.

What does it mean to not take other people's words personally? It means you embrace the reality and the profound truth that every word anyone ever utters is completely about them. Really? Yes, really.

Your mind may have already gone to work to disprove what I just said: that what other people say is about them. For example, you may be thinking, "My fifth-grade art teacher told me my crayon reproduction of Vincent Van Gogh's *Starry Night* was abominable! How was that about her?" Or, "My first wife told me she left me because I didn't make enough money. That's about me!"

Well, first, a teacher who insults a student's artwork needs to find another profession more suitable to their skills, which in this case are seriously lacking in the empathy and wisdom department. A teacher saying your art is abominable does not, and cannot, make it so.

Her perceptions (and everyone else's) are based on many factors, including their history, biases, opinions about art and maybe even their negative feelings toward the student. To further drive home the point, there's no doubt that Van Gogh heard a French version of this a time or two. When he was criticized or ridiculed, it was never about him and his art but rather the observer or perceiver.

And your wife leaving you because you didn't make enough money? If you believe her decision was about you, you're unnecessarily making yourself miserable. If you don't believe me, think about the thousands upon thousands of people at this very moment who wish the spouse they're married to made more money, or is under- or unemployed. People's choices are 100 percent about them, 100 percent of the time.

When you grasp the truth that what other people say and do is not personal it will forever change your life.

Admittedly, your friends and family may have repeatedly given you certain feedback such as "You're a loud talker" or "You're a slow walker" or "You drive really fast." Feedback like this is based on observations of facts and perceptions. And these facts or perceptions may have validity or may say something that's true about you.

Facts can be verified, and perceptions can be considered and measured if they're relatively simple to quantify. For example, it's possible to determine if you talk louder or walk slower or drive faster than most people. However, if a person has a problem with your loud talking, slow walking, or fast driving, it's about them, not you. Some people love loud talking, slow walking, and fast driving. And even if you agree with their assessment of you, what you choose to do about it is completely up to you.

Talking to people who have a strong habit of taking things personally feels like walking on eggshells. You find yourself analyzing every word before it passes from your lips to their ears, praying they won't find a way to transform what you just said into a highly disrespectful insult. It's like two people having two different conversations at the same time.

REMEMBER

When you understand that what people say is about them and not about you, you've mastered the skill of not taking things personally. This skill can make you exponentially happier and easier to communicate with.

Scanning What You Heard for Agreement

One of the ways you can stay curious while listening is by focusing on what you agree with. When you're in an argument or a heated conversation, you tend to zero in on what you don't agree with, what you don't like, or what you're going to say just as soon as the other person stops talking.

For example, while you're discussing the next family vacation, your spouse says they would love to go to Antarctica. They prefer to travel by rail for the land portion of the trip, they want to take your cute little Chihuahua, Boss, along, and they want to make the trip in August (one of the coldest months of the year in Antarctica).

As you listen to your spouse's captivating plans, you find that you're all in, except for one teeny, tiny part. You absolutely can't agree to taking Boss along on this frozen expedition. The little fellow can't stand the cold and routinely rips off his weatherproof dog boots with his teeth before his paws even touch the grass. You're deeply concerned about how he would weather, so to speak, this epic journey.

If you're like most people, even though you love the sound of your spouse's Antarctica adventure, you begin your reply with something like this: "No, we're not taking Boss." It's unfortunate to lead with what's a no go for you because now you and your spouse will probably proceed directly to locking horns in a battle over why Boss can't go to Antarctica, rather than planning and dreaming about your next adventure together.

The beauty of scanning for agreement is that when it comes time to respond to your spouse, you'll have the foresight to begin by telling them that their plans sound amazing. That you'd love to go to Antarctica in August by rail, and that you'd like to talk more about the possibility of taking Boss. Notice how Boss came at the end? An added bonus you'll get from using this tool is that you'll probably reach "Yes, let's get a dog sitter for Boss while we go on vacation" faster and easier.

REMEMBER

Scanning for what you agree with helps you give your response the best possible start by leading with the positive rather than with the negative.

Distinguishing Your Reality from Their Reality

When your listening boundary is nonexistent, isn't working well, or has shriveled up from lack of use, you may unknowingly and unwittingly believe what others believe even when it's not true for you. How does that happen?

For example, say you just told your mother that you made a reservation to do a half spa day for your birthday next week. Your mother replies, "Well, that's pretty selfish, don't you think?! What did your husband say about you wasting half the day getting pampered and spoiled?" Ouch!

If you struggle to separate your mother's reality from your own, you will automatically believe that you're selfish because she said so. When your listening boundary is strong and working well, you hear your mother's words and decide whether they're true for you, or not. If you don't believe you're selfish, your ability to separate your mother's reality from yours protects you from the intense, painful emotions of believing something about you that isn't true for you.

TIP

A handy tool to use when you're listening is to ask yourself if what you heard is true for you, not true for you, or if you're not sure and you need more information. If what they said is true for you, then you both agree. If what they said isn't true for you be sure not to *take it in* — believe it — as if it is true for you. If you do, you'll experience painful negative emotions. If you're not sure if it's true for you, ask clarifying questions. See "Asking clarifying questions" section later in this chapter for more information.

TIP

Other people get to believe what they believe. You get to believe what you believe.

When you believe what other people think or believe rather than what you think and believe, it's hard to know whom to believe! And worse, you'll be unnecessarily unhappy. You suffer when you live your life according to other people's thoughts and beliefs instead of your own.

REMEMBER

When your listening boundary is strong, you don't abandon what you believe to be true for what another person believes is true and you don't take on unearned blame, guilt, or shame.

Avoiding Upset and Misunderstanding with Good Listening

One of the secrets of having a black belt in the listening boundary is that your boundary skills protect you from communication that's not relational, not delivered well, mean-spirited, or even offensive. How can that be?

When you know how to listen well and how to correctly process what someone said, you avoid taking in what isn't true for you. For example, if someone calls you stupid and you don't consider yourself stupid, there's no reason for you to believe you're stupid or to have any strong feelings about their name-calling. You may have some thoughts and feelings about the person who called you stupid, but you can clearly see that what they said is about them, not you.

When you have a functional, healthy listening boundary, you avoid overreacting or misinterpreting what someone said without first checking it out or asking clarifying questions which I explain in the section "Asking clarifying questions" later in this chapter).

Seeing that someone's words don't equal your interpretation

A speaker's words and your interpretation of them are two different things. An easy tool to use when you want to distinguish what a speaker said from what you perceived or thought they said is to get a piece of paper, draw a line down the middle, and write at the top of the left column "Facts/Data" and at the top of the right column "Thoughts/Perceptions."

Then, to the best of your ability, write down exactly what the speaker said without using any perception or judgment words in the Facts/Data column. In the right column (Thoughts/Perceptions), write down all your perception words related to what was said.

For example, say that your teenager is an hour late getting home. You've been worried about him, so you're sitting in the living room waiting impatiently for his return. When he walks in the door, he says hello, mumbles a weak apology, and tells you he's really tired and he's going straight to bed. You're convinced he's been drinking.

Wisely, you decide that it's probably best to let him go to bed and discuss the broken curfew in the morning. But you're worried sick that he was drinking. So you get out your paper and write the two columns: Facts/Data and Thoughts/Perceptions.

The facts and data are:

>> He said he was really tired.

>> He said he was going straight to bed.

>> You understood his words.

>> He walked in a straight line and didn't stagger.

>> He said he was sorry for being late.

>> You didn't smell alcohol.

Your thoughts and perceptions are:

>> He tried to go to bed in a hurry to avoid being found out.

>> He's going to be an alcoholic just like his father.

>> He apologized but he didn't mean it.

>> He was out with John, and everybody knows John's a drinker.

>> He's going to have a hangover in the morning. Then you'll know for sure!

>> You're probably going to have to send him to rehab.

Can you see how none of the facts and data in this situation support the thoughts and perceptions?

Noticing that what you experience with your senses can often have no correlation to your thoughts, perceptions, and judgments can take your listening boundary to the next level. If you rely on the facts of what someone said, you won't make the mistake of reacting to what you perceived or made up. Your responses will stay closer to the actual data and facts.

TIP

If you believe someone is impaired or has been using mind-altering substances, avoid having a conversation with them. It won't be productive, and they may not remember anything about it. You can simply say, "I'll talk to you some other time. I can't talk to you right now." Don't blame them for your not wanting to talk, and don't tell them that you don't want to talk because they're wasted. Make your reasons for delaying a conversation about you, not about the other person.

Asking clarifying questions

Asking clarifying questions is one of the most powerful skills you can develop when it comes to listening.

Clarifying questions confirm that you're listening well, and they also send a message to the speaker that you want to understand what they're saying. And who doesn't want to be understood? When you begin noticing that there's often a wide gap between what someone says and what you perceive, you naturally find yourself asking more clarifying questions.

For example, in the scenario about the curfew-breaking teenager in the previous section, seeing that someone's words don't equal your interpretation, you have two options for how to talk to your son about what happened the night before. The conversation will be more helpful and productive if you ask him to tell you more about why he was late getting home. You can ask him directly, "Were you drinking last night?"

On the other hand, if you take your perceptions as true, you're more likely to accuse, interrogate, or talk *at* him, rather than staying curious and asking questions.

TIP

Here are a few examples of high-quality clarifying questions:

» Can you repeat what you just said? I want to make sure I got it right.

» Tell me more!

» What did you think about that?

» I'm not sure I know what you mean. Can you say that again?

Notice that each of these questions is open-ended rather than a yes-or-no question. Open-ended questions naturally invite the speaker to elaborate and expand.

Taking a pause when needed

If you've ever been told to take a deep breath or count to ten before you say or do anything, you're already one step ahead when it comes to knowing how to take a pause when needed. One of the smartest things you can do when you're agitated, upset, angry, or triggered while listening to another person is to take a break.

Here are six steps for taking a healthy, respectful time-out:

1. **Recognize that you're emotionally overwhelmed or flooded with painful, negative emotions.**

   You may feel hot, have an elevated heart rate, feel shut down, or become highly reactive.

2. **Communicate to the other person that you need to take a time-out.**

   Tell them, "I'm overwhelmed (or I'm not in a good place to have this conversation) right now, and I need a time-out."

3. **Tell the other person how long you need for the time-out and where you'll be.**

   Add enough time to your estimate to give yourself plenty of space to process what's happening for you and to get yourself grounded and centered again.

4. **Take more time, if needed.**

   If you realize while taking the time-out that you need more time, let the other person know as soon as possible.

5. **Be accountable about your commitment.**

   Return at the time you stated.

6. Reengage about the hot-button topic.

When you return, either ask the other person if they would like to reengage about the issue or schedule a mutually agreeable time in the future to talk about it.

Remember these time-out do's and don'ts:

>> *Do* take ownership of your need for a time-out rather than relying on the other person to suggest it.

>> *Do* reengage about the hot-button topic after a time-out.

>> *Do* use time-outs productively. The purpose of time-outs is to calm yourself and get grounded.

>> *Don't* use time-outs to avoid or delay talking about a topic that's difficult or painful for you.

>> *Don't* say, "You're upset, and I think you need a time-out." Take ownership of your emotions and your need for a time-out.

>> *Don't* refuse to accept the other person's request for a time-out by physically following them, continuing to talk to them after they've requested a time-out, or refusing to let them leave.

TIP

If you decide to experiment with taking a respectful time-out, always err on the side of taking too much time rather than too little. For example, if you think you can reasonably return in an hour, say you need two hours instead. When you have more space than you think you need, the added time cushion may help you feel calmer faster. And if you return to the conversation sooner than you agreed to, it may be a pleasant surprise to the other person.

Naming Listening Boundary Violations

When it comes to listening, it may seem like there's not a whole lot you can do to violate someone's boundaries while they're speaking. But humans have brilliant, clever minds that are sneakily adept at creating strategies for pushing back and resisting when we experience something we don't like. Listening is no exception.

Being intentionally distracted

Thanks to the widespread availability of digital devices, the many ways you have to entertain yourself, and the access that other people have to you through these devices, you're constantly lured to scroll, click, and watch. You live in the most distracted time in human history.

When your devices — or anything else — distract you from listening to another person when they're speaking, that's a problem. And it's even worse when you intentionally distract yourself to avoid listening.

Here are a few examples of being intentionally distracted:

» Being on your phone constantly while in the presence of another person, with no good or mutually agreed-upon reason

» Looking around frequently in a public place like a restaurant or sports arena and not looking at or talking to the person you're with

» Being on your computer to avoid connecting with or speaking to another person

» Playing with pets (or children) to avoid connecting with others

Keeping yourself distracted while another person is speaking sends a message to the speaker. Unfortunately, the message will be based on what the speaker makes up or assumes, which may have no connection to what's really happening.

It's reasonable to assume that the message the speaker gets from your behavior isn't positive. At best they may think you're improving your vocabulary by playing Words with Friends. At worst they may think you don't care about them. And if the speaker is someone you love, this isn't a message you want to send.

TIP

If devices have taken over your relationship or your family, consider having device-free moments built into your daily routine. For example, you can create an agreement with your partner that meals or walks in the park are device-free. And even if your partner doesn't agree, you can create a boundary for yourself to be device-free whenever you want.

Refusing to listen

Refusing to listen can take the form of interrupting another person or simply being unwilling to receive information someone is attempting to convey to you.

This can happen with verbal as well as written communication. Ignoring texts, phone calls, or emails is a form of refusing to listen. To be fair, sometimes it's completely appropriate to ignore certain forms of communication — like answering your phone while you're driving. However, frequently ignoring communications from someone you have a close personal or professional relationship with is harmful to the long-term health and sustainability of the relationship.

Leaving in the middle of a sentence

Have you ever been in the middle of a conversation when suddenly, out of nowhere, the other person leaves the room or the house? Most of us have experienced this at least once, and it can be infuriating and painful.

Walking away without warning during a conversation is an obvious (and unskillful) way to avoid communication. It's harmful not only to the conversation when it occurs, but also to the relationship over the long term. When walking away becomes a pattern, it creates reluctance or even unwillingness on the part of the person who's left behind to engage in important or difficult conversations. Finding ways to stay in conversations, even when they're difficult, creates trust and builds strong, enduring bonds.

TIP

If you get overwhelmed during conversations, use the six steps outlined earlier in this chapter under "Taking a pause when needed."

Changing the subject abruptly

Changing the subject abruptly is a less-than-desirable skill that few people have mastered, but the ones who have can leave you feeling left behind in their dust.

A person may change the subject without warning for many reasons, including being uncomfortable with the subject matter, being asked a question they don't want to answer, being unwilling to participate in the natural give-and-take of conversation, or simply being bored.

TIP

One of the cleanest ways to change the subject during a conversation is to say, "There's something else I'd like to talk about. Would it be okay with you if I change the subject?"

You should avoid changing the subject abruptly. It's usually an unwelcome and one-sided move that stops the flow of communication, the subject matter, the speaker, or all three. And if you're interacting with an abrupt subject changer, you can use simple tools (see Chapter 6) to steer the conversation back to the original topic before it takes a one-sided detour.

REMEMBER

If the other person says *no* to a change of subject, you need to respect their answer. It doesn't mean you have to stay in the conversation. It just means that for now you can't change the subject without violating their boundary.

Rolling your eyes and other nonverbal communications

Making facial expressions or gestures, turning away physically when someone is speaking, and other forms of nonverbal communication are boundary violations if the intent is to shame, ridicule, or insult another person.

Rolling your eyes when someone is talking can signal that you don't believe what they said is true. It can also suggest that you're holding the speaker in contempt or looking down on them.

Nonverbal communication can quickly create disconnection and conflict because the meaning of a nonverbal cue is almost impossible to figure out without knowing its intent. Staying conscious of what you're thinking and feeling during interactions with others and maintaining an attitude of respect and curiosity prevents you from sending nonverbal communications that harm rather than help connection and understanding.

Chapter **12**

Nonnegotiable Boundaries

I f personal boundaries had short, descriptive titles that perfectly explained what they are and how they work, nonnegotiable boundaries would be called *The Buck Stops Here* or *case-closed* boundaries.

That's because *nonnegotiable* means that you're not open to discussing or negotiating a boundary you set.

In this chapter, I define nonnegotiable boundaries and identify the four primary ones. I show you that not only are physical and sexual boundaries nonnegotiable (meaning that a *no* to physical or sexual touch means *no*), but also that you can set other nonnegotiable boundaries — such as ultimatums — in any relationship. I explain why it's important to be selective when you choose your nonnegotiables — especially because declaring a nonnegotiable boundary and not following through with it damages your self-trust and credibility with others.

Identifying the Four Nonnegotiable Boundaries

By definition, a *nonnegotiable boundary* is a limit you set that is not open to discussion or modification and is completely within your power to do. Another word to describe nonnegotiable boundaries when they apply to relationships is *deal-breakers*.

There are four nonnegotiable boundaries: Two apply specifically to your body, and two are related to interpersonal relationships.

The four nonnegotiable boundaries are:

» Physical boundaries: who, when, where, and how another person can touch you or how close they can get to you and your personal belongings

» Sexual boundaries: with whom, when, where, and how you engage sexually

» Saying *no*

» Ultimatums in relationships

Nonnegotiable physical and sexual boundaries, along with saying *no*, are the most common nonnegotiables. Nonnegotiable relationship boundaries (or ultimatums) are the least common and are often preceded by broken agreements or other relationship crises.

Defining a physical boundary

Your nonnegotiable physical boundaries include:

» How close another person gets to you physically

» Who, when, where, and how another person may touch your body

» Who, when, where, and how another person may access your personal belongings

Anytime you express a limit or say *no* to physical closeness, touch, or certain kinds of touch, your boundary is nonnegotiable. No one has a right to touch another person's body without their permission. (See Chapter 8 for more information about how physical boundaries work.)

TIP

If you want to teach children healthy personal boundaries, never force them to hug or touch another person, including a relative. Although giving Grandma a hug and a kiss may be a family tradition that goes back eight generations, when you demand that a child touch an adult, you're teaching them that they don't have a right to say *no* to unwanted touching.

Determining a sexual boundary

Like physical boundaries, your sexual boundaries are nonnegotiable. Your body is your domain, and you get to decide when, where, how, and with whom you engage sexually.

Unfortunately, there's still too much misunderstanding and misinformation about sexual boundaries — specifically, sexual boundaries related to women's bodies. Some cultures and religions believe that a woman's body belongs to her husband.

I've heard from several female clients that their pastors told them to have sex with their husband anytime he wants sex. This directive was intended as a solution to the husband's compulsive sexual behavior or his use of pornography. Being told by a clergy member that your husband has a right to sex on demand is not only sexual abuse, but also spiritual and religious abuse.

WARNING

Believing that you can change another person by either having sex with them or withholding sex from them is delusional. No one is powerful enough to cause another person to do or to not do anything.

You're free to choose the beliefs that align with what's true for you, but viewed through the lens of healthy functional boundaries, granting someone the right to another person's body is emotional, physical, and sexual abuse.

The level of entitlement, strong emotions, and misinformation surrounding sexual boundaries requires a detailed definition of what nonnegotiable sexual boundaries mean.

Here's what nonnegotiable sexual boundaries look like:

>> If you don't want to have sex with someone, that's a nonnegotiable boundary you have a right to set with that person, regardless of their relationship to you. You're not obligated to have sex with your spouse or partner — ever.

>> If you don't want to have sex at a certain time of day or at the time you're approached for sex, that's a nonnegotiable boundary you have a right to set regarding *when* you want to be sexual.

>> If you don't want to have sex in a particular place, that's a nonnegotiable boundary you have a right to set regarding *where* you want to be sexual.

>> If you don't want to engage in a certain type of sexual contact or participate in a certain type of sexual activity, that's a nonnegotiable boundary you have a right to set regarding *how* you want to be sexual.

Saying "no"

Despite being a word with only two letters, *no* is a complete sentence, a confirmation that saying *no* is a nonnegotiable boundary.

Does a *no* ever turn into a *yes*? Sometimes it does. But in the moment that someone says *no*, it means their *no* should stand, and not be challenged. You can be curious about their reasons for saying *no*, but you shouldn't attempt to persuade, manipulate, pressure, or intimidate a person to change their answer to a *yes*, or even a *maybe*.

TIP

When you resist another person's boundary, they'll defend it, which causes them to become even more committed to it. One of the best-kept secrets about respecting other people's boundaries is that when you honor someone's boundary — including a *no* — your acceptance builds trust and may even create the conditions that allow the boundary to soften or change in the future.

Establishing an ultimatum

Merriam-Webster defines an *ultimatum* as "a final proposition, condition, or demand." Ultimatums have a reputation for being final, forceful, and often threatening statements. However, ultimatums that meet the following two conditions are also nonnegotiable boundaries:

>> You have the power to create the boundary yourself, without the participation of another person.

>> Your ultimatum is not an obvious threat, nor is it intended to be a threat.

Here are a few examples of ultimatums that are also nonnegotiable boundaries:

>> If you have another affair, I will file for divorce.

>> If you ask me again to change the numbers on our financial statement to make them look better to the bank, I will turn in my resignation.

>> If you don't get help for your alcohol problem, I will end this relationship.

>> If you leave my son alone in your apartment again I won't allow him to visit you without my supervision.

>> If you take more than [x dollars] out of our joint account again without discussing it with me first, I will legally separate my money from yours.

Notice that for each example of nonnegotiable boundaries, the first condition is met. You have the power to create the boundary, or carry out the "consequence." You have the power to file for divorce, end a relationship, or move your money into a separate account. However, no one except the person who states these boundaries knows their intention.

If the primary intention of a nonnegotiable boundary is to frighten, threaten, or cause the other person to change their behavior, it's not a true nonnegotiable boundary. Establishing nonnegotiable boundaries means you're 100 percent sure you'll follow through with the action you describe in the boundary.

TIP

Nonnegotiable boundaries that describe what another person will do rather than what you will do aren't nonnegotiable boundaries. For example, "If you pay the electric bill late again, you have to put it on autopay" isn't a nonnegotiable boundary because it states what another person will do, rather than what you will do. You can't make anyone do anything.

For more information about establishing ultimatums, see Chapter 2.

Selecting Your Nonnegotiable Relationship Boundaries

When choosing nonnegotiable relationship boundaries, you should follow three important guidelines:

>> Understand that nonnegotiable boundaries are the least used of all personal boundaries. That's because they express a final, nonnegotiable limit where there's no possibility of compromise.

>> Never set a nonnegotiable boundary without knowing that you're completely committed to following through on the action you say you will take.

>> When it comes to creating nonnegotiable boundaries, go slowly and be mindful. Otherwise, you're likely to create a nonnegotiable that you don't honor, which will cause you to lose self-trust as well as credibility with others.

REMEMBER

You're the ultimate decider about your nonnegotiable boundaries. No one has a right to tell you what your boundaries, including your nonnegotiables, are.

Realizing very few nonnegotiable relationship boundaries exist

Life offers many opportunities to set physical and sexual boundaries or to say *no*. These relationship boundaries are the most common of the four nonnegotiable boundaries. However, setting nonnegotiable relationship boundaries happens infrequently. In fact, if you haven't experienced a significant relationship challenge or crisis, you may not have any nonnegotiables in your relationship.

Before creating a nonnegotiable boundary, I recommend you ask yourself two questions:

>> Am I absolutely unwilling to discuss — or negotiate — this with the other person?

>> Am I 100 percent committed to following through on the action I said I would take?

If you answer *yes* to both questions, you most likely have a thoughtful, sound nonnegotiable boundary.

TIP

Nonnegotiable boundaries are sometimes misused to get important needs met. For example, if you need more connection or closeness in your relationship, you may tell your spouse that if they don't spend at least an hour a day with you, you'll divorce them. You're free to create this nonnegotiable boundary, but you may discover that you're not prepared to follow through. A better solution is to define what connection and closeness look like for you, make a specific request, and create an agreement. You can do this by working the six steps of the boundary-setting process, starting with Chapter 13.

Getting clear about your commitment to a nonnegotiable boundary

Because nonnegotiable boundaries make a strong, powerful, and final statement, you must be undeniably clear about your commitment to any nonnegotiable boundary you create — especially nonnegotiable relationship boundaries.

If you have any hesitation about the boundary or your ability to follow through with the action you say you will take, don't set the boundary. Wait until you're calm, crystal clear, and certain that you can trust yourself to follow through.

TIP

When you're experiencing strong emotions or uncertain that you're doing the right thing, it's always better wait to set a nonnegotiable boundary than to set it and not follow through.

Choosing nonnegotiables wisely

Selecting nonnegotiable relationship boundaries gets tricky when you're feeling strong emotions, you're triggered, or you're simply out for revenge.

In those situations, you'll be tempted to set boundaries you'll call nonnegotiable that sound like this:

>> If you run another stop sign, I'm never going to ride in the car with you again.

>> If you don't tell Uncle Joe to stop calling me "toothpick" I'm never going to visit him with you again.

>> If you look at me like that again, I'm going to divorce you.

>> If you don't double my salary, I'm going to quit.

>> If you don't tell your mother to stop serving brisket at her Sunday lunches, I'm never going again.

Of course, you can decide to stop riding in the car with a reckless driver or leave a job because you don't get a raise. However, in most cases, these sorts of statements are outbursts of emotion rather than thoughtfully created limits.

REMEMBER

You become untrustworthy to yourself and others when you don't follow through by taking action on a nonnegotiable boundary you set. That's why it's important to choose your nonnegotiable relationship boundaries carefully and rationally.

4
Creating Personal Boundaries

Discover the six steps for identifying, creating, and maintaining effective personal boundaries and get started with Step 1.

Investigate what you experienced so you can get clear about your reality in Step 2.

Identify needs that aren't being met in a problematic situation you're working on and name the outcome you want in Step 3.

Find out where your power lies in Step 4 so you can easily identify what action to take.

Take action to create the boundary you want to set in Step 5.

Review your results and find out what to do if a boundary didn't work in Step 6.

IN THIS CHAPTER

» Creating boundaries in six steps

» Working the first step of the boundary-setting process

» Acknowledging anger, stress, and emotional pain

» Choosing a situation to address

» Focusing on one incident at a time

Chapter 13

Step 1: Know What Isn't Working

What if I told you that you can create any boundary — with yourself or with anyone else — using the same six steps every time? This may seem hard to believe because boundaries are often divided into categories or implemented according to the type of relationship involved. For example, you set boundaries in the workplace, boundaries with family members, boundaries in intimate relationships, and boundaries with friends.

There's no doubt that the boundaries you create in various contexts and relationships are based on the different levels of closeness you have with the people involved and the privacy you want in those contexts (see Chapter 3). However, creating boundaries in each relationship or context is accomplished in exactly the same way. Knowing the six steps for identifying, creating, and maintaining effective personal boundaries streamlines and simplifies the process.

In this chapter, I introduce and explain the six steps for creating healthy, effective personal boundaries. Starting with Step 1, you determine what's not working for you in a given situation or relationship. I describe common signs that may suggest you need to set a boundary, how to identify a situation where you may want to create a boundary, and why it's best to work on one issue or incident at a time rather than trying to tackle a long-standing pattern or problem all at once.

Using the Six Steps for Creating Boundaries

One of the best-kept secrets about boundaries is that once you master the fundamental steps for identifying, creating, and maintaining healthy, effective boundaries, you can use these same steps to create any boundary you want to create.

Here are the six steps:

1. **Know what isn't working.**
2. **Get clear about your reality.**
3. **Clarify your needs and the outcome you want.**
4. **See where you have power before you take action.**
5. **Take action to create a boundary.**
6. **Evaluate your results and see what went wrong.**

These steps are described in detail in this chapter as well as Chapters 14 through 18. They're meant to be worked sequentially, starting with Step 1 and working each step until you get to Step 6.

REMEMBER

Step 6 specifically addresses a boundary that isn't successful. Part 5 of this book has info about addressing boundaries that don't work. If a boundary is successful, you won't always need to work Step 6, but it's included in the process because eventually you'll need it! A boundary may be unsuccessful for many reasons, so don't assume it's because you did something wrong or made a mistake. For example, if you create an agreement with someone (which is a boundary) and they break the agreement, their breaking of the agreement is their responsibility — it's never yours.

Like so many things in life, these steps are simple, but they're not always easy.

For example, when you get to the step of clarifying your needs and the outcome you want (Step 3), like many people you may make the mistake of focusing exclusively on outcomes that require another person to change or to behave differently. This option always appears to be the easier path to getting needs met because it doesn't require you to do anything! I agree that there may be situations where the only way you can get the outcome you want is if someone else changes. However, your boundary work is more effective when you stay open to other options, especially options that you have the power to create. I share more about how to do this in Chapter 15.

TIP

Focusing exclusively on getting another person to change in order to get your needs met is one of the most common pitfalls of boundary work. It's understandable to want another person to be respectful, honest, cooperative, affectionate, and so on. You can make a request of the other person to change, but your boundary work is much more effective when you also explore what you have the power to do when someone is disrespectful, dishonest, uncooperative, or cold (rather than affectionate).

Rest assured that once you understand the steps and know how to avoid the pitfalls, you'll identify and create boundaries with more ease, effectiveness, and even joy!

Getting Started with Step 1

Whenever you need to create a boundary, Step 1 (know what isn't working for you) is your starting point in any given situation.

You may already know that your boss texting you at all hours of the night and on weekends isn't working for you. (I can completely understand why that wouldn't work for you!) But there may be other situations where knowing what's not working for you isn't as obvious.

For example, you may have a vague feeling that something's not right about a situation, but you're not sure what it is. Or maybe you've got negative feelings about something (or someone), but you don't know why, or you can't quite put your finger on what's wrong. In the following sections, I show you how to recognize potential boundary issues by paying attention to specific experiences in your day-to-day life, including:

>> Anger or other negative emotions

>> Stressful situations

>> Arguments with partners, family, friends, coworkers, and others

>> Broken agreements

>> Painful patterns in relationships

>> Negative feedback or consequences from others

When you're feeling angry or stressed, or your relationships are in conflict, you're likely to feel overwhelmed and unsure about what to do or how to proceed. That's why you need an easy-to-follow process like the six steps for identifying, creating, and maintaining healthy, effective boundaries.

Taking time to be specific about what's not working for you gets your boundary-setting process off to the best possible start.

Seeing That Anger Can Signal You Need a Boundary

The emotion of anger is one of the best clues that you may need to set a boundary. For example, if you're angry because one of your friends repeatedly interrupts you when you're talking, this is a great topic to explore as a potential boundary. Keep in mind that the boundary probably won't involve stopping your friend from interrupting because you don't have the power to change their — or anyone else's — behavior. (See Chapter 16 for more information about seeing where you have power to take action, and where you don't).

TIP

Because it's possible that anger may be about something that doesn't require a boundary, I recommend that when you notice you're feeling angry, you ask yourself, "Is there a limit I need to set here, or is there a boundary I need to create?" If the answer is *yes*, you should work the six steps.

Anger sometimes manifests as resentment. My favorite definition of resentment comes from the work of Pia Mellody, author and Senior Fellow of Meadows Behavioral Healthcare, who defines it as "victim anger." Essentially, resentment is when you're not only feeling angry, but also seeing or perceiving yourself as a victim. Resentments are often unconscious or unspoken expectations about the way other people *should* behave or the way things *should* work.

Resentment is an even stronger indicator of the need to create a boundary than anger. Seeing yourself as a victim means you believe that someone is doing something to you that causes you to feel uncomfortable, threatened, or even unsafe. And while it may be true that you need to protect yourself, feeling like a victim creates a sense of powerlessness. Boundary work — when it's done effectively — eliminates the feeling of powerlessness because you're taking empowered action on your own behalf. This is why doing boundary work focused specifically on your resentments can be extremely helpful.

To see how anger or resentment can be a sign that you need to set a boundary, imagine that your best friend is routinely 20 minutes late when the two of you make plans to meet for lunch or a cup of coffee. You've known your friend for 15 years, and they're 100 percent reliable about one thing: being late.

You're starting to notice that your friend's tendency toward tardiness is getting on your nerves, to the point that you don't have the same positive feelings about getting together. Sometimes you even dread meeting your friend because you know they're going to be late. You feel like your time is being disrespected. Your irritation and anger are starting to get in the way of your connection. When your friend shows up 20 minutes late to lunch again, you notice that you have to force yourself to smile or talk to them in a casual, relaxed way.

Based on what you're thinking and feeling in this situation, do you think it's time to set a boundary? I think it is! You find out exactly how to do this by working the six steps.

Identifying Points of Stress or Emotional Pain

Another way to determine where a boundary may need to be set is to notice any areas of stress or emotional pain in your life.

I once had a business coach who said, "Where there's stress, there's no system." I think it's more accurate to express that thought this way: "Where there's stress, there's no *effective* system." I added the word *effective* because the truth is, the results you're getting are always determined by the system you've put in place at the moment. The problem is, it may not be the system that creates the results you want. Knowing that an effective system reduces stress is helpful in both your professional and personal life, and requires creating parameters, limits, or boundaries.

For example, if you experience regular stress around getting to the train on time each morning to get to work, you have a system problem. If your current habit is to get out of bed at 7:30 a.m. when you have to catch the train at 7:50 a.m. to make it to work on time, your getting-up-in-the-morning system is working to create stress in your life. But it's not working to help you feel calm and relaxed as you walk to the train station. Creating a new getting-up-in-the-morning system that reliably gives you a calm, relaxed walk to the train station is an example of implementing a self-boundary.

REMEMBER

Creating a *self-boundary*, or a boundary for yourself, is accomplished using the same six steps you use for creating boundaries with everyone else.

Emotional pain in the form of sadness, hurt, jealousy, or loneliness is another sign that you may need to set a boundary. For example, if you're in a relationship that isn't as affectionate or respectful as you'd like it to be or doesn't feel *mutual* (meaning there's an imbalance of giving and receiving), you may often feel sad or lonely in the relationship.

The pain you feel doesn't necessarily mean you need to end the relationship. It can point to areas in the relationship where you may want to create agreements or set limits so that you get more of your needs for affection, respect, or balance met.

To help identify potential areas of stress or emotional pain, ask yourself:

>> Do I experience stress or emotional pain in any of my current relationships?

>> Are there parts of my daily schedule or my daily routine that create stress for me?

>> Do I regularly encounter certain situations where I frequently experience emotional pain?

After you single out those relationships or situations, write a short description of each one that pinpoints the issues that are causing you stress or emotional pain. This information helps you identify potential areas of your life where a boundary may be the solution.

Focusing on a Specific Incident or Situation

Remembering a specific incident or situation that didn't go the way you wanted is a great place to start when you're exploring where you may need to set a boundary. Not experiencing what you wanted and the uncomfortable emotions that went along with that situation are clues pointing you in the direction of uncovering what didn't work for you — Step 1 for creating a healthy boundary.

Recalling an argument

Take a moment to remember the last time you had a serious disagreement or argument with someone — preferably someone you have a close relationship with — or an argument that involved something very important to you like money or parenting. These are the arguments that will disturb and bother you the most.

Does the argument feel unresolved because you're still having strong feelings about it? Or does the argument feel unresolved because you didn't reach a mutual understanding with the other person, or because you know the same situation is likely to be repeated in the future? If you answered *yes* to any of these questions, this argument is worth exploring to find out if there's a boundary you want to create.

Another way to reflect on a past argument to determine if you need to set a boundary is to rate or assign the argument a number on a scale of 1 to 10, with 10 being the absolute worst argument and 1 being so unimportant you forgot about it. If the number is a 7 or higher, ask yourself:

>> What upset me about this argument?

>> Was there anything I said during the argument that made me feel uncomfortable?

>> Is there something I did or said during the argument that I would do differently if I could redo it?

>> What did the other person do or say that causes me to give this argument a high rating?

>> What do I wish had happened instead during this conversation?

>> Is there anything about the argument that would cause me to need or want to set a boundary?

If you still have strong feelings about the argument or you have specific and detailed answers to most of these questions, this argument warrants a deeper look as an issue that may require a boundary.

Dealing with an annoying person

Is there someone in your life you can count on like clockwork to annoy you? If your answer is *yes*, I recommend that you first rule out the possibility that you're experiencing a classic case of "one finger pointing out and the other three fingers pointing back at you." In other words, many times what annoys you about someone else is the same trait or characteristic that you can find in yourself. The fancy psychological term for this phenomenon is projection. *Projection* means I project (or put) onto you what I don't see, don't want to see, or don't like about myself.

That being said, some people can be truly annoying! And if you routinely have to interact with an annoying person in your daily life, creating a boundary to manage the situation may be just what you need. For example, you can limit how much time you spend with them, how much access they have to you, or the ways you're willing to interact with them.

If the annoying person you're dealing with is a family member, you may think you just have to accept their annoying behavior. I want you to know that you have a choice. You can give them a pass, but you can also create limits and boundaries with them. No one is exempt from boundaries — including family members.

Experiencing severe consequences in the workplace

If you've been in trouble at work for chronic tardiness or absenteeism, poor performance, or unprofessional interactions with coworkers or a supervisor, the boundaries you need to set are with yourself.

A simple truth about boundaries is that if you repeatedly fail to place limits on yourself, other people or institutions will show up to do it for you. Your employer, a licensing board, or even the legal system will take up the slack in any areas where you don't rein yourself in. For example, if you're unable to abide by ethical conduct guidelines or meet the obligations of your job, you may lose your license, or your employer may place you on probation or fire you.

If you carefully study the information presented in this book and follow the recommendations in it, you can make significant improvements to your boundaries. However, if you repeatedly struggle to set self-boundaries (limits on yourself) in order to avoid severe consequences, find a mental health treatment provider to work with. A therapist or counselor can help you identify why this is a struggle for you, and work with you to implement strategies to improve your situation and quality of life.

Struggling to resolve an issue or disagreement

I hope you're as relieved as I was to know that John Gottman, PhD — world-renowned for his work on marital stability and divorce prediction — discovered through his 50 years of research with couples that 69 percent of problems in a relationship are unsolvable. This statistic explains a lot, doesn't it? Unsolvable problems can include personality traits of your partner that annoy you or other long-standing issues around money, sex, or relationships with in-laws.

This surprising statistic may lead you to believe that 69 percent of the time your long-term relationships will be an unending string of disagreements or arguments, but it doesn't have to be that way. If you have a recurring argument or disagreement with someone — your spouse or anyone else — you may need a boundary, even for those unsolvable relationship problems. For long-standing disagreements, boundaries can change your approach to the issue or help you create an agreement that reduces the impact of fundamental differences between you and another person that cause upset or stress.

TIP

You can reduce the stress created by fundamental differences between you and other people by embracing the reality that different doesn't mean wrong or bad. For example, there are effective and less effective ways to load a dishwasher, get from point A to point B, or clean out the hamster cage. But there's no wrong way.

Examples of common disagreements in long-term relationships include:

» The amount of time spent with family members on special occasions or holidays

» How to parent minor children still living at home

» The frequency of contact with a parent, friend, or family member

» The frequency or perceived quality of sexual interactions

» How much money to spend, save, donate to charity, or give to adult children

» The timing of getting married, moving, or becoming pregnant and starting a family

Anytime you struggle to resolve an issue or recognize you have a chronic disagreement with someone — about money, time spent together, parenting, or anything else — creating an agreement that both honors and manages differences is key. You can do your part to find a workable solution by seeing what's not working for you using Step 1 of the boundary-setting process.

Taking care of a boundary that's overdue

Have you ever let something you didn't like go on for so long that it reached a boiling point and you finally exploded? We've all been there. The good news is, the explosion is your clue that a limit is in order or overdue.

Say your mother has had a key to your apartment for years. She comes over to your apartment a couple times a month when you're at work to tidy up or clean your bathroom. You never asked her to tidy up and clean your apartment. She never asked if it was okay with you, and you never created an agreement with her about it.

Now you're infuriated! You've wanted to ask her to give your key back for years. You've thought about changing your locks without telling her so she can't get into your apartment anymore. You're dating someone, it's starting to get serious, and your friend is asking questions — wondering what's up with you and your mother. You're worried that if you don't do something soon, it's not only going to ruin your new relationship but will also make your relationship with your mother even worse.

You want to ask your mother for the key back and tell her that she'll need to check with you in the future when she wants to come over to your apartment to visit you. You're terrified, but you know you've got to do it. In this situation, the boundary you want to set is with your mother. What's not working (your focus in Step 1) is her having a key to your apartment and showing up unannounced.

TIP

When you need to take care of a boundary that you've neglected or that's overdue, a great way to begin the conversation is to say, "I need to clean up something with you." When you begin this way, you send a message to the other person that you're not blaming them, and you're taking responsibility for your role in the problem or difficult circumstance. Taking responsibility is a form of accountability, which is one of the most highly desirable traits any person can have.

Experiencing a broken agreement or commitment

One of the most frustrating, painful experiences you can have with boundaries is when an agreement or commitment is broken. If you don't have good information about how boundaries work or tools for setting boundaries, when an agreement or commitment is broken, you may believe the problem is that boundaries don't work. You may feel helpless and give up because you don't know what to do.

Take my word that you can do something to improve a situation or get your needs met even when someone breaks an agreement or commitment. In Chapters 18 and 19, I show you why an agreement may not have worked, and I give you tips that help you determine whether you want to renegotiate a broken agreement and what to do next.

Processing One Incident or Situation at a Time

When you want to set a boundary or create an agreement with someone, it's vitally important to process only one incident or situation at a time. No matter how many times you've experienced the problem, and no matter how long the problem has been causing you repeated distress, I strongly recommend that you address only one incident or situation — a concrete and memorable example. Focusing on one situation or incident at a time makes your boundary work more effective.

If you combine multiple incidents, situations, or patterns for Step 1 of the boundary-setting process, you won't be able to make meaningful progress as you work through the remaining steps. In Step 2 of the process (see Chapter 14), you catalog specific information about the incident or situation. You describe what you experienced with your five senses of sight, sound, smell, taste, and touch, what you thought or perceived, and the emotions you felt.

When you try to process a pattern of behavior or a long-standing problem rather than focusing on a single incident that illustrates the pattern, you're dealing with a jumble of data (or facts), perceptions, and emotions that you won't be able to easily sift through or make sense of. You get more clarity by keeping your focus on one situation or incident at a time. At the same time, you're making progress on resolving the unwanted repetitive patterns of behavior the incident represents without the need to process all of them.

If you feel frustrated about keeping your focus on one incident when you've been experiencing the same problem for years or decades, you're in good company. Someone has told me more than once, "But you don't understand! I've been married to this person for 32 years, and they've been [fill in the blank with a bad, unattractive, or infuriating behavior] the whole time. I can't just focus on one incident. This is a pattern. It's been going on for years, and it's a BIG problem!"

I hear you. It's tempting to want to lump similar incidents or behaviors together and work on them as a pattern. It's also tempting to combine situations into one "issue" because when put together, they show a pattern, which feels more serious and urgent than a one-off incident. In other words, if something happens only once, it's not nearly as significant or problematic as when it's repeated a second, third, or fourth time. There's no denying that's true.

And while a pattern of behavior can be a bigger problem than a single incident, I still recommend that you choose one specific incident that illustrates the pattern. When you get to Step 2 of the boundary-setting process, where you identify your reality about the incident, you're going to get very detailed and very granular. If you focus on your spouse's 32-year pattern rather than a recent example of that pattern, you won't be able to fully work the remaining steps, and you'll feel confused and overwhelmed. (Keep in mind that you can always address additional incidents related to the pattern of behavior by working the six steps again at a later time.)

REMEMBER

Regardless of how many issues or behaviors may be problematic for you, choose only one specific incident where the behavior occurred to work on. Focusing on the specific data of one situation simplifies your boundary work.

Another reason I recommend working on one incident in a behavior pattern is that in Step 3, you identify an outcome that you want in the situation. If you focus on a pattern rather than a specific incident, it's more difficult to identify a specific outcome other than "I want this to stop — now!"

When you explore incidents individually, you see more options for how you can respond, beyond just making a pattern stop. Making the pattern stop may be completely out of your control, but your response to the pattern is fully within your control.

You also gain more experience with the boundary-setting process by addressing one incident at a time. With practice, you become more skillful at identifying responses to problems that have plagued you, and your boundary-setting muscles grow stronger.

Chapter **14**

Step 2: Get Clear about Your Reality

Whenever you've got a problem that requires — or that you think may require — a boundary, the first thing you need to know is what isn't working for you in that situation. Seeing what isn't working is the first step of the six-step process for creating boundaries. (See Chapter 13 for an overview of the six steps and how to identify what isn't working for you.)

Once you have a clear picture of what's not working for you in a given situation, the next step is to get more granular about what you experienced. Step 2 of the boundary-setting process — getting clear about your reality — asks you to identify the facts of the situation, your thoughts about the facts, and your emotions. The facts, along with your thoughts and emotions about them, are your reality.

Exploring and knowing your reality as it relates to the problem you're working on is a critical component for creating effective boundaries. Not being clear about exactly what happened or what you experienced is like taking your car to the repair shop and telling the mechanic it isn't working, but having no facts or details that explain what's wrong with it. Without facts and details, a mechanic won't know how to repair your car. Without facts and details about the problem or situation you're working on, you won't know how to resolve it.

In this chapter, I give you three specific questions to ask yourself about a situation that's been a source of upset or conflict. I explain the important distinction between facts and data you experience through your five senses and what you think about what you experienced. I explain the crucial connection between thoughts and emotions, and you discover why emotions aren't a direct result of what you experienced with your five senses, but rather a result of what you thought about what you experienced.

REMEMBER

When you work the six steps of the boundary-setting process you don't need to know in advance what boundary you'll set. You're simply exploring a problematic situation or incident to discover whether you need to set a boundary and what that boundary might be. Although you may be confident and clear about exactly what boundary you want to set before working the steps, it's never a requirement.

Identifying the Data

The starting point for knowing your reality is identifying the facts (or data) of a situation or event. When you're awake, you're constantly receiving incoming data from your five senses:

>> Sight

>> Sound

>> Smell

>> Taste

>> Touch

REMEMBER

Data consists of the cold, hard facts of a situation. When you're identifying data, don't use perception words like *rude*, *late*, *mean*, or *angry*. If your descriptions of the situation are open to interpretation or may be viewed differently by another person, you're not providing data.

To illustrate how you get clear about your reality, I use the following fictional scenario as the problem to work for Step 2 of the boundary-setting process. This problem is what you identified in Step 1 — knowing what isn't working (see Chapter 13).

> You go to dinner with your family, and you notice that your sister-in-law is less talkative than she usually is. You don't think much about it at first. At some point during the evening, your brother pulls you aside and tells you that your

sister-in-law is upset with you because of something you said at Thanksgiving dinner a few weeks ago. He tells you that she's so upset, she won't go to the Christmas party at your parents' house next week unless you apologize to her.

You don't remember saying anything that may have upset your sister-in-law at Thanksgiving. You ask your brother what she told him you said, and he says he doesn't know. He just knows that she's upset, and she wants an apology before the Christmas party. Dumbfounded and confused, you tell your brother you need to think about it and get back to him.

TIP

When you're identifying the data for Step 2 of the boundary-setting process, it's not necessary to break down each of the five senses into separate categories. I describe them separately to illustrate the importance of sticking to the information as facts.

In the following sections, I show you how to look at and break down the incident with your brother and sister-in-law into data.

Describing what you saw

Remembering that describing data means focusing only on the facts of what you can see, hear, taste, smell, or touch, start what you saw:

>> You *saw* your brother and sister-in-law (and anyone else who was there) at dinner.

>> You *saw* your brother pull you aside to talk to you.

>> You *saw* your brother's face as he talked to you.

You may notice that your observation that your sister-in-law was less talkative than usual isn't included in the list of what you saw.

Your observation can't be considered a fact because *less talkative* is your perception of the situation, not a fact. The only way your observation can be categorized as a fact is if one of the following is true:

>> You observed your sister-in-law for the entire dinner (without looking away), and you didn't see or hear her say anything.

>> You recorded the exact amount of time she talked, and you have a record of the amount of time she talked at every dinner before that.

General descriptive terms like *less, more, better, worse, faster,* or *slower* are indicators that what's being described is your perception rather than a fact. Unless you have specific, quantifiable data such as "she was going 50 miles faster than the speed limit," the statement is one of perception rather than fact.

Requiring this level of detail and specificity about knowing your reality may seem over the top. But as you clarify the importance of distinguishing facts from perceptions, not only do you appreciate the benefits of understanding the difference, but you also see how you can avoid painful, negative emotions by understanding the difference between data, thoughts, and emotions.

Knowing what you heard

Staying with the requirement that you focus only on what the facts of the situation are, here's what you heard:

>> Your brother asked to talk to you privately.

>> Your brother said your sister-in-law is upset with you and wants an apology before the Christmas party.

>> If you heard your sister-in-law speak, you can include that you heard her talk.

>> You heard your brother say that he doesn't know what upset your sister-in-law.

You should avoid turning secondhand information into data. *Secondhand information* (information someone tells you about another person or situation) should never be considered fact until you've verified it with the other person in question. For example, if your sister tells you that your mother said she's going to cut you out of her will, it's not true until you call your mother (if you really want to know) and say, "Mom, Chloe told me you're taking me out of your will. Is that true?"

Explaining what you felt (through your sense of touch)

In some situations, part of the data you need to record may include what you felt with your sense of touch. Data about touch or physical contact can include:

>> Feeling an object through your sense of touch

>> Being touched by another person

- » Someone placing something on your body

- » An object inadvertently touching your body (for example, something that falls on you from above)

- » Someone touching your body with an object

- » Being physically or sexually attacked or touched in an abusive way

When you apply these criteria to the sister-in-law example, you can see that data from your sense of touch most likely isn't a factor.

Adding other sensations (smell or taste)

In most situations you work through using the six steps, you won't have sensations of smell or taste to analyze. In the scenario of being at dinner with your brother, you probably smelled and tasted the food you ate. If that information is important to your experience of the situation, you can include it. If not, it's fine to omit.

When it comes to what you smell (scents or odors) in general, remember that the sense of smell — like the sense of taste — is wide open to interpretation. Not everyone perceives smells in the same way. For example, two people can smell a particular kind of food or plant and describe what they smell in two completely different ways.

When you identify a smell as part of data, it's best to describe what you smelled as "*it* smelled like . . .," rather than "*I* smelled . . .," unless you knew for a fact what you were smelling. In other words, if you saw fire and smelled smoke, you can say, "I smelled smoke." But if you didn't see fire, it's best to say, "It smelled like smoke."

You may have noticed that saying "It smelled like smoke" is a perception rather than a fact. In some situations, including a perception as part of the facts of your reality is unavoidable. When a sense perception is a significant factor in the problem or issue, you need to include it in both the facts and your thoughts.

For example, if your partner made an agreement with you that they won't smoke cigarettes and they came home from work smelling of cigarette smoke, you wouldn't have any way of talking about the issue without relying on a description of what you smelled.

HOW BOUNDARY WORK IMPROVES CRITICAL THINKING

One of the biggest mistakes people make when they're thinking through a problem or an issue is confusing what they think with what they experienced, or the facts. Separating data and facts from your thoughts and emotions will significantly improve not only your boundaries skills, but also the quality of your ability to analyze your thoughts.

The benefits of separating perceptions, thoughts, and emotions from data are that:

- **You become a keener observer of the distinction between data and perception in all situations.** This will significantly reduce the negative emotions you experience based on believing your thoughts or perceptions are facts, or the truth.

- **Your thinking becomes clearer and more accurate.** You won't confuse data (facts) with thoughts or perceptions which most people do on a regular basis.

- **You won't make the mistake of unknowingly turning secondhand information into data (or facts).** For example, in the situation where your brother told you your sister-in-law wants an apology, what your brother said to you is data. However, your sister-in-law wanting an apology isn't a fact until she tells you directly that she wants one.

- **Your new critical thinking skills improve your boundary work.** For example, if you think it was outrageous or ridiculous for your brother to ask you to apologize to your sister-in-law, your thoughts aren't facts. If you work the six steps on this problem based on believing your thoughts are facts, your boundary work won't be grounded on a firm foundation of knowing, for a fact, that your sister-in-law asked for an apology.

Pinpointing Your Thoughts about the Data

The second part of Step 2 is to identify the thoughts you have about the data.

Thoughts can include perceptions, opinions, beliefs, and judgments. In this part of Step 2, I encourage you to give full expression to all the thoughts you have about the problem you're working on, no matter how judgmental, silly, or outrageous they seem. Write all your thoughts on a piece of paper. Later in this section, I help you narrow down your thoughts to choose the one that has the most meaning, energy, or power for you.

Giving free rein to your perceptions and judgments

Continuing with the situation where your brother told you that your sister-in-law is upset about something you said and wants an apology, consider the possible thoughts or perceptions you may have. You'll notice that the following list of potential thoughts contains many possibilities that wouldn't likely come from one person. This list is designed to illustrate the wide-ranging variety of responses people may have in this situation.

Potential thoughts you may have about what your brother said to you about your sister-in-law include:

>> I didn't do anything wrong.

>> I've thought back to all my interactions with her at Thanksgiving dinner, and I can't think of anything I said that would be upsetting to her.

>> I can't believe she would be so upset she would want me to apologize to her.

>> I'm not going to apologize to her. I don't care if she comes to the Christmas party.

>> She's such a drama queen. It's her fault that my brother doesn't come to as many family events as he used to.

>> We used to have such a great relationship. I wish she had come to me directly and told me she was upset rather than going through my brother.

>> I'm so worried about this. I don't want to ruin the Christmas party. I need to apologize to her right away.

>> I wonder who else knows about this.

Avoiding self-censorship

When you're exploring your thoughts, perceptions, or judgments about the situation you're working on, don't censor or try to "clean up" what you're really thinking.

To help you feel as free as possible as you write down all your thoughts on paper, I can admit that several times over the years when I've processed difficult thoughts or problems in my journal, I've written just one word on a single page. A word that can't (and shouldn't) be printed in this book.

When you're recording your perceptions, opinions, thoughts, or judgments, be as authentic as possible. No one needs you to be nice. You're not a bad person because you think Uncle Leo is a jerk or your sister is a racist. Your writing is your private information. It's not for public consumption, plus it helps you feel better to get it all out. (See Chapter 3 for more information about private information.)

TIP

If you've had the unfortunate experience of someone looking at your diary or journal without your permission, don't use this violation of your privacy as a reason not to put your thoughts down on paper. You can keep your writing in a locked safe or box, in a password-protected document on a computer, or on a secure note-taking app on a tablet or cell phone. If these suggestions don't ease your fears, clients who want the ultimate in privacy share with me that they sometimes take a photo of what they write, then burn or shred it. Whatever works for you is the way to go.

Choosing your most powerful thought

After you've compiled all the thoughts you have about the problem you're working on, choose the thought that has the most meaning, energy, or power for you.

In this part of Step 2, it's important to choose one primary thought because some thoughts may conflict with other thoughts, and some may have very little energy or meaning for you. Narrowing down your thoughts to the most important one also helps you more easily identify your emotions, which I explain in the next section.

TIP

If it's not obvious to you which thought holds the most power, one of the best indicators is your physical or body sensations associated with the thought. For example, if a thought makes you feel angry, you may feel your heart rate increasing or you may feel more heat in your body. More intense body sensations suggest that the thought that created it is stronger.

Recognizing Your Emotions

Knowing what emotions you're feeling is an important part of getting clear about your reality in any situation. The last part of Step 2 is to identify the emotions you're feeling based on the data of the situation and your thoughts about the data.

Many people struggle to identify their emotions. If that's true for you (and even if it's not), I recommend using the following list to help you pinpoint exactly what you're feeling. You can choose one of the primary words (in bold type) or a secondary word for the emotion that best matches how you're feeling about the situation.

- >> Affection (love)
- >> **Anger**
- >> Apprehension (fear)
- >> Compassion (love)
- >> Contrite (guilt)
- >> Desire (passion)
- >> Elated (joy)
- >> Embarrassment (shame)
- >> Enthusiasm (passion)
- >> Excitement (joy)
- >> Exposed (shame)
- >> **Fear**
- >> Frustration (anger)
- >> **Guilt**
- >> Happy (joy)
- >> Hope (joy)
- >> Humbled (shame)
- >> Hurt (pain)
- >> Irritation (anger)
- >> **Joy**
- >> Lonely (pain)
- >> **Love**
- >> Overwhelm (fear)
- >> **Pain**
- >> **Passion**
- >> Pity (pain)
- >> Regret (guilt)
- >> Remorse (guilt)
- >> Resentment (anger)
- >> Sad (pain)

>> **Shame**

>> Tenderness (love)

>> Threatened (fear)

>> Warmth (love)

Adapted from the work of Pia Mellody

Merriam-Webster defines *emotion* as:

> A conscious mental reaction (such as anger or fear) subjectively experienced as strong feelings usually directed toward a specific object and typically accompanied by physiological and behavioral changes in the body.

Emotions and feelings are often used interchangeably, although technically they mean different things. *Emotions* have a mental or thinking component (which I discuss later in this chapter), while *feelings* are the physiological responses of the body that may or may not have a connection to thoughts.

For example, when you're driving down the freeway and you must brake suddenly or quickly swerve to avoid hitting another car, you have a variety of bodily sensations or feelings before you register any thoughts. On the other hand, you may sometimes notice a physical sensation and only later connect that sensation to an emotion like anger or fear.

REMEMBER

For simplicity and because the words emotions and feelings are often used interchangeably, when I refer to *feelings* I mean bodily, physical, or physiological sensations.

Seeing the connection between thoughts and emotions

One of the biggest misconceptions people have about emotions is that they're caused by external or events, like what someone said to you or how they behaved.

The reality is, there's a far more powerful connection between your thoughts and your emotions than there is between your emotions and data (what you experienced or facts).

If you're skeptical about the significance of the thoughts-emotions connection, here's a simple story that illustrates the point:

You're steering a boat down a long, winding river. Up ahead you see another boat coming toward you right down the middle of the river. As the boat gets closer, you notice it's headed straight toward your boat, and you naturally begin to feel nervous.

You quickly begin maneuvering your boat toward the right side of the river so you can avoid a collision with the other boat. You think, "The captain of that boat must be crazy or drunk! Who do they think they are, taking up all the space in the middle of the river?" You feel outraged, afraid, and angry. You may even feel like a victim of the other boat's captain.

You manage to get as far to the right bank of the river as possible just in time. When you pass the other boat, you see that no one is on board. No one is steering the boat.

At that moment, your outrage, fear, and anger completely disappear. You may even laugh out loud. Why? Because you no longer believe someone in charge of the boat was being reckless, negligent, or foolish. You can no longer think of yourself as the victim of the boat's captain.

TIP

Anytime you're feeling a negative emotion, ask yourself, "What thoughts am I thinking right now that may be the source of my emotions?" You find clarity and get to the truth of situations faster by looking first to your thoughts, rather than external events and circumstances.

You may say, "Yeah, but it's normal to feel scared if you think a boat is going to crash into you." And you'd be right. Your natural and appropriate fear would propel you to take the same action — maneuvering your boat to the side of the river. However, you wouldn't feel outraged and angry unless you think someone, or something, is the cause of the boat coming straight at you.

THINK ABOUT IT

The facts of the situation (or data) never changed. But your perceptions (thoughts) did. When your thoughts about why the boat was coming your way changed, your negative emotions disappeared.

Pausing to consider the source of your emotions

Take a closer look at the connection between thoughts and emotions by returning to the situation described earlier in this chapter where your brother told you that your sister-in-law wants an apology from you.

These are some of the thoughts you may have about what your brother told you, followed by the associated emotions you likely feel based on each thought:

>> I didn't do anything wrong.

  - Anger

>> I've thought back to all my interactions with her at Thanksgiving dinner, and I can't think of anything I said that would be upsetting to her.

  - Fear

  - Sadness

>> I can't believe she would be so upset she would want me to apologize to her.

  - Embarrassment

  - Shame

>> I'm not going to apologize to her. I don't care if she comes to the Christmas party.

  - Anger

>> She's such a drama queen. It's her fault that my brother doesn't come to as many family events as he used to.

  - Anger

  - Resentment

>> We used to have such a great relationship. I wish she had come to me directly and told me she was upset rather than going through my brother.

  - Sadness

  - Guilt

>> I'm so worried about this. I don't want to ruin the Christmas party. I need to apologize to her right away.

  - Guilt

  - Pain

>> I wonder who else knows about this.

  - Fear

  - Embarrassment

Seeing how your emotions are dependent on your thoughts illustrates the importance of slowing down to identify your reality by distinguishing between data, thoughts, and emotions.

Compiling Your Answers to Step 2

For this last part of Step 2, you record the emotions you feel and add them to the data and the thoughts you identified earlier.

Using the main scenario in this chapter, your final work for Step 2 may consist of the following information:

>> **Data:**

- Your brother pulled you aside to talk to you.

- Your brother told you that your sister-in-law is upset about something you said (he doesn't know what it was).

- Your brother told you that your sister-in-law wants an apology before the Christmas party.

>> **Thought (the one with the most power for you):**

- We used to have such a great relationship. I wish she had come to me directly and told me she was upset rather than going through my brother.

>> **Emotions:**

- Sadness

- Anger

- Embarrassment

Once you've compiled all three components of the problem you're working on, you have identified your reality and completed Step 2 of the boundary-setting process.

Chapter **15**

Step 3: Clarify Your Needs and the Outcome You Want

For Step 3 of the boundary-setting process, you determine what needs aren't being met in the situation or problem you identified in Step 1. (Refer to Chapter 13 for more information about figuring out the problem you want to work on.) Then you describe the outcome you want in that situation. Knowing what needs aren't being met helps you clarify your ideal outcome, which gives you direction for the steps that follow.

In this chapter, I explain how knowing what your needs are is an essential part of the boundary-setting process. When you don't know what your needs are, you can't meet them yourself or ask another person to help you meet them.

I also give you a list of common personal and relationship needs to help you identify the needs that aren't being met in the situation or problem you're working on. You get specific guidance for how to think about and explore all the potential outcomes so you can choose the one that's the best fit for your situation.

Discovering Unmet Needs

To show you how you begin working Step 3, here's an example of a problem in a relationship. Say your partner has a habit of leaving their dirty clothes on a chair in the bedroom you share. Sometimes they leave their clothes in the chair for three or four days before moving them to the laundry basket, which drives you crazy!

When you ask yourself what needs of yours aren't being met in the clothes-in-the-chair situation, your need for order can be one unmet need. Cooperation may be another, meaning you'd like your partner to cooperate with keeping your home clean and tidy, which helps you feel more calm and serene.

Based on your need for order and cooperation, one of the possible outcomes can be that you'd like your partner to put their dirty clothes in the laundry basket rather than placing them on the bedroom chair.

When you think about your partner's annoying habit, consider all the thoughts that may be running through your mind:

>> If they weren't such a slob, they would put their dirty clothes in the laundry basket as soon as they take them off.

>> They leave their clothes on the chair because they think I'm going to pick them up. I used to do that, but not anymore. I'm not their maid!

>> I think they leave their clothes on the chair just to annoy me. They're trying to get back at me because they think I should cook at home more often.

If you get sidetracked by these thoughts and emotions about the clothes-in-the-chair situation instead of focusing on your unmet needs, the *outcomes* you may want (based on the corresponding thoughts) would be:

>> My partner will stop being such a slob.

>> My partner needs to know I'm not their maid, and I'm not going to pick up their clothes anymore.

>> I'm going to make sure they never see how annoyed I am about their clothes in the chair, so they won't have the satisfaction of thinking they've gotten under my skin.

The problem is, even if your partner stops being such a slob (which you'd need to carefully define), or you stop picking up their clothes, or you don't let on how annoyed you are about their clothes-in-the-chair habit, you still won't have the outcome you truly want — the outcome that meets your need for order and cooperation. You want the bedroom chair to be clothes-free — all or most of the time!

TIP

Choosing an outcome in the boundary-setting process isn't an exam or a test. There's no single, perfect outcome for any problem or situation. Stay curious and experiment, trusting that every time a boundary doesn't work out the way you want, you're learning and growing.

Realizing the Connection between Needs and Boundaries

Needs are the basic, essential elements for a safe, stable, and fulfilling life. The most fundamental human needs are the need for safety, food, and shelter. Higher-level needs like the need for achievement or personal growth aren't required for survival, but they're vital for a fulfilling life.

Since personal boundaries are about protecting you (and others), it's easy to see how needs and boundaries are related. Boundaries — limits you create for yourself (or *self-boundaries*) and agreements you make with others — help you get your needs met.

Here are a few examples of the relationship between needs and boundaries:

>> You live in a high-crime neighborhood, so you lock your door every time you leave your home, or you don't walk outside after dark. Your choices to lock your door or to not walk outside after dark are self-boundaries you set to get your need for safety met.

>> One of your friends doesn't reach out or initiate contact as much as you do. You need a comfortable balance of give-and-take in relationships, also known as *mutuality*. You think about options for how you may get this need met, and you decide that for the next couple of months you'll experiment with reaching out less to see what it feels like to have more balance in the relationship. Your choice to decrease your level of contact is a boundary you created to get more of your need for mutuality met.

>> Your partner is chronically late getting ready when the two of you have plans to leave the house at a certain time. You talk to your partner and create an agreement that you'll wait for them for 10 minutes past the previously agreed-on time to leave. After that you'll leave, and your partner can take their own car or a rideshare. Creating this agreement (a boundary) helps you meet your need to be on time to events or activities.

You have two primary ways to get needs met using personal boundaries. You can take action yourself to get a need met (first two examples in the list), or you can create an agreement with someone (last example).

Reviewing Maslow's hierarchy of needs

Abraham Maslow was an American psychologist best known for creating a theory of psychological health he called the *hierarchy of needs*. Maslow's theory suggested that humans must have certain basic needs met before they can move on to fulfilling higher-level needs.

Maslow divided his hierarchy into five sections, beginning with the basic level of physiological needs:

>> Physiological: food, water, shelter, sleep

>> Safety: physical (bodily) safety or security, health, employment

>> Love/Belonging: family, friendship, sexual intimacy

>> Esteem: self-esteem, achievement, respect

>> Self-Actualization: achieving one's full potential, self-fulfillment

Note: Maslow's hierarchy of needs is often represented in a pyramid format with physiological needs at the bottom of the pyramid, as shown in Figure 15-1. However, there's no evidence that Maslow represented the hierarchy using a pyramid.

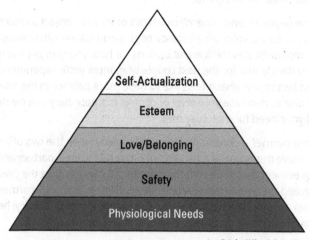

FIGURE 15-1:
Maslow's
hierarchy of
needs.

© John Wiley & Sons, Inc.

Maslow didn't intend the hierarchy of needs to be rigid or linear, meaning that you can't meet higher-level needs unless all your lower-level needs are met. For example, it's possible that someone may not have all their safety needs met but still have a meaningful, healthy family life. But before any of the higher levels can be attained, the basic needs of food, water, shelter, and sleep (physiological needs) are required to sustain life.

When you identify the needs that aren't being met in the situation you're working on, it can be helpful to review Maslow's hierarchy to see where your identified needs appear on the list. For example, discovering that your need for safety is repeatedly unmet in certain relationships is important information about the nature and quality of that relationship.

WARNING

Because safety (as a form of protection) is the foundation for effective personal boundaries in intimate relationships, chronic lack of safety in any relationship should never be ignored.

Be aware that personal boundaries create safety through:

>> Protecting yourself from intellectual, emotional, physical, or sexual harm

>> Protecting others from any intellectual, emotional, physical, or sexual harm that you may cause, intentionally or unintentionally

Exploring common relationship needs

In most situations, another person is involved when you want or need to set a boundary. To help you identify what needs aren't being met in the problem you're working on, here are some of the most common relationship needs:

>> Acceptance

>> Attention

>> Autonomy (independence)

>> Closeness

>> Communication

>> Companionship

>> Compassion

>> Consistency

>> Cooperation

- » Empathy
- » Harmony
- » Humor
- » Inclusion
- » Intimacy
- » Kindness
- » Love
- » Mutuality
- » Nurturing
- » Participation
- » Partnership
- » Physical touch
- » Reliability
- » Respect
- » Security
- » Support
- » Trust

REMEMBER

Although this list doesn't include every need humans can have, you can refer to it when you're identifying your unmet needs in the situation you're working on for Step 3.

TIP

If you want to find out if a new relationship has the potential for becoming deeper and more intimate, identify your top three to five relationship needs from the previous list. Then begin noticing whether you experience these needs being met in the new relationship. No one is responsible for fulfilling your needs, but you may find that some people fulfill your most important needs better than others.

Identifying What Needs Aren't Being Met

The first part of Step 3 is to identify your unmet need(s) in the problem you're working on. The second part of the step is to name the outcome you want. Using the list in the previous section, Table 15-1 provides examples of how common relationship issues can be related to unmet needs.

TABLE 15-1

Naming Unmet Needs

Problem	Unmet Needs
Friend or partner is chronically late.	Consistency, cooperation
Someone broke an agreement.	Trust, security, reliability
Someone close to you speaks to you in a harsh, critical, or emotionally/verbally abusive manner.	Acceptance, kindness, respect

To complete the first part of Step 3, review the problem you're working on and identify at least one need that's not being met. You can identify as many needs as you want, but I recommend that you narrow your final selection to the two or three most important needs (refer to Table 15-1). Knowing what your most important needs are helps you create the best description of the outcome you want.

REMEMBER

When you're identifying the outcome you want, be sure to clearly define the outcome or what the fulfilled need looks like. For example, don't say, "I want my partner to be more orderly," without adding "by putting their clothes in the laundry basket and not leaving them on the chair in the bedroom."

Getting Clear about the Outcome You Want

Envisioning a specific, or even measurable, outcome is vital to the success of your boundary work.

In the clothes-on-the-chair scenario earlier in this chapter, I explain how being sidetracked by thoughts and emotions about your partner's bad habit prevents you from getting clear about the outcome you want.

If you choose a broad, hard to define outcome like curing your partner of *slobbism* (a word not yet in the dictionary, but it can happen!) or pretending that their habit doesn't annoy you, you won't accomplish the simple, measurable outcome you want. You just want your partner's clothes off the chair.

Knowing how to identify outcomes

While the following sections can help you brainstorm outcomes for a given situation, if you're not sure about the specific outcome you want in the situation you're working on, I recommend that you:

1. **Think about the problem or issue you're working on.**

2. **Review the list of needs you identified that aren't being met.**

3. **Look for a connection between the problem, the unmet need(s), and potential outcomes.** (See Table 15-2 for example).

TIP

Anytime you struggle to formulate the outcome you want in your boundary work, review the list of needs you identified earlier in this step and ask, "What helps me feel [the unmet need]?" Answering this question helps you generate more ideas about the outcome you want.

TABLE 15-2   **Identifying Potential Outcomes for Solving the Identified Problem**

Problem	Unmet Needs	Potential Outcomes
Friend or partner is chronically late.	Consistency, cooperation	The friend or partner is on time. You create an outcome that decreases or eliminates the impact of their chronic lateness.
Someone broke an agreement.	Trust, security, reliability	The broken agreement is repaired or fixed. You identify an outcome that protects you from future broken agreements.
Someone close to you speaks to you in a harsh, critical, or emotionally/verbally abusive manner.	Acceptance, kindness, respect	The person speaks to you in a kind, respectful manner. You end conversations with the person when they become harsh, critical, or abusive. You stop communicating with the person.

Allowing yourself to imagine the perfect outcome

Believe it or not, many people have an automatic off switch when it comes to saying what they want. When you're exploring all the possible outcomes of the situation you're working on, I suggest you take a sky's-the-limit approach. Why? Because you never know what's possible.

Here are the kinds of thoughts that stop you from imagining what you want:

>> They wouldn't do that.

>> That would hurt their feelings.

>> That's a lot (or too much) to ask.

>> We've always done it this way. I can't rock the boat.

Sometimes what stops you from imagining what you want isn't your conscious thoughts, but habitual ways of thinking that you're not even aware of. These thoughts have hardened into beliefs like the following:

>> I don't deserve it.

>> Asking for what I want is selfish.

>> I never get what I want.

>> I shouldn't ask for that. I have it a lot better than most people.

Don't let these thoughts and beliefs get in your way. Ask yourself what's the most fabulous outcome that you can imagine. You may not get it, but it's better to aim for 1,000 and get 50 than to aim for zero and get exactly that.

TIP

When you're exploring outcomes, ask yourself, "If there are no limits or if I can't fail, what's the outcome I want?" This type of question bypasses your habitual ways of thinking and viewing the world so you can see more options and experience more freedom.

Brainstorming all possible outcomes

One of the smartest things you can do when you're exploring outcomes is to think of all the possibilities, no matter how absurd or outlandish they seem. Giving your mind free rein will keep it open and creative.

For example, in the clothes-in-the-chair scenario, here are a few possible outcomes:

>> Ask your partner if they'll put their clothes straight into the laundry basket when they take them off.

>> Remove the chair from the bedroom.

>> Create an agreement with your partner that every time you remove their clothes from the chair, they'll take you to your favorite restaurant for dinner.

>> Pick the clothes up yourself and put them in the laundry basket.

>> Put the laundry basket behind the chair and toss the clothes into the basket.

>> Hire a maid to come in every day and move the clothes from the chair to the laundry basket.

>> Put a folding screen in front of the chair so you can't see it.

>> Train your dog to take the clothes from the chair to the laundry basket.

>> Start sleeping in another bedroom so you don't have to look at the chair.

As you read this list of possible outcomes, your mind may become more open and creative about all the potential solutions. To be fair, you can rule out some of these options immediately. For example, if you don't have a dog, you have to cross that option off the list. Hiring a maid can get expensive, so that outcome may need to go as well, unless it's affordable for you and you love the idea!

Notice that only two of these outcomes require the participation of someone else — in this case, your partner. You have the power to make all the other options happen if you choose to, including hiring a maid. *Note:* Recognizing where you have the power to determine the outcome is crucial to the next step of the boundary-setting process (see Chapter 16).

Discovering the hidden desire underneath the outcome

Sometimes your desires are hidden underneath the outcomes you want, and it's helpful to identify them.

My favorite example of a desire hidden under a stated outcome is the woman whose outcome is for her husband to make more money. If she's working through the boundary-setting process based on this particular outcome, it's clear that she needs to make a request because her husband making money requires his participation. She doesn't have the power to make money for him.

Digging a little deeper, it turns out that what she really wants is a bigger home. Her family, including two toddlers, is squeezed into a two-bedroom house. Plus, a baby is on the way, and she (understandably) wants more space. She's convinced that the way to get a bigger house is for her husband to make more money.

But is it true that to get a bigger house you need more money? In general, you can say that you need more money to live in a bigger house. But that's not absolutely true.

For example, if this family is living in the most expensive area of town, they can likely buy a bigger house for the same price in a less expensive area of town. Maybe they live in a new house with top-of-the-line everything, and they can move to an older, larger house that needs a few updates but is more than adequate for their space needs.

In this example, the hidden desire underneath the outcome is to live in a bigger home. Imagine the difference between approaching your partner and asking them to make more money versus telling them that you would love to live in a bigger house. There's no way to know how your partner would respond to either option. But asking them to make more money has a distinctly shaming tone (even if it's unintended), while sharing your wish for a larger house expresses a desire that creates the possibility of collaboration and mutual agreement.

If you discover that your original outcome is hiding the true outcome you want, take some time to brainstorm all possible options for the new outcome you identified. This helps you clarify and improve your boundary work.

TIP

If you want to dramatically improve the quality of your thinking, check in regularly with the truthfulness of your thoughts by asking, "Is this really true?" You may be amazed at the number of times you answer, "Absolutely not!" And the more you see the untruths in your thoughts, the more open and creative your mind becomes.

Seeing the limits of people-dependent outcomes

One of the most common mistakes people make when identifying the outcome they want is relying too heavily on people-dependent outcomes.

People-dependent outcomes are outcomes that require the participation of another person. In the example of the woman who wants a bigger house, she needs to make a request of her husband that they move to a bigger house. Her request is the first part of the agreement-making process. All agreements require the participation of another person.

When you're exploring the possible outcomes you want for a particular problem, I strongly suggest that you identify all the ways *you* have the power to solve the problem. If you're willing to take the necessary action to achieve the outcome you want without making a request or creating an agreement, you'll get the outcome you want much easier and faster. Relying on an agreement to accomplish what you could accomplish on your own is essentially an unforced error. Why depend on another person to give you what you want or need when you can give it to yourself?

Because boundary issues often involve problems with other people, it can be tempting to look to the other person as the solution to the problem. For example, if your partner has repeatedly lied to you about their gambling habit and that's the issue you're working on, you may choose the outcome "They'll stop lying to me about their gambling habit."

While this outcome is understandable and even logical, it's not the best choice in this situation. I can practically hear you saying, "But you said brainstorm all possible options and the sky's the limit!!" Yes, I did say that. You can want your partner to stop lying about their gambling habit, but if this is a long-standing issue, you'll make far more progress by focusing on what's in your circle of control. (More about the circle of control in Chapter 16.)

If you stick with the outcome "They'll stop lying to me about their gambling habit," the only way you can get this outcome is by making a request and creating an agreement. You can ask your partner to stop lying, and they may even say, "Sure, honey, I'll do that." But what are the chances that this agreement is for real?

In this situation and others like it, you feel more empowered, create better outcomes, and make more progress by focusing on outcomes you have the power to create without making a request. You can't stop someone from lying to you, but you can decide how to respond to their deception and its consequences.

REMEMBER

Choosing to take action yourself rather than making a request isn't about not having needs or wants or being stubbornly independent. You can make a request of anyone about anything. However, if you have the power to create an outcome yourself, you must be willing to do it if the other person says no. Understanding the connection between self-responsibility and making requests is one of the principles of healthy interdependence in relationships.

Choosing the easiest outcome

Choosing the easiest among all possible outcomes may seem obvious, but it's worth mentioning. In the clothes-in-the-chair example, it's probably easier to ask your partner to place their clothes in the laundry basket than it would be to train your dog to do it.

However, be sure that when you decide to choose the easiest outcome, you're not settling or sacrificing. For example, just because you're apprehensive about making a request of your partner to move their clothes to the laundry basket, that doesn't mean you should choose to pick the clothes up yourself. If the easiest option leaves you feeling angry or resentful, or fills you with dread, choose another outcome.

Avoiding vague outcomes

When identifying the outcome you want in the situation you're working on, be as clear and specific as you can. Using the clothes-in-the-chair example, imagine the outcome you choose is to ask your partner to put their clothes in the laundry basket, and they agree to do that. The first day they put their clothes in the basket, but the next day they don't. They can say they did what you asked them to do. And sadly, they would be right because vague outcomes create vague results.

Other examples of vague outcomes include:

>> My friend will call me more often.

>> I will go to bed earlier.

>> My partner will be more affectionate.

>> My partner will talk to me more.

Except for the second example, each of these outcomes requires you to make a request of someone to create an agreement.

Here are examples of more specific outcomes that improve the quality of your solution:

>> My friend will call me once a day.

>> I will go to bed by 10:30 p.m.

>> My partner will touch me once a day.

>> My partner and I will talk and check in with each other 15 minutes a day after the kids go to sleep.

When you create clear, specific descriptions of the outcome you want, you know when the outcome has been accomplished, you craft better requests, and you avoid the misunderstandings that are a consequence of vague agreements.

REMEMBER

Vague and unclear outcomes lead to vague requests, which create vague agreements. These are the types of agreements that usually fail or lead to conflicts and arguments about whether the agreement was honored.

Including a high level of specificity

Although you can improve a stated outcome by getting clearer and more specific, you can significantly increase the quality of your outcome by adding a higher level of specificity and detail.

Using the examples in the previous section, here are highly specific descriptions of possible outcomes:

>> My friend will call me once a day before 9:00 p.m.

>> I will be in bed by 10:30 p.m. with my phone in another room and the lights turned off.

>> My partner will touch me once a day before we go to bed (or in the morning at a specific time).

>> My partner and I will talk and check in with each other for 15 minutes a day (using the guidelines the therapist gave us) after the kids go to sleep and before we watch any TV.

Establishing deadlines, if necessary

Not all outcomes require deadlines. However, some outcomes are significantly improved when you add dates, time frames, or the frequency of a certain action.

Here are a few situations where adding a deadline or time frame to the outcome you want makes them more specific and measurable:

>> You want your car to be repaired within the next two weeks.

>> You want to find out whether a family member has an alcohol or drug problem. You want the family member to be assessed by a trained professional within the next month.

- >> You want to decide where your kids will go to summer camp. You need to have a conversation with your ex to discuss all the options, and you want the decision to be made within the next three weeks.

- >> You want to put 10 percent of your household income into a retirement account every month.

- >> You want to go back to school next fall. To make sure you're prepared for the admissions exam, you ask your family to not interrupt your weekly 7:00 p.m. to 8:00 p.m. study time for the next two months.

REMEMBER

When the outcome you want requires an agreement, keep an open mind about deadlines and time frames. For example, say you want to book the hotel for your summer vacation by the end of March, but your spouse wants to wait until after April 15 (Tax Day in the U.S.). If the person you're making an agreement with proposes a different deadline or time frame that doesn't negatively impact the outcome, stay flexible about the date(s) as part of the overall process of creating an agreement.

You can include a deadline for any boundary that is time-sensitive or involves a situation you would like to resolve sooner rather than later. Including a deadline in the outcome you want, when applicable, improves clarity, makes the boundary more actionable, and increases the likelihood that a commitment or agreement won't be dropped or forgotten.

Chapter **16**

Step 4: See Where You Have Power Before Taking Action

My native city of Houston, Texas, has weathered untold numbers of hurricanes. Six of the eight most destructive storms Houston has experienced have happened since I was born, including Hurricane Harvey, which produced 50 inches of rain in just five days.

I've never known one person who was cynical or doubtful about the power of hurricanes, but I've met a few stubborn people who were determined to weather a storm even after they'd been told to evacuate. The power you have when you know a hurricane is coming is to stockpile water, canned goods, candles, and batteries, or board up your home and leave town if you receive evacuation orders. Then, you wait and see what happens.

Imagine what you would do if you believed you had power over a hurricane. Would you go outside and tell the hurricane to cease and desist, go in a different direction, or simply simmer down and act right? Or would you go about your life as though a hurricane wasn't coming?

If you saw someone respond in one of these ways to an approaching hurricane, you'd think they were a bit off their rocker. The truth is, sometimes people act exactly like this when it comes to their own personal power. They believe they have power when they don't, or they don't take action on their own behalf by using the power they already have.

In this chapter, I show you why it's important to understand what's in (or isn't in) your circle of control as you're working through Step 4 for creating a boundary. I explain the two types of power and how to avoid the inevitable pitfalls of not knowing or accepting where your power lies. You get clear about the power you have to create the outcome you want (the outcome you identified in Step 3; see Chapter 15), and you choose the level of power that best fits your situation.

Understanding the Circle of Control

Control is another word to describe power. You (and everyone else) have a *circle of control* that contains everything you have power over.

To get a picture of your own circle of control, imagine a circle drawn on a piece of paper. Right above the circle are the words "My Circle of Control."

Written inside the circle are three categories of control:

>> What I say

>> What I do, or my behavior

>> What I think

You may be wondering, "Is that it? Are these the only three things I have control over?" The simple, and perhaps disappointing, answer is yes. Read the following sections to find out why.

Knowing what isn't under your control

You may notice that emotions aren't on the list of categories of control. Emotions aren't in your circle of control because your emotions are almost exclusively determined by what you think. And if you explore the inner workings of your mind more closely, you can see that even your thoughts aren't 100 percent under your control.

If you're skeptical or you strongly disagree that you have limited control of your thoughts, scan your memory for any thought you've ever had that you didn't want, didn't like, were embarrassed about, or found deeply disturbing.

For anyone who didn't find one of these thoughts, keep looking — or submit your application for sainthood today! For the rest of us, ask, "If I could choose (had control of) my thoughts, would I choose these unwanted, embarrassing, or disturbing thoughts?" Probably not.

TIP

If the idea that you have limited control over your thoughts is new or deeply upsetting to you, try to think of your thoughts as clouds appearing in your head, floating through, and then disappearing again. Thoughts are natural cosmic events. Your power lies in the attention you give them and how much power you allow them to have over you.

Before we move on to what is in your circle of control, think about behavior. Have you ever wanted to stop eating sugar, end your social media addiction, go to bed before 3:00 a.m. most nights, or get more than 500 steps a day, but you just can't make it happen? Yes! We've all been there. And because you've been there, you know that what you do, or your behavior, isn't always 100 percent in your control.

I don't say any of this to discourage or depress you. I only want to drive home the truth about your circle of control and what you have power over so you won't waste time trying to control things you have no power over. People spend excessive amounts of time engaged in activities outside their circle of control, despite the fact that trying to control what you can't control doesn't work — ever!

TIP

If you want to completely transform your perception of what you don't control, try this thought experiment anytime you feel frustrated by your lack of control: "I have absolutely no control over [fill in the blank]. This gives me the freedom to [fill in the blank]." For example: I have absolutely no control over my spouse's ice cream consumption. This gives me the freedom to focus on improving my own eating habits, or to feel more connected to my spouse now that I'm not judging, criticizing, and trying to change them.

Seeing the truly tiny size of your circle of control makes it easier to accept how vast and unlimited the space outside the circle is.

Here's a (very) short list of what's *not* in your circle of control:

>> What anyone else thinks, says, or does

>> Traffic

>> What time the sun rises and sets

- » Wars or international conflicts
- » The length of the wait in the checkout line at the grocery store
- » Weather or natural disasters
- » When you hear back about the job you applied for
- » What time your flight takes off
- » When (or where) you get a flat tire
- » How long you wait on hold for the next customer service representative

REMEMBER

The better you get at recognizing what you do and don't have control over, the more peaceful and happier you are.

Focusing on what's under your control

When you know and accept the inherent (fundamental or basic) limitations of your circle of control, you open up massive space and opportunity to turn your focus to yourself and what you want to create or accomplish. Getting clear about what's in your circle of control helps you craft a life that's more interesting, fulfilling, and productive.

THINK ABOUT IT

If you've spent a good portion of your life trying to control situations or people you had no control over, you may be amazed by how much extra time, energy, and resources you have when your attention is focused solely on what's in your circle of control. For most people, minding their business is a full-time job.

Here are some examples of what's in your circle of control:

- » How you manage your body or your health, including:
  - • What you eat
  - • How much movement (exercise) you get
  - • How much you sleep
  - • How you take care of and maintain your physical health
- » How you care for your physical possessions
- » How much time you spend with other people or alone
- » How much money you spend
- » Where you live
- » How you parent your children

REMEMBER

It's only logical that if you have a circle of control around what you have power over, then everyone else also has their own circle of control around what they have power over. If you struggle to accept the limits of your circle of control, here's an exercise that may help:

1. Draw a circle on a piece of paper and write above the circle "My Circle of Control."

2. On another sheet of paper write a list of everything you're worried about.

3. Review your list and place a "C" next to each item you have control or power over.

4. Place any item marked with a "C" inside your circle of control.

5. Repeat this exercise every day for 30 days.

6. At the end of 30 days, review your circle of control and daily lists to discover the limits of your circle of control, paying special attention to the items not in your circle of control.

7. Make note (either mentally or on paper) of key insights or takeaways.

Getting clear about what's in your circle of control (and what's not) is crucial to seeing where you have power to create the outcome you want. In the next section I define what power is in the context of setting boundaries. I also explain the two primary types of power to show you which type you should avoid.

Exploring Two Kinds of Power

Merriam-Webster defines power as the "ability to act or produce an effect." Before I tell you about the two kinds of power, pause for a moment and ask yourself what the word *power* means to you.

» Is power a desirable or undesirable quality?

» Is power negative, positive, or neutral?

Your answers to these questions are influenced by many factors, including your gender, your past experience with power and authority figures (or with someone's abuse of power), and what you've been taught about power.

Common synonyms for power include:

» Authority

» Dominance

>> Force

>> Leverage

>> Supremacy

These words illustrate that for many people the word *power* evokes negative thoughts and feelings.

You may remember a time when someone had power over you or a time when you felt powerless. If you've ever spent much time with someone who seemed to enjoy having power over others, you may think that all power is bad. The problem with believing that all power is bad or undesirable is, you won't see the positive qualities of power.

TIP

One of the ways to quickly identify words that describe negative power is by seeing the inherent power imbalance or vertical relationship structure embedded in the term. For example, each of the five words in the previous list implies a hierarchy or vertical structure where one person has more power than another.

Here are additional synonyms for power, focused on its positive aspects:

>> Ability

>> Competence

>> Energy

>> Influence

>> Sovereignty

>> Strength

These two lists illustrate that power manifests in different forms. For example, having dominance is very different from having influence. To distinguish between the two types of power, the first list describes *power over*, and the second list describes *authentic personal power*.

Cultivating authentic personal power

To get an idea of what authentic personal power looks like, glance over the second list of synonyms in the prior section.

Here's an even clearer picture of what it looks like when you operate from a position of authentic personal power (rather than *power over*):

- ≫ You understand that your circle of control (power) is limited to what you think, say, and do. Everyone else and everything except what you think, say, or do are outside your circle of control.

- ≫ You understand that you're responsible for knowing what your needs are and getting them met.

- ≫ You don't use manipulation, control, intimidation, force, or revenge to get your needs met.

- ≫ You understand that you're responsible for your intellectual, emotional, physical, and sexual well-being and for your happiness. You don't believe anyone other than you is responsible for making you happy, and you don't hold other people responsible for your emotions.

- ≫ When you require help to get a need met, you ask for help in a direct (rather than an indirect or manipulative) way.

- ≫ You make requests of others rather than issuing demands or ultimatums.

- ≫ You're aware of your inherent worth and value.

- ≫ You're aware of and accountable (but not responsible) for the impact of your behavior on others.

- ≫ You're willing to accept powerlessness, when appropriate.

REMEMBER

In the messiness of human interactions, there's an enormous amount of confusion and misinformation about personal responsibility. You aren't responsible for anyone else's thoughts, emotions, or behavior, and no one else is responsible for your thoughts, emotions, or behavior. Believing that you or anyone else has this level of awesome power is synonymous with believing that you (or others) are godlike. You impact others, but you aren't the cause of their responses or reactions to you, and no one is responsible for your responses or reactions.

To help you cultivate more authentic personal power, here are nine questions or suggestions that correspond to the characteristics in the previous list:

- ≫ **Ask yourself, "Is this in my circle of control?"** If the answer is no, turn your attention to accepting and going with the flow of reality or taking action, if appropriate.

- ≫ **Ask yourself, "What are my needs? How can I get these needs met?"** Begin with finding where you have the power to meet a need, rather than looking to another person to fulfill a need you have the power to fulfill yourself.

>> **Be curious about whether you use manipulation, control, intimidation, force, or revenge to get your needs met.** If you find that you're engaged in one of these losing strategies, ask yourself, "What are some healthier ways to get my needs met?" Then experiment with those alternative strategies.

>> **Remind yourself often that you, and only you, are responsible for making yourself happy.** Ask yourself, "How can I take responsibility for my emotional, intellectual, physical, and sexual well-being and my own happiness?"

>> **Experiment with direct phrasing and clear requests.** If you need some-one's help, ask them directly. For example, you can say, "I need to drop my car off at the repair shop next Tuesday at 8:00 a.m. Would you be willing to pick me up and take me to work after that?"

>> **Become a detective of your day-to-day experience and see if you're making demands or issuing meaningless ultimatums.** If you find areas where you're making demands or issuing ultimatums, be curious about where these urges originate, and try to make small improvements to eliminate demands and ultimatums to get your needs met. (See Chapter 2 for more information about ultimatums.)

>> **If you struggle to see your inherent worth or value, make a list of all the positive qualities about yourself that you're proud of.** If you can't think of anything, make a list of the positive qualities of someone you deeply love and care for. If you believe the other person is inherently valuable and worthy (as well as human and imperfect), see if you can extend this same sentiment to yourself.

>> **Don't take responsibility for another person's negative response to you.** You're responsible for your behavior, but you're not responsible for how others respond to you. Don't assume you know the impact you have on someone else unless they tell you directly.

>> **To grow your ability to accept powerlessness, continually remind yourself of what's in your circle of control and what you have power over.** This helps you see that although powerlessness can feel frustrating or even hopeless, it can also be freeing and liberating.

Rejecting "power over"

Power over is a strategy to get your needs or wants met by using force, manipula-tion, intimidation, coercion, and other negative and harmful means.

REMEMBER

The only adult relationships where one person can legitimately claim authority or power over another person are relationships with a hierarchy of power (teacher-student and employer-employee relationships, for example). However, even these hierarchical relationships may have limits on power defined by rules, regulations, or codes of ethics, along with the freedom the person with less power has to leave or end the relationship.

Power-over strategies are counterproductive, and ultimately ineffective, ways to relate to another person. They're counterproductive because they're often great at getting short-term results, but they create disconnection or alienation in the long term. Power-over strategies are ineffective because the cooperation or agreement they achieve is largely rooted in fear or avoidance, and isn't genuinely or wholly given.

Here are a few examples of what a power-over strategy looks like:

>> Telling another adult what to do

>> Using threats or intimidation

>> Withholding approval, affection, information, resources, and so on for the sole purpose of persuading another person to do what you want them to do

>> Ostracizing, excluding, or shunning another person in situations where they would naturally or typically be included

>> Relating to others in highly transactional ways to achieve a specific outcome (for example, giving gifts or anything of value for the purpose of creating a "debt" the other person feels compelled to pay back)

TIP

Many women have negative responses to the word *power*. I believe this is because women have far more experience with power-over strategies than with authentic personal power. If you have negative associations with the word *power*, see if you can find examples of people who have used positive authentic personal power to influence or create something you value or appreciate.

Knowing the Pitfalls of Not Understanding Power

When you don't understand where your power to create the outcome you want lies, you lose precious time, stir up unnecessary drama, and experience painful negative emotions.

Wasting time

You waste time in two primary ways when you don't understand where your power lies.

>> You attempt to have power over things you have no power over.

>> You don't use the power you have to create the outcome you want.

Consider this example: Your brother has been giving money to your younger sister for years because she lacks a steady income and has addiction issues; she also mismanages her money. You call your mother, hoping to convince her to tell your brother to stop giving your younger sister money.

In this situation, not only do you have no active role, but you also have no power. Therefore, you're wasting your time. Your power lies in asking your sister directly if you can do anything to support her (without giving her money) or in talking to your brother if he's open to hearing your concerns.

TIP

Talking to one person with the hope of changing another person is called *triangulation*. The triangle consists of you, the person you're talking to, and the person you're talking about. Triangulation is an ineffective and relationship-harming strategy for solving problems. When you have a problem with something another person said or did and you genuinely want to resolve it, go directly to them and avoid discussing it with other people.

In addition to wasting time, you delay getting the outcome you want if you don't use the power you have to make it happen. For example, if your partner told you they would call the plumber about a leak in your house, and it's been two weeks and the leak is starting to cause damage, you lose precious time and potentially cause more damage to your home by not picking up the phone and calling the plumber yourself.

Creating unnecessary tension and conflict

Sometimes when you misunderstand what's in your control and what's not, you create conflict or tension — not just within yourself, but also with other people. This is especially true when you believe you have the power to create the outcome you want, but the outcome instead requires that you make a request of another person.

Say, for example, you want your adult son and his family to come to your house for Christmas dinner. Forgetting that you can't tell another adult what to do, you decide that the action you need to take to get the outcome you want (your son having Christmas dinner at your house) is to tell him what time you're serving Christmas dinner. You call him and say, "Joe, I wanted to let you know that we'll be having Christmas dinner at 2:00 p.m."

After a very long pause, Joe replies, "We've already got plans for Christmas day." If you could see the thought bubble above Joe's head, you'd see that he feels as though he's being treated like a child. Plus, he's irritated and frustrated that you expect him to do something he didn't agree to do.

You are devastated. You may think the problem is Joe (or his wife) and his utter disregard for family traditions. But the problem is that you forgot what you have power over. In this situation, your power lies in making a request — inviting your son and his family to your home for Christmas dinner.

REMEMBER

Some people think that boundaries don't apply to families. Your family is entitled to their opinion that boundaries don't apply to them, and you're entitled to your opinion that they do.

Using ineffective strategies to get your needs met

When you use unworkable methods to accomplish pretty much anything, your efforts aren't likely to yield the results you want. Here's a list of the most common unproductive and ineffective strategies, followed by the effective strategies in the boundary-setting process:

» Telling another person what to do. The effective strategy is to make a request.

» Believing that an expectation obligates another person to do what you think they should do or what you want them to do. The effective strategy is to make a request.

» Failing to take action to create the outcome you want when you have the ability to do so. The effective strategy is to take action.

» Hoping or expecting another person to read your mind and do what you want them to do. The effective strategy is to make a request.

» Making a request of another person when you have the power to create the outcome yourself, and being unwilling to take the action you're asking the other person to take. The effective strategy is for *you* to create the outcome you want.

TIP

When you want to make a request of someone to do something you can do yourself, honestly ask yourself what's the true outcome you're seeking. In other words, if you want a bouquet of flowers that you have the power to give yourself, but you want to make a request that your spouse give them to you, the outcome you actually want is to receive flowers from your spouse. If the true outcome you wanted was flowers, you would give them to yourself.

Experiencing a host of negative emotions

Finally, consider all the negative emotions you experience when you either assume you have power where you don't or fail to use the power you have.

Here are just a few of the negative emotions you may feel:

>> Anger

>> Despair

>> Frustration

>> Helplessness

>> Pain

>> Resentment

>> Sadness

WARNING

Boundary problems play a role in many mental health problems, including anxiety and depression. Highly anxious people feel chronically unprotected and may be unable to set limits that would decrease or eliminate their anxiety. People who suffer from depression often struggle to use the power they have to take action on their own behalf, or they overestimate the power others have over them.

Getting Clear about Where Your Power Lies

The sole purpose of Step 4 in the boundary-setting process is to discover where your power lies so you can take the most effective action.

You have four possibilities for where your power lies (or *points of power*) in the situation you're working on. These options, described in detail in the following sections, include:

>> You have the power to create the outcome you want, and the outcome doesn't require making a request of another person.

>> You need help to create the outcome you want.

>> You need to make a request of another person to create the outcome you want.

>> You're powerless to create the outcome.

Once you're clear about where you have power to create the outcome you want, you can move on to Step 5 (see Chapter 17).

Knowing you have the power to create the outcome

Having the power to create the outcome you want is often the simplest and easiest solution, provided you're willing to follow through with the required action.

Here are a few examples where you have the power to create the outcome:

>> Saying *no* to an opportunity, a request, an invitation, and so on

>> Deciding to take time away from a situation or a relationship (including separation or divorce)

>> Changing your mind

>> Renegotiating a previously made agreement

>> Doing anything you have the resources (ability, money, time, and so on) to do, provided you're not breaking an agreement

Seeing you need help to create the outcome

Getting the outcome you want sometimes requires seeking help from other people. Seeking help is different from making a request because you have the power to find and get the help you need without the agreement of another person.

Situations where you may need help to get the outcome you want include:

>> You're considering divorce and want information about parental rights, division of property, and so on.

>> You're unhappy at your job and you need career counseling to explore how to match your current skills with other job opportunities.

>> You have a health concern and want to get more information from a relative(s) about their health history.

The outcome you want may require help from a friend or family member, or you may need to consult with a doctor, accountant, financial planner, contractor, real estate agent, or another professional.

Creating the outcome with a request

Some outcomes can be accomplished only through making a request of another person. An outcome that requires the participation of another person is accomplished in three steps:

1. **Make a request.**

2. **Receive a *yes* (or agreement) from the other person.**

3. **Follow through on the actions that are part of the agreement.**

Making a request is only the first step of the agreement-making process. I explain in detail how to make requests and create agreements (along with what to do if someone says *no* to a request) in Step 5 (see Chapter 17), but for now here are a few examples of situations that require agreements:

>> You want to go somewhere or do something with another person. This can be anything from having lunch, to taking a yearlong trip around the world together.

>> You want to go to couples therapy with your partner.

>> You want to sell a home that is the legal property of you and another person.

>> You want someone close to you to get help for a serious mental health issue or addiction.

>> You want to receive a gift for a specific occasion (or no occasion except that it's Monday!).

The bottom line is, any outcome you want that requires another person to say or do anything needs a request.

Recognizing when you are powerless

The final option for seeing where you have power is knowing when you're powerless to create the outcome you want. This means you can't take any action on your own or make any request to achieve the outcome.

Seeing that you're powerless can be frustrating. At the same time, admitting and accepting powerlessness is an essential skill for understanding what is (and isn't) in your circle of control.

Examples of situations where you may be powerless include:

>> A loved one who has a terminal illness

>> An addicted family member or friend for whom you've already said and done everything that's in your power to do

>> Someone crashes into your car while you're driving, gives you their insurance information, and you find out later they're not insured

TIP

Even in powerlessness, you can take action. Find ways to let go and surrender the outcome through prayer, or offering the situation to your higher power, God, or the universe.

Identifying Multiple Points of Power

Exploring all the potential solutions to the issue you're working on keeps your mind open and shows you the various options for where your power lies. In certain situations, you may be able to take action to get the outcome you want *or* make a request of another person to create an agreement. Both options lead to an acceptable outcome.

These are a few examples where you have more than one point of power:

>> You want to have flowers on your dining table every week. You can get the flowers yourself, or you can ask someone else to get them.

>> You want a new suitcase. You can buy the suitcase yourself, or you can ask someone else to buy it for you.

>> You want to see more movies or go to more concerts. You can go to more movies and concerts on your own, or you can ask someone to go with you or take you.

>> You want your lawn mowed at least twice a month. You can mow it yourself, hire someone, or ask someone else to do it.

Occasionally, someone tells me after they worked this step that they checked the box for all four points of power: They had the power, they needed help, they needed to make a request, and they were powerless. That's an open mind!

While that situation is uncommon, it's true that most of the time you can choose "I am powerless." That's because even when you have the power to create an outcome on your own, an unexpected event can prevent you from following through. You're also powerless over how (or whether) someone responds to your requests.

That being said, for clarity and to create the best probability of getting the outcome you want, you need to choose just one option among the points of power. The next section can help you find the best one.

TIP

If you have a tendency to focus on changing other people to get your needs met, exploring all possible points of power is especially helpful for you. Your default choice will be to make a request, in hopes that the other person will behave differently. Take the time to see if another option may achieve the outcome you want.

Choosing the Best Option for Your Situation

Now that you've identified all your points of power, you can choose the one option that's best for you and your situation.

Here are some guidelines for choosing the best option, especially when you're unsure or confused about how to proceed:

>> In general, choose the option to take action yourself if you have the power to create the outcome. This is often the easiest and fastest route to the outcome you want.

>> If you have the power to create an outcome, and the outcome can also be accomplished through making a request, choose to take action yourself unless it's extremely important to you that the other person participate.

>> If the outcome you want requires the participation of another person, the only option you can choose is to make a request. If you need another person to do anything, they must agree to do it. And the only way you can create an agreement is by making a request.

WARNING

Never decide to take an action yourself if you know that you will be resentful. Resentment is victim anger. If you make a choice that causes you to feel like a victim, you become a victim of your own choice. When you have freedom to choose, you can't be a victim. (For more on avoiding resentment and victimhood, see Chapter 7.)

Once you've chosen the best option for where your power lies for the issue you're working on, you're ready to move on and take action to create a boundary (Step 5).

Chapter **17**

Step 5: Take Action to Create a Boundary

As tempting as it may be to jump straight to the action step when you want to set a boundary, I highly recommend taking the time to complete the preliminary steps first.

If you jump into action before working through the previous four steps, you're likely to repeat what you've done in the past. If that's been working for you, be my guest! But if you'd like to do something different, experiment with another option, and get better results, give yourself the gift of slowing down to work all the boundary-setting steps in order.

REMEMBER

As a brief reminder before you take action to set a boundary, you should: know what isn't working for you, identifying the problem that you believe may require a boundary (see Chapter 13); get clear about your reality, using the data from your five senses, your thoughts, and your emotions (see Chapter 14); clarify your needs and the outcome you want (see Chapter 15), and see where you have power before you take action (see Chapter 16).

The next step, Step 5, is where you consider everything you discovered from working the first four steps to decide exactly what action you're going to take to create your boundary.

In this chapter, I show you why you need to match what you have power over with the action you plan to take, and I provide instructions for how to do it. I explain in detail how to create high-quality agreements, which starts with making specific, clear requests and ends with two yeses. Finally, I discuss why it's dangerous to proceed with your plan of action if you're not 100 percent confident that you'll follow through or if you're trying to use boundaries or agreements to punish someone or retaliate.

Aligning Your Action with Your Points of Power

Each of the steps for creating boundaries builds on the prior steps. In Step 4, you identified where you have control or power in the problematic situation you're working on. In Step 5, you use what you discovered about where your power lies to create a plan of action. In other words, you match where you have control or power to the action you take.

REMEMBER

You have the following four options for identifying where your power lies (your *points of power*) in a situation you're working on:

>> You have the power to create the outcome you want, and the outcome doesn't require making a request of another person.

>> You need help to create the outcome.

>> You need to make a request of another person to create the outcome you want.

>> You're powerless to create the outcome.

After you identify your point of power for the problematic situation, you take action to create a boundary that matches where you have power.

>> If you identified in Step 4 that you have the power to create the outcome you want (without seeking help or making a request), all you need to do is proceed with taking the action you want to take.

>> If you identified in Step 4 that you need help to create the outcome you want, you proceed with making a plan to get the help you need.

>> If you identified in Step 4 that you need to make a request of another person to create the outcome you want, the next step is to craft your request and make a plan for presenting it.

>> If you identified in Step 4 that you're powerless over the situation you're working on, your only action is to find ways to let go or surrender the outcome since it's not in your control. Admitting powerlessness is an essential skill for accepting what is (and what isn't) in your circle of control (see Chapter 16).

The next sections help you see how you can put your plan into action.

Making a plan to take action

Once you identify your point of power in the situation you're working on, it's time to make a plan for taking action.

Here are some examples of plans of action based on the four possibilities of where your power lies in the situation you're working on:

>> **You want to leave your current job.** You have the power to tell your employer that you're quitting. You decide when you want to give notice, arrange to meet with your employer, and have the meeting.

>> **You want is to manage your money better.** Because you don't have the information or skills to be a better manager of your money, you don't have the power to create the outcome you want without getting help. You need to do research, gather information, or make an appointment with a financial planner. You decide to find a financial planner and make an appointment.

>> **You want is to go to couples therapy with your partner.** Since this outcome requires the participation of another person, you must make a request. You make a plan to craft your request, then tell your partner you'd like to go to couples therapy, and ask if they're willing to go.

REMEMBER

When you make a request to create an agreement with someone — like going to couples therapy — the agreement is only the first of several steps needed for achieving the outcome you want. After the agreement to do couples counseling is made, you need to choose a therapist to work with and decide who will contact the therapist. You work through each component of the overall process using the same method of identifying what you want or need (Step 3), knowing where you have power (Step 4), and either taking action yourself or creating an agreement (Step 5).

>> **You want is for your adult son to stop hanging out with friends you think aren't good for him.** You have no power to decide whom your adult son hangs out with, which means you're powerless. Your plan of action can be to do whatever helps you accept your powerlessness in this situation. Your actions can also include continually reminding yourself that his friends are his business or connecting with other parents who are dealing with similar situations.

Seeing where you need accountability to follow through

Accountability is the willingness or obligation to accept responsibility for your actions. Why would you need accountability to follow through with a boundary you want to create? The simple answer is that boundary setting can be difficult, and sometimes scary!

For example, if you made an agreement with someone who has repeatedly broken the agreement and you haven't said or done anything about it, you're probably going to struggle to get the courage to talk to them about it. Or maybe your situation involves needing to consult with an attorney, accountant, or doctor, and the mere thought of picking up the phone or writing the email pushes you to the brink of a panic attack.

When I think about accountability, I'm reminded of a phone conversation I had several years ago with a man who'd been avoiding sending an email to an accountant about some paperwork he needed to complete. This email was one item on a long list of items that were overwhelming and paralyzing him.

As we were talking, I asked him if he was near a computer, and when he replied that he was, I said, "Why not send the email right now?" Because he had an open mind and was a highly teachable person, he went to the computer and returned to our conversation less than a minute later. He accomplished the thing he'd been putting off for weeks almost instantly due to the power of accountability.

Adding accountability to your plan may mean the difference between having a plan of action and taking action.

TIP

Here are some examples of how you can add accountability to your action plan for a boundary you need to set:

>> If you need to have a difficult conversation with someone about a repeatedly broken agreement or want to make a bold request, you can tell a friend about your plan to have the conversation on a specific day and commit to giving them an update as soon as you have the conversation.

>> If you've been avoiding taking action on something that's overdue or causing you stress, you can let someone know the first action you plan to take (choose one that's simple and feels easy to you) and the date you plan to do it, and then follow up with them once you've completed it.

>> To create an even higher level of accountability, you can use methods like paying a self-imposed fine or enforcing another consequence you find undesirable or even painful. (But don't hurt yourself!) Adding these high-stakes forms of accountability is especially helpful in situations where a problem has persisted for a long time, or longer than you would like. (For more information about creating higher levels of accountability, see Chapter 19.)

Crafting an effective request

When you need to create an agreement with another person to get the outcome you want, the only way you can do that is to make a request. Crafting an effective request isn't difficult, but if you neglect key components like being specific or making sure your request is in the form of a question, the agreement you create may not be successful.

These are some best practices for crafting an effective request:

>> **Express your request in the form of a question.** For example, "Would you be willing to go to couples therapy with me?"

>> **Make your request clear and specific.** For example, "I would like to see you more often. Would you be open to having lunch together once a month?"

>> **Avoid telling the other person what they should think, say, or do.** For example, don't say, "You need to clean up after yourself. Would you do that?" Telling another person what you think they should do prior to making a request may sabotage the request. No one wants to hear what they need to or should do. Also notice that the request to "clean up after yourself" is vague and open to perception and interpretation. One person's clean space may be another person's pigsty. That's why this request isn't specific enough to create a high-quality request or agreement.

TIP

Including a statement of the outcome you want prior to making a request can be a powerful addition to crafting an effective request. For example, if you want to go to a movie with a friend, you can say, "I would love to go to a movie with you next week. Would you like to go?"

REMEMBER

Requests must end with a question mark. If you believe you made a request, but it didn't end with a question or a question mark, you didn't make a request.

Seeing possible actions even in powerlessness

As frustrating as it can be, you're powerless in some situations. Being powerless means you can't do anything to get the outcome you want on your own, or by getting help or making a request.

Here are the examples from Chapter 16 of situations where someone is powerless:

>> A loved one who has a terminal illness

>> An addicted family member or friend for whom you've already said and done everything that's in your power to do

>> Someone crashes into your car while you're driving, gives you their insurance information, and you find out later they're not insured.

Here are some actions you can take in situations where you're powerless to get the outcome you want:

>> Explore ways to let go, release, or surrender.

>> Review what's in your circle of control (see Chapter 16) and focus on accepting the situation, and what you can control.

>> Pray or take part in any practice that supports you in letting go of what's outside your circle of control.

WARNING

You must be completely honest with yourself when you see that you're powerless to create the outcome you want. If you have the power to create an outcome but you choose not to take action, you're not powerless. You're simply choosing to do nothing. If you proceed as though you're powerless when you're not, you disempower yourself and make yourself a victim of your unwillingness to take responsibility for what you have the power to do.

Being Honest about Your Commitment to Your Plan

When you're in the process of creating a boundary in a situation where you have a sense of urgency or very strong feelings, avoid rushing into action without thinking it through. The consequences you may experience from acting on urgency, strong emotions, or even doubts can cause delays, create more problems, or sabotage what you're trying to accomplish. It's easy to get in a hurry and commit too soon to a course of action you're not 100 percent committed to.

For example, imagine your spouse came home drunk at 2:30 a.m. two days ago and you're very upset about it. You worked through the first four steps and the outcome you want is to be separated from your spouse for two weeks. In Step 4 (see Chapter 16), you identified three possible solutions: You can sleep in the guest bedroom, leave your home and stay somewhere else, or ask your spouse to leave your home for two weeks.

You have the power to take action on the first two options (sleep in the guest bedroom or stay somewhere else), but the third option (asking your spouse to leave for two weeks) requires an agreement. You prefer to leave and stay somewhere else. Before you tell your spouse your plan, ask yourself if you are 100 percent confident that you will follow through.

TIP

When you're considering setting a boundary that requires you to follow through with a certain action you've never done before, avoid blurting out your boundary immediately, especially when you're feeling strong emotions. Unless it's an emergency, wait at least 48 hours before announcing your intention to set the boundary. Having a time buffer helps protect you from setting a boundary you're not ready to commit to. (See the sidebar, "Avoid the temptation of hollow threats," later in the chapter.)

Doubting means you need to delay action

If you're getting ready to take action to set a boundary and you start second-guessing yourself or having doubts, it can be because:

» You're feeling uncomfortable because what you're getting ready to do is a new behavior for you.

» You're worried about pushback or resistance to your boundary or the request you plan to make.

» You're not sure that what you're getting ready to do is right for you.

If you're feeling uncomfortable about the simple fact that you're doing something different or because you're afraid of the reaction you may get, those are not good reasons to delay or abandon your plans. If setting boundaries is new and different behavior, not only will it feel uncomfortable to you, but it will also feel uncomfortable for others. That's one of the primary reasons people experience pushback and resistance. (See Chapter 6 for more information about how to navigate and manage pushback on your boundaries.)

On the other hand, if you're feeling unsure that what you're getting ready to do is the best decision for you and the issue isn't urgent or an emergency, take a pause. Your boundary work is always more successful when you're clear and determined about your plan of action.

TIP

If you're not sure whether your doubts are warranted, talk to a trusted friend, mentor, life coach, or therapist to get their feedback. Getting an objective perspective helps you figure out whether your hesitation is warranted and healthy, or unwarranted and fear-based.

Delaying action if you have overwhelming emotions

WARNING

When you're in the middle of a storm of overwhelming emotions like anger, rage, sadness, fear, or grief, it's never the best time to take action on a boundary. The only exception is when an emotion is related to an immediate situation of physical danger or harm. In other words, if someone is physically attacking you or another person and you're feeling terrified, your primary focus must be on protecting yourself or the other person.

Aside from threats to physical safety, being in the grip of overwhelming emotions often causes people to act in ways that aren't reasonable, rational, or warranted. If you just found out that your partner of 32 years is leaving you for another person, it's normal to feel shocked and outraged.

In situations like this, it's tempting to go into full-scale boundary-setting attack mode so you can feel more in control or powerful. The danger of setting boundaries when you're under the influence of strong emotions is that your boundaries are more likely to be punitive or vengeful (more on this later in the chapter). Or you won't follow through with your boundaries because you weren't in your "right mind" when you set them.

If you want to give your boundaries the best possible chance of success, wait until your emotions have settled down and you're able to rationally assess the situation and all your options. Then you can take action if that's what you decide to do.

TIP

One of the simplest ways to find out if you're experiencing strong emotions is to measure your heart rate. If it's above 100 beats per minute (bpm), you're in a stressed state. You can measure your heart rate manually by pressing your index and middle fingers on your opposite wrist and counting the number of pulses you feel in one minute. Alternatively, you can use a pulse oximeter or any wearable device that measures heart bpm.

Trying to change another person is a red flag

Over the years, I've observed that many people have blind spots when it comes to knowing whether their motivation to set a boundary comes from their need for self-protection or self-care, or from a desire to change another person.

Whenever you attempt to create a boundary for the sole purpose of changing another person's behavior, or because you believe a boundary you already want to set (for your own reasons) may also cause someone to change, you're not engaged in boundary work. You're engaged in control, manipulation, or both. The purpose of boundaries is to protect you and others, and never to change or influence someone to do what you want them to do.

Here are a few signs that your boundary work is focused on changing another person rather than taking care of yourself:

>> You want to go to your friend's birthday party, but you decide to skip it because your friend said something that hurt your feelings last week. Your reason for not going to the party is that you want her to realize how upset you are about what she did.

>> You decide to sleep in another room, apart from your spouse. When you're explaining to your friends or therapist why you made the decision, you say, "My spouse hates it when I sleep in the other room."

>> You lowered the spending limit on the credit card your spouse uses that's part of your joint account. You took this action because they consistently spent over the card's prior limit, and you felt disrespected and unappreciated as the primary breadwinner. Your reason for lowering the spending limit without telling your spouse is that you hope they'll appreciate you more when they find out they can't spend as much as they used to.

Here's how each of the previous scenarios may look if the focus is on creating a powerful, healthy outcome rather than trying to change another person:

>> Instead of skipping your friend's party (which you really don't want to do), you review what happened and see that what you want is to feel connected to her. You make a plan to talk to her and let her know that something is standing in the way of your connection and ask her if she's willing to talk with you about it.

>> You honestly consider your reasons for wanting to sleep separately from your spouse. If you determine that sleeping separately is healthy for you at this time, you take responsibility for your choice rather than making your decision about your spouse and their feelings.

>> You spend some time thinking about feeling disrespected and unappreciated because of your spouse's overspending and what you would like from them — being as clear and specific as possible. You craft a request and present it to your spouse.

Knowing When You Have an Agreement

Agreements are boundaries because when two (or more) people enter into an agreement, they've mutually decided that certain limits apply to both of them.

You can also think of agreements as contracts. In business contracts, two or more people have written parameters of what each party will or won't do, and then sign the document and agree to follow through on their promises as defined in the contract. Violating the contract results in consequences, which are often written into the contract.

TIP

Forgetting agreements — even important ones — is more common than you may think. Consider creating an *agreement journal* to record agreements you make in important or long-term relationships. You can write down the date the agreement was made and a short description of it, followed by the initials of everyone who is a party to the agreement. Even if the other person isn't interested in recording and initialing the agreement, you can write it down for your own reference.

Creating a boundary with "yes" or "I agree"

When you make a request and the other person answers with *yes* or *I agree*, you have an agreement, also known as a *boundary*.

To increase the likelihood of getting to *yes* or *I agree*, I recommend following these guidelines:

>> Choose a time when you and the other person are peacefully coexisting and you have minimal distractions. Ideally, both of you are relatively calm.

>> Ask the other person if they're available or open to talking about something important.

>> Be willing to take *no* for an answer. If the other person isn't ready to have a conversation, try to schedule another time to talk.

>> If the person is open to talking, phrase your request using a version of:

- I would like. . . . Would you be willing to do that?

- What I would like is. . . . Is that something you can agree to?

- Would you be open to. . . ?

Here are a few things to avoid when you present requests:

>> Making requests when you or the other person is feeling highly anxious, triggered, or angry

>> Presenting requests when you're not willing to accept the other person's *no* — to your request to have a conversation or to the request related to the boundary you want to create

>> Continuing to talk to the other person when they tell you they're not available for a conversation or they're not in a good place emotionally to talk about anything important

>> Insisting on resolving the issue immediately, even when the other person tells you they need time to think about your request

Negotiating an agreement

Creating agreements requires clarity, forethought, and basic knowledge of how to negotiate with another person. Once you've crafted the request you want to make, present your request to the person you want to create an agreement with. The other person may say *yes, I agree*, or *no*, or they may propose an alternative solution.

If the answer to your request is *yes*, you've created an agreement — congratulations!

If the other person says *no* to your request, here are some questions you can ask:

>> Would you be willing to say more about why this is a *no* for you?

>> What would you be willing to agree to?

>> Is there something else you'd like to propose that would change your *no* to a *yes*?

>> Are there any conditions or scenarios in which you would say *yes* to this request?

REMEMBER

Stay humble about the fact that you may have no idea why the other person said *no* to your request. Rather than assume you know their reasoning, ask questions to stay genuinely curious, and remind yourself that you're listening to know and understand them. This is a perfect opportunity to practice your listening boundaries! (See Chapter 11 for more information about listening boundaries.)

What if the person you made the request of proposes an alternative solution or agreement? In this case, you're on the receiving end of a potential new agreement. You're free to say *yes* or *no*, or to propose another alternative solution.

Here are some do's and don'ts for negotiating an agreement:

>> *Do* stay open to the possibility that negotiating an agreement may give you a higher-quality agreement than if the person had simply said *yes* to your original request.

>> *Do* focus on the reality that creating a negotiated agreement likely guarantees higher commitment or buy-in.

>> *Don't* say *no* to an alternative proposal simply because you're feeling reactive or angry, or because you just want to be right.

>> *Don't* enter into any agreements when you feel unsure, overly emotional, obligated, or guilty, or believe that you will have resentment.

TIP

When making requests, ask yourself how attached you are to getting the outcome you want by using a rating scale of 1 to 10, with 10 being the most attached. The higher the number, the more difficult it will be for you to receive a *no*. In other words, the stronger you feel about getting what you want makes it more disappointing to not get it. One of my mentors Pia Mellody (author and Senior Fellow of Meadows Behavioral Healthcare), suggests that when you're highly attached to an outcome, you can tell the other person, "I'm very attached to the outcome of this request. I really want you to do what I'm asking you to do. But I know you have a right to say *yes* or *no*, or negotiate with me, and I don't have a right to get everything I want." That takes courage!

Refraining From Taking Retaliatory or Vengeful Action

Sometimes when you're dealing with a crisis or strong, raw emotions, you're tempted to use boundaries to retaliate, take revenge, or punish.

I remember hearing a story about a woman whose husband had behaved badly in some way. It just so happened that the title to his very expensive red sports car was in her name. Because she was so distraught, angry, and hurt (and because she could), she sold his car to someone for $1.

Another revenge story that comes to mind involves someone who found out that their recent ex was getting ready to take an amazing trip with their new love interest. The jilted partner somehow managed to impersonate the ex and completely reroute their entire travel itinerary.

These stories may make your inner teenager practically giddy imagining the dollar bill presented to the misbehaving husband for the sale of his red Ferrari, or the look on the ex's face when they arrived in Paris, Texas, rather than Paris, France.

The hidden truth about retaliation and revenge is that the person who takes revenge is unknowingly reinforcing the power the other person holds over them. Revenge can be devilishly fun, but it often sets in motion other events that are undesirable, and often painful.

When you know how to respond to irritations, difficult situations, or crises with healthy, functional boundaries, you may daydream about a fun way to get even, but you know there's a better way. When you replace retaliation with good boundaries, you avoid drama and *counter-revenge* (the other person taking revenge on you). Best of all, you can create a solution that allows you to sleep at night, and one that you won't regret.

THINK ABOUT IT

Sixteenth-century poet George Herbert said it best: "Living well is the best revenge."

Like revenge, punishing people is a tempting use of boundaries. I once heard a story about a father who refused to talk to his adult daughter for months while they were living in the same house. The daughter wasn't a criminal, drug addict, or loafer. She'd simply made the mistake of displeasing her father in some small way, and she was punished for it.

You're free to misuse boundaries in this way, but there are consequences. Imagine the consequences to the long-term health of this father-daughter relationship. When you make yourself a punisher rather than a boundary creator, you place yourself in the position of judge, jury, and even God.

TIP

If you have a habit of retaliating, seeking revenge, punishing, or making hollow threats, experiment with telling yourself, "Wait for 24 hours before doing anything. If you still want to [fill in the blank with your choice of options] after 24 hours, then be my guest."

AVOID THE TEMPTATION OF HOLLOW THREATS

If you've ever said, "If you . . . one more time, I'm going to . . . ," you're probably no stranger to hollow threats. These kinds of statements have a tendency to be full of hot air.

When you make a threat that you don't follow through with, not only do you lose credibility with the other person, who sees that you don't always keep your word, but you also lose credibility with yourself. It's a lose-lose situation.

When emotions are running high or you've had an unusually terrible day, you're more likely to make hollow threats. If you're prone to making threats you rarely follow through with, the information in this book can help you avoid lashing out prematurely and give you alternatives to making threats that create far better outcomes.

Seeing the danger of losing self-trust

Taking revenge, punishing, and making hollow threats all come with the potential danger of losing trust in yourself.

Many people place a significant amount of importance on the trustworthiness of others, but self-trust is even more important than trusting another person. When you trust yourself, you're confident that if someone in your life turns out to be untrustworthy, you'll do what you need to do to take care of yourself.

There are two primary consequences of low self-trust when it comes to you and your boundaries:

>> You may delay or neglect to set a boundary because, based on your track record, you don't believe you'll follow through.

>> You don't believe you can care for, protect, or stand up for yourself.

TIP

If you've lost trust in your ability to stand up for or protect yourself, ask yourself if you're able to protect or stand up for another person (for example, a child or loved one). If your answer is *yes*, then trust that you can care for, protect, and stand up for yourself. You just haven't applied this known ability or skill to yourself yet.

Avoiding losing credibility

Credibility is the quality or power of inspiring belief. Another word for credibility is believability (yes, it's a real word!). Anytime you say one thing but you do another, you lose credibility — with yourself or another person.

When you substitute revenge, punishment, or threats for healthy personal boundaries, you're practically guaranteed to lose credibility. On the other hand, when you use healthy personal boundaries to resolve everything from minor upsets to devastating relationship crises, you become someone who is trustworthy and credible to yourself and to everyone else.

After working through Step 5, you may find that you need to evaluate an agreement or revisit an action you took — depending on your results, how the other person responds, or how the situation develops. But for now, rest assured that you've done everything you can to create the outcome you want. Congratulations!

Chapter 18

Step 6: Evaluate Your Results and See What Went Wrong

I wish I could tell you that every time you set a boundary or create an agreement it will be successful the first time. But boundaries — like everything else in life — take time to figure out, practice, and experiment with.

Even when you're an experienced boundary setter, some of your boundaries may not work (at least the first time) for many reasons. Sometimes they're simply outside your control, like an agreement that's broken by another person.

However, I always bristle when someone sets a boundary that doesn't work and then declares, "Boundaries don't work." When a boundary isn't successful or an agreement is broken, it's not because boundaries don't work. That's like saying bikes don't work if you fall off your bike when you're learning how to ride it.

If you fall off a bike when you're learning how to ride, it's usually because you made a riding error despite having good instructions, you weren't taught good riding skills, or someone (or something) came along and knocked you off your bike.

These are the same reasons boundaries sometimes "don't work." Boundaries are more likely to be unsuccessful when you're figuring out how to create them, when you make a mistake despite having good information and skills, or when someone breaks an agreement that causes a boundary to fail.

In this chapter, I assure you that if you create a boundary that doesn't work, it's not the end of the world. There's still hope! In fact, the more you experiment with boundaries, the more mistakes you'll make and the more your boundaries will improve.

I show you how to figure out why a boundary you created wasn't successful, and how to evaluate the quality and clarity of a boundary. I give you four options for proceeding after a boundary bust so you can decide what's the best fit for your particular issue and situation.

Identifying What Didn't Work

Anytime a boundary isn't successful, the first thing you need to do is review and examine it so you can find out why it didn't work.

There are five primary reasons boundaries don't work:

>> You didn't follow through with a boundary you had the power to create (a boundary that didn't require an agreement with someone else).

>> You didn't make a request of another person for the purpose of creating an agreement.

>> You thought you had a clear agreement with someone, but you and the other person had different understandings or interpretations of what the agreement meant.

>> You made an agreement with another person but discovered that they weren't fully committed, weren't sincere, or didn't buy in to the agreement.

>> You made an agreement with another person that was clear, specific, and measurable, but one of you broke it.

I explain each of these reasons in detail in the following sections.

THINK
ABOUT IT

If you think I'm being cruel when I suggest that you'll make mistakes with your boundaries, I want you to know what the inventor of the incandescent light bulb, phonograph, and motion picture camera said about failure. Thomas Edison said, "I have not failed. I've just found 10,000 ways that won't work."

Admitting you lacked follow-through

If you worked through all the steps for creating a boundary but you didn't take action to create it, ask for help, or make a request, the problem is the lack of follow-through.

The good news about poor (or no) follow-through is, you're in the driver's seat! That's because you don't need the participation of any other person. You can easily regroup, recommit, and follow through by taking action as soon as possible.

THINK ABOUT IT

If you have a pattern of not following through with taking action to create a boundary or with making requests to create agreements, investigate your pattern of behavior to find out what gets in your way. Having clarity and overcoming any mental or emotional blocks improves your future boundary work.

TIP

Before you move forward based on an assumption that you've "fixed" a boundary, I recommend that you build in an extra step of accountability when you recommit to your original plan of action. A simple way to support yourself with accountability is to tell a friend about your plans and commit to letting your friend know as soon as you complete your plan of action. When you add accountability to your plan, you exponentially increase the likelihood of following through. (See Chapter 17 for more information about adding accountability to your boundary-setting process.)

Misunderstanding the meaning of an agreement

One of the most common reasons agreements don't work is because they were open to interpretation. In other words, when an agreement isn't clear and specific, it's more likely to be misunderstood and misinterpreted.

Here are a few examples of agreements that are highly vulnerable to misinterpretation or misunderstanding:

>> **We agree not to raise our voices when we talk to each other.** This agreement is open to interpretation because *raise our voices* isn't clearly defined and is a matter of perception. It also doesn't take into account that each listener may have completely different hearing abilities.

>> **We agree to spend more time together.** This agreement is open to interpretation because *spend more time together* isn't clear or specific.

>> **We agree to save more money.** This agreement is open to interpretation because *more money* isn't defined by a percentage, dollar amount, and so on.

>> **We agree to keep a cleaner house.** This agreement is open to interpretation because *cleaner* is in the eye of the beholder and isn't defined in the agreement.

>> **We agree to do a better job of parenting.** This agreement is open to interpretation because *better job* isn't defined by describing exactly how the two people who created the agreement can improve their parenting.

When someone uses unclear or vague words like *more*, *better*, or *soon*, ask them what more, better, or soon means or looks like. For example, if your spouse says they're going to take you to World of Barbie "soon," you can say, "That sounds wonderful, you know how much I love Barbie! When is soon? I need to start packing." I'm not saying they'll get more specific about when they'll take you to World of Barbie, but I do recommend you ask because you'll create an agreement that will get you there much faster.

Seeing that you didn't have an agreement after all

It's disappointing to believe you had a solid agreement with someone only to discover that what you thought was an agreement really wasn't.

Here are two examples of how you don't actually have an agreement:

>> You realize that the person you made the agreement with wasn't sincere, lacked commitment, or had no intention of honoring the agreement. If you make an agreement with someone who lacks commitment to the agreement, it won't take long to find out. When a person lacks commitment, sincerity, or buy-in, there's a higher-than-average likelihood they either won't or can't honor the agreement.

>> You see in hindsight that when the agreement was made, you didn't make a request in the form of a question and didn't receive a *yes* from the other person. Because you didn't receive a *yes*, you didn't create an agreement.

Imagine the outcome you want for the issue you're working on is for your partner to "take you out to dinner once a month." Provided that you don't have a certain restaurant in mind, or a particular day or time of the month you'd like to go, this is a clear and specific outcome.

However, if you create the agreement using any of the following statements, you don't have a true agreement:

>> You're going to take me to dinner once a month.

>> I'd like you to take me to dinner once a month.

>> I would love to go to dinner with you once a month.

>> Damien takes Suzy to dinner once a month. Isn't that nice?

Even if your partner looks at you and says, "Okay" or "That sounds great," you still don't have an agreement. Why? Because you didn't make a request in the form of a question.

TIP

If you tell someone you'd like to do something with them and you believe they agreed to do it without explicitly saying *yes* or *I agree*, ask them directly, "Do we have an agreement?" If they answer in the affirmative, you're good to go.

In this scenario, you can create an agreement by saying:

> I would love for you to take me out to dinner once a month. Would you be willing to do that?

Notice that this request begins with you stating the outcome you want, and it ends with a question. After your partner hears the question, they can respond by saying *yes* or *no*, or negotiating an alternative agreement with you. If both of you agree by stating two yeses or *I agree*, you have an agreement.

REMEMBER

Creating an agreement requires making requests, and all requests end with a question mark. If your request isn't a question or doesn't end with a question mark, you aren't creating an agreement.

Experiencing a broken agreement

Not only are broken agreements unsuccessful boundaries, but they're also boundary violations by the person who broke the agreement. However, broken agreements shouldn't be considered boundary violations if:

>> You see in hindsight that the agreement was open to interpretation and was misunderstood or misinterpreted.

>> The agreement was created with a demand rather than a request.

REMEMBER

If you create a boundary with another person using a demand rather than a request, you haven't created a boundary or an agreement.

Whether you or the other person broke the agreement, you need to explore the reasons the agreement was broken and decide how you want to proceed. The options for dealing with broken agreements range from doing nothing to creating a new agreement. New agreements created after broken ones should include a higher level of accountability if the new agreement is broken in the future. In Chapter 19, I explain in detail how to explore your options and proceed after a boundary is broken.

Evaluating the Quality and Clarity of an Agreement

When an agreement you created is broken, you should review the original agreement and ask yourself the following three questions:

- » Was the agreement specific enough?
- » Did I state a demand (rather than make a request)?
- » Was the other person committed or sincere?

Lack of specificity, making a demand instead of a request, and not having a fully committed agreement are all examples of boundaries that need improvement.

Reviewing the specificity of the agreement

When you're evaluating the quality and clarity of an agreement, begin by finding out whether the agreement was specific enough.

Highly effective and specific agreements include the following key components:

>> **Provide time frames.** When you create an agreement, use specific time quantities like minutes, hours, days, months, and years, or include periods of time like *within the next two weeks*.

>> **Specify quantities.** Identify quantities when agreements include matters of time, money, or anything you can measure.

>> **Avoid vague words like *more, better,* or *soon*.** Define what more, better, and soon mean or look like to you by using specific and measurable quantities or qualities.

- *More* can be defined using a specific amount of time, money, or anything measurable.

- *Better* can be defined by describing what you'd experience with your senses — sight, sound, taste, smell, or touch — if something or a certain situation improves.

- *Soon* can be defined by stating a specific time frame like *within the next day/week/month/year*.

TIP

If you're not sure whether a term or phrase is unclear or vague, ask yourself if you can see, hear, taste, smell, or touch it. If you can't connect the term or phrase with something you can perceive with your five senses, chances are, it's too vague.

If the original agreement lacked time frames or specific quantities, or contained vague words or terms, this was the likely cause of the broken agreement.

Mistaking a demand for an agreement

If you issue a demand rather than make a request, unfortunately you don't have an agreement. One of the easiest ways to avoid mistaking a demand for an agreement is to recognize that a demand doesn't contain a question, but a request does.

Creating an agreement with another person requires:

» Making a request that ends with a question mark

» Receiving a *yes* or *I agree* from the other person or negotiating an agreement that ends with both of you answering *yes*

Getting real about buy-in or sincerity

When you create an agreement with someone who isn't all in on the agreement, or who lacks buy-in or sincerity, it shouldn't be surprising when the agreement fails or is broken.

In all fairness, you may have had no idea that the other person wasn't fully committed, and even if you had an inkling that they lacked sincerity, it's not your fault they broke the agreement.

However, it's important to be mindful of situations in the future when you have an intuition or hunch that this person isn't all in. You may be particularly vulnerable to ignoring your intuition or going into denial when an agreement is important to you and you're highly invested in a particular outcome.

For example, if your spouse has a significant gambling problem that's causing you emotional and financial stress, you may be more likely to ignore your intuition that your spouse isn't fully committed to agreeing to stop gambling. Broken agreements are sometimes a wake-up call that agreements aren't the best solution for a problem and it's time to explore other options for getting your needs met.

TIP

If you're in a relationship with someone who has a habit of breaking agreements due to low or no commitment (or you're the person who breaks agreements), try adding time between making a request and receiving a response. For example, after you make the request, say, "I prefer not to have your answer now. Would you let me know tomorrow?" With additional time to consider a request, a person with low or no commitment may be less inclined to say *yes* when they'd prefer to say *no*.

Here are a few reasons people make agreements when they're not fully committed:

» They want your approval and tend to say *yes* to most of your requests.

» The two of you have recently experienced a major relationship crisis and the other person believes that if they don't say *yes* to your request, you will leave them, or there will be a major unwanted consequence.

>> They tend to avoid conflict; rather than state their authentic *no,* they go along to get along.

>> They want the conversation to end, so they say *yes* to make that happen.

>> They're a bad actor who frequently enters into agreements with no intention of honoring them.

WARNING

You have both the right and the freedom to say *yes* to a request for the sole reason that you're afraid the other person won't like you or will end the relationship. However, if you say *yes* when you really mean *no,* you deprive the other person of knowing who you are — the authentic you. You also put the relationship at risk when you enter into agreements you're not fully committed to. These low or no buy-in agreements are the most likely agreements to be broken, and broken agreements break trust. It's better for you and the long-term health of your relationships to say *no* or negotiate an alternative agreement.

Deciding How to Proceed

Now that you know what went wrong with your boundary, it's time to decide what to do next.

You have four options for proceeding after a boundary isn't successful:

>> Recommit to the original action or agreement.

>> Start over with a revised agreement.

>> Start over with the boundary-setting process beginning at Step 1 with a new problem you now have due to the unsuccessful boundary.

>> Decide to do nothing.

To resolve or "fix" the broken boundary, you need to choose one of these options. The following sections examine each option to help you decide how to proceed with the agreement.

Recommitting to the original action or agreement

In some situations, recommitting to the original action or agreement is the most logical and reasonable option.

If the solution is a simple fix of taking action yourself to create the outcome you want, asking for help, or making a request, you can just recommit to the original plan.

Here are some scenarios where recommitting is often the best choice:

>> You didn't follow through on an action you had the power to take, including asking for help.

>> You created an agreement with someone, but you discovered that a miscommunication or misunderstanding caused the agreement to fail. For example, you made an agreement with your spouse that they would make a reservation at a hotel for three nights, but your spouse understood the agreement to be for a two-night reservation. (This is a good example of why it's helpful to keep an agreement journal, especially for important agreements. See Chapter 17 for more information about agreement journals.)

>> You broke an agreement initially, but you want to recommit by telling the person you created the agreement with that you'll follow through with what you agreed to do by a certain date or time.

TIP

When you break any agreement, the most effective, responsible, and accountable action you can take is to admit your mistake, apologize for breaking the agreement, and either offer to immediately follow through with the agreement or ask the other person how they'd like you to repair or resolve the broken agreement.

However, recommitting to the original agreement isn't always the best choice. I don't recommend recommitting in either of these circumstances:

>> The person who broke the agreement has broken the same agreement more than once.

>> You have strong unresolved feelings about the broken agreement. Your strong emotions may be a sign that you need a higher level of commitment or accountability to feel comfortable recommitting to the agreement. (See Chapter 19 for more information on how to make a plan for accountability.)

REMEMBER

Repairing an agreement means to make it right. When you break an agreement, you can repair it by following through with the terms of the original agreement or asking the person you made the agreement with how they'd like you to fix or repair it.

Starting over with a revised agreement

If an agreement you made was unclear, not specific enough, or simply not workable, you may want to start over by creating a revised agreement.

Follow these steps for starting over with a revised agreement:

» Review the guidelines earlier in this chapter for evaluating the quality of the original agreement you made.

» Review your agreement and identify the changes you need to make.

» Craft a revised request that includes the changes, additions, or improvements you identified.

» Present your request and create a revised agreement, if possible. Remember, the other person must say *yes* to your request to create a revised agreement.

TIP

When you want to start over with a revised agreement, begin by telling the other person what, if anything, you should have done differently to avoid the broken or unsuccessful agreement. Then you can say, "I'd like to create a new agreement with you," and present your request. Leading with describing your role in the broken agreement (if any) means you're taking responsibility and being accountable.

Revisiting the steps to resolve a new problem

One of the advantages of having a step-by-step process for creating boundaries is that you can always start over with a new problem or issue and work through the steps on the new issue.

For example, if you created an agreement with your partner to pick up your son from school every Friday but last week they forgot for the third time in two months (broken agreement), you should consider the latest broken agreement a new issue or problem to work, beginning again with Step 1 — knowing what isn't working (see Chapter 13). The most recent broken agreement should be considered a new problem because your partner not picking up your son from school is a serious issue and they've repeatedly broken the agreement. You would be unwise to recommit or revise the original agreement, and doing nothing isn't an option.

The description of the new problem in this situation may be:

>> My partner said they would pick up our son every Friday, but they forgot for the third time.

>> My partner isn't reliable. This is the third time they've forgotten this commitment.

>> My son is starting to ask me who's picking him up from school. I think he's getting anxious and worried because this has happened three times.

Identifying (and working the steps on) a new problem created by a broken agreement is always a better choice than revising the original agreement, especially when the broken agreement significantly changes either the way you see a situation or what you think and feel about the person who broke agreement.

Continuing with this example, when your partner forgot to pick up your son from school for the third time, starting over with a revised agreement isn't a wise choice. You can make more progress by identifying the new problem or issue you have based on the broken agreement, and work Steps 1 through 5 on the new problem.

WARNING

Avoid creating agreements with anyone who has repeatedly broken agreements. When you need to create a boundary with a chronic agreement breaker, focus on outcomes you have the power to create rather than outcomes that require requests that lead to agreements.

Making a conscious, considered choice to do nothing

When you're exploring your options for any boundary-setting decision you need to make, doing nothing is always an option. Whether you didn't follow through with taking action or making a request, or you're facing a broken agreement, you can always choose to simply drop the issue.

Here are several reasons you can safely choose to do nothing, or to not proceed after a boundary is unsuccessful:

>> You have more information than you had before creating the boundary, and that information changes how you see the situation or impacts your level of interest or motivation to do more work on that particular boundary.

>> The person you made the agreement with is someone you no longer have a desire to have a relationship with.

>> You decide you prefer to take a wait-and-see approach for now.

>> Even though the boundary was unsuccessful, the original problem has improved, and you don't have the same level of need, interest, or energy to revise the boundary.

>> You realize that the way you originally saw the situation was mistaken or distorted. For example, you realize in hindsight that you took action based on believing your thoughts about what happened rather than the actual data (or facts) of the situation. Because you now see the situation in a new light, you have no further need to create a boundary.

Before you decide to take no action after an unsuccessful boundary or a broken agreement, ask yourself these questions:

>> If you do nothing about the failed boundary (or broken agreement), will you have a resentment? In other words, will you see yourself as a victim if you do nothing?

>> Are you willing to take responsibility for your decision to change your mind? Are you willing to be responsible for your choices?

>> Are you willing to refrain from blaming another person for your decision not to proceed?

If you answer *no* to the first question and *yes* to the next two questions, it's safe for you to choose to take no further action. You're making an empowered decision because you're taking responsibility for your choice without believing you're a victim or blaming anyone.

If you say *yes* to the first question (meaning you'll have a resentment if you do nothing), you can choose to do nothing but it's not the wisest decision. I recommend reviewing your boundary work to see if there's an action you're able and willing to take instead. You can also review Chapter 7 to find out more about resentments.

REMEMBER

When you make a free and conscious choice to do something but tell yourself you "had to" do it, you're making yourself a victim of your conscious choice. Unless you're being threatened with harm, you're making a free choice. When you're free to choose an action, you can't be a victim by taking the action you chose.

5

Figuring Out What to Do When Boundaries Don't Work

Discover how to navigate or renegotiate broken agreements.

Elevate your boundary work to the next level when you face challenging situations.

Chapter 19

Renegotiating a Broken Agreement

B roken agreements are frustrating and painful. You may be tempted to think you did something wrong if an agreement you created with another person didn't work. To navigate through a broken agreement easier and with more confidence, approach it as an opportunity to examine and improve your boundaries skills.

Broken agreements occur for many reasons. The most common reasons agreements fail are:

» The agreement wasn't clear, measurable, or specific enough.

» One or both people who created the agreement forgot it.

» One of the agreement makers wasn't fully committed to the agreement.

» The person who broke the agreement has a pattern of breaking commitments or agreements.

TIP

Forgetting agreements is more common than you may imagine. It's one of the reasons I highly recommend keeping an agreement journal for important agreements you make with a partner, family member, or child. (See Chapter 17 for more information about agreement journals.)

In this chapter, I give you tips for how to decide whether you want to renegotiate a broken agreement. It's always your choice! I also explain the connection between increasing your self-protection and renegotiating an agreement, and what to do if you struggle to protect yourself even when people repeatedly break agreements with you. I show you how to change your requests and agreements to improve the chances that a new agreement you create is successful.

REMEMBER

When the details of an agreement are revised or renegotiated those agreements can be referred to as *new*.

Deciding Whether to Renegotiate a Broken Agreement

Even though broken agreements are highly undesirable, not every broken agreement must be renegotiated. You get to decide whether the agreement is worth renegotiating.

For example, say you made an agreement with your partner to pick up your dry cleaning so you'd have the clothes you need for a trip you're taking the next day. Your partner calls you from your child's soccer practice, and when you ask about the clothes, they admit they forgot them. The dry cleaner is open for another hour, so there's still time to pick up your clothes. In this situation, renegotiating the agreement doesn't make sense and won't get you what you need — your clothes for the trip. In this case, rather than revisiting your agreement, you'd be better off getting in your car and picking up the clothes yourself.

On the other hand, if you have an agreement with one of your clients that they will pay you every 30 days and they haven't paid you for 60 days, you may want to revisit and potentially renegotiate the agreement with your client.

Rating the importance of the issue

When you're trying to decide whether to renegotiate an agreement, one of the quickest and easiest ways to know what to do is to rate how important the issue is for you using a rating scale of 1 to 10, with 10 being the most important.

For example, high-level issues or broken agreements such as theft, chronic deception, or betrayal are issues that most people would rate between an 8 and a 10. These are situations that require serious and decisive responses.

Low-level issues you would rate as less than a 4, like being 10 minutes late picking up a child from school one time, would call for a lower-level response, or no response at all.

Rating the importance of an issue helps you decide how you want to proceed. If you rate an issue higher than a 7, the next step is to renegotiate the agreement (see the section "Exploring Your Options," later in this chapter) or take the issue and your boundary work to the next level with a higher level of commitment and accountability. If you rate an issue lower than a 4, you may decide not to take any action, or to simply observe or monitor what happens next before taking action.

Choosing not to renegotiate an agreement

Just because an agreement is broken, that doesn't mean it must be renegotiated. For example, if you agree to meet a friend for lunch at noon and they don't show up until 12:20, it doesn't make sense to renegotiate the agreement with them. But it would be wise to make a mental note so that next time you make a plan to have lunch with your friend, you can consider if you want to change how you create agreements with them about having lunch. (See Chapters 16 and 17 for more information about crafting effective requests and agreements.)

Renegotiating an agreement is always an option, and any party to an agreement can choose whether to renegotiate. However, just because another person wants to renegotiate an agreement with you, that doesn't mean you're obligated to renegotiate with them. Before you decide *not* to renegotiate an agreement, focus on the importance of the issue and give it a rating. If you rate the importance of the issue higher than a 7, I recommend you renegotiate the agreement or take the boundary you want to create to the next level (see Chapter 20).

TIP

Choosing not to create an agreement with someone is also an option, no matter where you are in the negotiation or renegotiation process. The key factors to consider are whether you can feel safe without creating the agreement and whether you can forgo making an agreement without feeling resentful, or like you're a victim.

Dealing With People Who Repeatedly Break Agreements

I regret to report that some people are serial agreement breakers, boundary pushers, and boundary violators. The good news is, you've got solutions for dealing with them.

If you're dealing with someone who repeatedly breaks agreements, I don't recommend renegotiating an agreement. Renegotiating creates a new agreement, and the person you would be creating a new agreement with has already demonstrated they're not reliable about keeping agreements.

Creating a new agreement with a serial agreement breaker is a form of *amnesia* (memory loss). This kind of amnesia is common in relationships with people who have active addictions or certain mental health disorders, or are just garden-variety difficult people.

Rather than renegotiate with a serial boundary breaker, you're better off focusing your energy and attention on how you're going to get your needs met in a way that doesn't require you to rely on, or be dependent on, the other person behaving or following through in a certain way.

In Chapter 20 I show you how to take a boundary to the next level.

Increasing your self-protection

The two functions of boundaries are to protect yourself and to protect others. When someone has repeatedly broken an agreement with you, choosing to do nothing or to recommitting to the same agreement with them won't work.

Increasing your self-protection after someone repeatedly breaks agreements can take many forms. Ideally, what you choose to do is a logical and natural next step based on the specific agreement you made. What follows are two examples of repeatedly broken agreements and actions you can take to increase your level of self-protection.

Your partner has an alcohol problem, and when they drink, you don't want to be in their company. They have repeatedly broken an agreement not to consume more than one alcoholic drink during the evening. Options for increasing your self-protection include:

>> Choosing to not be in your partner's presence when they drink

>> Sleeping (or living) separately from your partner for a specific period of time, or until they make a sustained, positive change in their alcohol consumption

You loaned your extra car to a friend and made an agreement that they would return the car to you three months ago. They've asked twice to extend the return date, and you agreed. They still haven't returned the car. Options for increasing your self-protection include:

>> Telling your friend that if they don't return the car by next Friday, you'll take the car back

>> Going to their home or workplace immediately to retrieve the car using your extra set of car keys

Seeing an agreement breaker for who they are

Author, poet, and civil rights activist Maya Angelou said, "When someone tells you who they are, believe them the first time." The reason people repeat this quote so often is that humans have a habit of getting amnesia about who other people are — especially their loved ones and anyone they have a high investment in, or deep attachment to.

Seeing a person who has repeatedly broken agreements for who they are means you can reasonably expect them to continue to do what they've been doing. I sincerely believe that people can and do change, but expecting or hoping that someone who's proven to be unreliable with agreements will change is unrealistic at best, and delusional at worst.

I can't tell you how many stories I've heard about difficult relatives, spouses, or friends behaving badly only to find out that these same relatives, spouses, or friends have been behaving in the same bad ways for years, or even decades. The person telling the story about their bad behavior seems shocked and outraged. But there's no good reason for them to feel that way. When you see people for who they are and you stop expecting them to be someone other than who they've shown you they are (and knowing that change is possible), you can do a better job of taking care of and protecting yourself. You may also be more relaxed and at ease because you understand how to take care of yourself even when other people aren't being who you'd like them to be.

Getting help if the pattern is chronic

If your life seems to be an unending stream of relationships with people who are chronic agreement breakers or boundary violators, I recommend you seek professional help from a mental health treatment provider. Find someone who has a good grasp of the way boundaries work and understands childhood trauma.

The roots of persistent negative patterns like this are often found in harmful childhood experiences or trauma. Identifying and understanding how these patterns came to be helps you understand how you got here, reduces any guilt you feel, and grows your self-compassion. You don't have the power to completely stop people from breaking agreements with you or violating your boundaries, but understanding your history, along with the fundamentals of healthy boundaries, can help you significantly reduce the number of people in your life who break boundaries.

Exploring Your Options

If you decide to renegotiate an agreement that was broken, you have the following options:

>> Recommit to the original agreement.

>> Create a new agreement.

In this section, I describe how each of these options work, and why you may choose one option over another.

Recommitting to the original agreement

One of the simplest ways to renegotiate a broken agreement is to simply recommit to the original agreement. Recommitting to an agreement is often the best choice in the following situations:

>> The person who broke the agreement is usually reliable, dependable, and rarely (if ever) breaks agreements.

>> You don't know or have very limited experience with the person who broke the agreement, and you want to give them a second chance. This option should be chosen only if you're free of negative feelings like anger or resentment.

>> You're not 100 percent sure about the details of the original agreement. For example, you made an agreement to walk at the local park with a friend, but they go on a different day than you agreed to and call you to ask where you are. You're not sure if you were clear about which day you agreed to. Because there was an apparent misunderstanding you recommit to walk at the park another day.

REMEMBER

Because all broken agreements involve what did or didn't happen in the past, when you recommit to an agreement that was broken, the finer details of the renegotiated agreement typically aren't the same as the original agreement. For example, when you recommit to go to a movie tomorrow instead of tonight, you go on a different day but the reason you committed the agreement in the first place — to go to a movie together — is the same.

Here's an example of recommitting to an agreement that was previously broken:

> You made an agreement with a friend that you would go see a movie last Saturday afternoon. The plan was for your friend to pick you up at your apartment at 2:00 p.m. so the two of you could ride together and split the cost of parking. When your friend hadn't arrived by 2:10, you texted to see if they were on their way. They replied that they completely forgot and were at the mall on the other side of town and wouldn't be able to pick you up in time for the movie. They apologized for forgetting and asked if you could go tomorrow instead.

> In this situation, you have several options: going to the movie by yourself, agreeing to go with your friend tomorrow, not going to the movie at all, or going with someone else at a completely different time. You decide to recommit to going to the movie with your friend who will pick you up to go to the movie tomorrow.

REMEMBER

Recommitting to the agreement isn't the best choice for an agreement that has been broken more than once. For repeatedly broken agreements, you must do something different to get different results. This can be accomplished through renegotiating the details of the agreement, creating a higher level of commitment or accountability, or finding another solution that doesn't require an agreement.

Creating a new agreement

Sometimes agreements don't work or are broken because they weren't clear or because the other person wasn't fully committed to the original agreement. In either case, the best option is to create a new agreement.

The following are examples of unclear agreements:

>> **We agree to have a conversation about the dog's barking problem.** This agreement is unclear because there's no specific time frame for having the conversation.

>> **We agree to save some money over the next six months for a vacation.** This agreement is unclear because the amount of money isn't specified.

>> **We agree to hire a plumber to fix the leak in the bathroom.** This agreement is unclear because you don't know who's going to find or contact the plumber.

Options for creating new agreements to replace these unclear agreements include:

>> **We agree to have a conversation about the dog's barking problem by next Saturday.** This agreement is clear because both the topic and the time frame of the conversation are included.

>> **We agree to open a new savings account and deposit at least $1,500 in it over the next six months for a vacation.** This agreement is clear because it includes the amount of money, the time frame to save the money, and the account in which the money will be saved.

>> **We agree to hire a plumber to fix the leak in the bathroom. I'll research plumbers, and we'll choose one based on my research. Once the plumber is chosen, you'll call them to schedule an appointment. We agree that the appointment will be scheduled within the next two weeks.** This agreement is clear because you know who will do the research, who will decide which plumber to hire, who will schedule the appointment, and what the time frame for scheduling it is.

Most people who break agreements because they weren't fully committed or didn't buy in won't tell you this directly. If you suspect that an agreement you made was broken due to lack of buy-in from one (or more) people, review it for these signs that point to a lack of commitment:

>> At the time the agreement was made, the person who eventually broke the agreement gave nonverbal cues or made negative comments that suggested they weren't "all in" or that they weren't happy about the agreement, despite saying that they agreed.

>> The agreement involved a long-standing pattern of behavior that has caused repeated conflict in the relationship. The person who eventually broke the agreement may have complied to avoid conflict or to simply end a tense conversation.

>> The person who broke the agreement has engaged in past deceptions that involve the subject of the agreement. For example, you asked your spouse to stop smoking. They said they would, but they've lied to you more than once about whether they continue to smoke. They agreed because they want to please you and they know smoking is unhealthy, but they haven't (yet) made meaningful efforts to stop.

If you think someone created an agreement with you (which they eventually broke) without having buy-in, avoid creating a new agreement with them until you've explored one or all of the following options:

>> Ask the other person if they felt like they couldn't say *no*. If they say they didn't feel like they could say *no*, ask them what caused them to believe that. The purpose of your questions is to find out more about their thoughts and perceptions about the agreement, not to blame or scold.

>> Ask the other person if they would like to make another agreement instead. For example, if they agreed they would call you by 9:00 every night when they're out of town, but they consistently break the agreement, what can they commit to that would work for them?

>> Ask yourself how important the issue is to you on a scale of 1 to 10, with 10 being the highest importance. If you rate the issue lower than a 5, examine how important creating the agreement is to you. If you can be happy without creating the agreement, can you let it go? If your answer is *no*, you need to explore other options.

Unless you threaten someone with bodily harm, an adult's perception that they're not free to say *no* or to negotiate with you is a reflection of their distorted thinking. It's not a reflection on the request you made or an agreement you proposed.

Requiring a higher level of commitment

When you recommit to the same agreement and that agreement is also broken, you must consider including a higher level of commitment in any future agreements you create regarding the same issue.

My favorite story about requiring a higher level of commitment comes from a couple I once knew who I'll call the McKleens. Mr. McKleen loved being an active parent and participant in his household. He went to the grocery store anytime a loaf of bread or a gallon of milk was needed. He changed diapers, went to pediatrician appointments, and rarely missed the children's sporting events. He was a great partner.

Mr. McKleen's can-do attitude also spilled over into doing the laundry. All went well until one day when he made the dreadful mistake of mixing the dark and light clothes. I'm sure you've attempted this dangerous experiment at one time or another, but on this particular occasion Mr. McKleen's mishap turned one of his wife's new blouses from a beautiful mint green to what appeared to be a splotchy, clumsy tie-dye job. Mrs. McKleen was furious!

Because she knew about creating agreements, she asked him not to wash her clothes anymore, and she did this in the cleanest (so to speak) way possible. She didn't resent that she would need to wash her own clothes. After all, her clothes — her responsibility. Her primary motivation was to avoid the terrible feeling of seeing her wardrobe reduced one piece at a time on each laundry day.

Mr. McKleen agreed he wouldn't wash his wife's clothes anymore. But for whatever reason — forgetfulness or thinking it was "no big deal" — he did it again. Mrs. McKleen repeated her request, and he again agreed not to wash her clothes.

For unknown reasons, this pattern repeated at least three or four more times. Thankfully, most of the time no clothing was ruined in the process, but it was still very upsetting to Mrs. McKleen. She sincerely didn't want her husband to touch her clothes!

At some point during the painful, multiyear laundry drama, Mrs. McKleen realized that she was going to have to turn up the heat. Maybe around the third time the agreement was broken, she told Mr. McKleen that she needed more than an apology. She needed responsibility, and she needed accountability. She asked him what he thought should happen the next time he "forgot" and "accidentally" washed her clothes.

To his credit, Mr. McKleen came up with a brilliant plan. He said that the next time he washed her clothes he would make a cash donation to a charitable organization he despised — an organization he genuinely didn't want to support. He also added to this new and much improved agreement that every time he broke the agreement, the amount of the donation would increase by $50. Brilliant!

TIP

High levels of commitment and accountability that create discomfort and even emotional pain can dramatically increase the effectiveness of an agreement. Monetary fines or other undesirable consequences serve as motivators for maintaining commitment to an agreement.

The case of Mr. and Mrs. McKleen's laundry woes may be an extreme one involving either a very forgetful or very hardheaded husband, but I'm happy to report that after having to write two checks to the despised charitable organization, Mr. McKleen officially swore off washing his wife's clothes, and the laundry nightmare came to an end.

It takes what it takes. And sometimes it takes an increasingly higher level of commitment to get the job done. You can't make someone be more committed, but you can build commitment and accountability into an agreement to increase the likelihood that the agreement will be honored.

THINK
ABOUT IT

Because many agreements are created by making requests, you may need to recraft a request to fix an agreement that didn't work or was broken. The most common reasons for recrafting a request are that the request wasn't specific enough, or accountability wasn't built into the agreement.

Adding more specificity

In Chapter 17, I talk about best practices for creating agreements, which includes being specific. Being specific means including time frames, dates, amounts of money, frequencies, or any other details that make an agreement clear and unambiguous.

One of the challenges around knowing whether an agreement is specific enough is that an agreement can appear to be specific, but when it's broken, the weakness of the details is revealed.

For example, if you make an agreement with your ex that the two of you will talk to each other about anything related to the safety of your children, you may feel confident that this is a clear agreement. However, you discover after the agreement is broken (from your perspective) that the two of you have different definitions of what safety means. Your ex took your kids on a vacation where they went scuba diving. For you, scuba diving is a risky activity, but your ex didn't see any connection between scuba diving and safety. If you want to create an agreement with your ex to discuss issues of safety as they relate to your children, you need to add specific language or even a list of situations or activities that each of you agrees is related to safety.

The following are some examples of vague or unclear requests:

>> **Would you be willing to spend more time with me?** This request is vague because it doesn't include a specific amount of time. If you spent 5 minutes together last week, this agreement would be considered fulfilled if the other person spent 5½ minutes with you this week. That's probably not what you had in mind when you made the request.

>> **I need more time to finish this project. Is that okay with you?** This request is vague because it doesn't include a deadline for finishing the project. If the person who assigned the project follows up by asking when it will be finished, the person working on the project can simply reply, "You told me it was okay for me to take more time."

>> **Would you stop spending so much money on power tools?** This request is vague because it doesn't specify an amount of money. If your spouse spent $1,000 on power tools last month and spends $999 on power tools this month, they are in compliance with this agreement, but it may not have been what you were aiming for.

>> **Can we talk about where we're going to spend the holidays this year?** This request is vague because it lacks a time frame for when the talk will occur.

By simply adding specificity, you can rephrase these vague and unclear requests as follows:

>> **Would you be willing to spend 15 minutes each evening with me?** This request is clear because it includes the frequency (each evening) and the amount of time spent together.

>> **I need another week to finish this project. I will get it to you by next Thursday. Would that work for you?** This request is clear and unambiguous because it creates a deadline for finishing the project.

>> **Would you be willing to limit your spending on power tools to no more than $250 a month?** This request is clear because it includes the frequency (monthly) and a specific dollar amount.

>> **I'd like to have a conversation with you by next Sunday about where we're going to spend the holidays this year. Are you agreeable to doing that?** This request is clear and unambiguous because it includes the time frame for the conversation and exactly what the conversation is about.

TIP

When you're adding more specificity to agreements, one option is to ask the other person what they feel comfortable agreeing to. For example, in the power tools agreement, the person making the request can ask the power tool user, "What do you think is a reasonable amount to spend on power tools each month?" You may worry they'll say, "Oh, I don't know. Maybe $3,000?" But remember, you're having a conversation. You're not obligated to agree to $3,000 just because you asked the question. On the other hand, they may say an amount that's less than what you want to propose. Hooray!

Making a plan for accountability

If you're in a situation like Mr. and Mrs. McKleen's laundry mess where repeated agreements don't yield the results you want, you need to add accountability into your agreements if you want to experience a better outcome. *Merriam-Webster* defines *accountability* as "an obligation or willingness to accept responsibility or to account for one's actions."

REMEMBER

Both parties to an agreement share accountability for the success (or failure) of the agreement.

Here are four ways to build accountability into an agreement:

>> Your spouse has repeatedly skipped doing yard work despite many prior agreements. You request that if the lawn doesn't get mowed and edged two weeks in a row, your spouse will hire someone to mow, edge, and maintain the yard once a week indefinitely.

» Your partner likes to gamble and has repeatedly spent more on gambling than the two of you agreed on (but not enough to jeopardize your financial well-being). You request that if they spend more than the amount you agreed on in the future, they will deposit the amount of money they overspent on gambling into your personal checking account. You can spend the money however you want.

» Your spouse has a habit of agreeing to pick up groceries at the grocery store but not making it home with everything on the list — not because an item wasn't available but because they overlooked it. When they get home and the missing item is brought to their attention, they shrug their shoulders as if to say, "Oh well, better luck next time." You request that in the future if they don't come home with everything on the list (unless it's not available), they will return to the grocery store the same day and get the missed item.

» Your friend agreed to stop smoking, but they have repeatedly broken the agreement. You request that if they smoke again and don't tell you, they will enroll in (and complete) a program to help them stop smoking within two weeks of the time you discover (or they tell you) that they smoked.

Accountability is a highly desirable relationship trait and is especially powerful in situations or relationships where trust has been damaged or shattered. Building accountability into an agreement increases the probability that the agreement will be honored and can even heal past broken agreements.

Chapter **20**

Taking a Boundary to the Next Level: Advanced Skills for Difficult Situations

Have you ever heard the definition that explains insanity as doing the same thing again and again and expecting different results? This definition perfectly describes what happens to you if you don't know what to do when a boundary doesn't work as expected.

You need to know how to take a boundary to the next level, rather than repeating what you already know doesn't work. For example, if you've made an agreement with your boss three times about not texting you on weekends but they continue to do it, making the same agreement with them for the fourth time would be . . . well, insane.

When someone has broken an agreement with you multiple times or they've repeatedly violated a boundary you set, you've got to know what to do next. Otherwise, you may think boundaries don't work. When a boundary isn't successful, it's not that the boundary didn't work or you did something wrong. It just means you have a bit more work to do. You may be frustrated or feel resentful that you need to do more work, especially when you weren't the person who didn't honor the boundary. But I can assure you that taking a boundary to the next level builds your boundaries skills and makes you more confident the next time you need to set a boundary.

Taking a boundary to the next level isn't just a way to increase your self-protection; it's also a form of self-care. When you're taking good care of yourself, you don't allow other people to repeatedly trample your limits or ignore agreements they've made with you.

In this chapter, I show you specific ways to manage and stop repeated boundary violations. You see why in any situation where boundaries are "forgotten," ignored, or essentially trampled, you must increase self-protection or account-ability to maintain the boundary or agreement. I also discuss how to tell another person that you're taking a boundary to the next level and explain why sometimes avoiding or completely eliminating contact with someone is best for everyone — but especially for you!

Dealing With Repeated Boundary Violations

Setting boundaries isn't a one-and-done endeavor. You've encountered many boundaries challenges up to this point in your life, and you may face many more in the future. Whether you take on a new role like becoming a parent, in-law, or supervisor, or you find yourself in a difficult situation you've never experienced before, you can use the principles in this book to create strong boundaries for the rest of your life.

In addition to the lifelong garden-variety boundaries you need to create, from time to time you'll likely need to set boundaries with chronic boundary violators. I hope these experiences are few and far between. However, if you're going through a particularly challenging season in your life, facing issues like a high-conflict divorce or a close family member who's in active addiction, you may have more opportunities than the average person to develop your skills for dealing with repeated boundary violations.

If you don't know how to take a boundary to the next level after someone repeatedly breaks an agreement or barrels through a boundary you set, you can expect to feel frustrated, resentful, and unprotected. Doing the work of stopping boundary violations and broken agreements takes effort and courage, but the rewards, in the form of calm, peace, and freedom, are well worth it.

Increasing your self-protection incrementally

Boundaries serve two essential purposes: They protect you, and they protect others (see Chapter 1). When you create a boundary with someone, either through letting them know your limits or by creating an agreement, you're protecting yourself.

For example, if you tell someone that you're available to talk on the phone until 10:00 p.m., you've let them know your limit around how late you're willing to talk on the phone. The same limit can be created by an agreement you make with another person that the two of you will wrap up phone conversations before 10:00 p.m. In both instances, you may be protecting yourself by making sure you get to bed by a certain time so that you get enough sleep. Or the self-protection may be that you're setting the 10:00 p.m. limit (rather than making an agreement) with someone you don't want to talk to later than 10:00 p.m. because you have good reason to believe they'll be drinking after that time, and you don't want to talk to them when they've been using mind-altering substances.

WARNING

Avoid talking to anyone who's been drinking or using other mind-altering substances. You can say, "Let's talk another time," or "I need to go. I'll talk to you later." Don't say, "You've been drinking (or taking drugs). I can't talk to you when you're under the influence." Remember that an altered person can't be relied on to have a rational conversation. If you want to tell them you won't talk to them if you think they're under the influence of alcohol or drugs, tell them when they're sober.

After you create a limit or boundary, if you experience repeated broken agreements or boundary violations, the most effective first response is to incrementally (gradually) increase your self-protection. What does this mean?

Imagine your spouse has a very bad habit of draining your joint checking account down to $199 and taking the cash to the nearest casino. This has been going on for so many years, you've lost count. You've tried almost everything to make them stop, and they've promised over and over not to do it again. But nothing has changed.

When you hear that you may be able to do something about this infuriating situation by using boundaries, you decide to create an agreement with your spouse that (hopefully) protects you from their financially reckless behavior.

So, you tell your spouse that you want to create an agreement that if they withdraw more than $200 from the ATM, they'll talk to you first to confirm that you agree they can make the withdrawal. They agree to your request, and because you received a *yes*, you create a boundary in the form of an agreement.

Unfortunately, the next Friday night your spouse goes to the bank and withdraws $340 without letting you know. You find out because you get an alert on your phone — something you set up because of their past behavior. When you call to ask if they just withdrew $340 from your bank account, they respond defensively, "Why are you always breathing down my neck about money?"

TIP

When you have reason to believe that someone has violated a boundary or done something that's upsetting for you, always begin your conversation with a question. Ask them to confirm what you believe to be the facts before you express your thoughts and emotions. "Did you withdraw $340 from the ATM just now?" is a better conversation starter than "What's wrong with you? I thought we agreed you would talk to me before you took more than $200 out of our account!" Stay curious. Allow room for the reality that what you think is true may not actually be true, or that there's more to the story.

As a result of this new information about your spouse's bank withdrawal and the broken agreement, you decide that you need to take your self-protection to the next level. In this case, self-protection is safeguarding your current and future financial well-being, which is jeopardized by your spouse's handling of money.

Your next level of self-protection may look like one (or more) of the following options:

» You tell your spouse that the next time they withdraw money without discussing it with you, you'll need to make some changes to how you're managing and handling money with them. (You don't need to know exactly what that looks like, but you do need to be confident that you'll follow through.)

» You start depositing your paycheck into a separate account that your spouse doesn't have access to and stop depositing money into any joint accounts.

» You separate all your financial accounts from your spouse's accounts.

» You request a postnuptial or marital property agreement that separates your property from your spouse's property, including all bank accounts.

» You initiate a temporary separation from your spouse to give yourself space to think about how you want to proceed in the relationship.

» You decide to file for divorce and end the relationship.

Notice that the list of options starts with a low-level response and ends with the highest-level response — ending the relationship. In most situations involving other people, ending a relationship is the highest-level response you can take unless they're engaged in illegal behavior and you report them to law enforcement. Increasing your self-protection incrementally can be accomplished in many ways, and you get to decide which response fits best for you.

REMEMBER

Your response to any broken agreement or boundary violation should be equivalent to the broken agreement or boundary violation. Low-level violations warrant low-level responses. High-level violations require high-level responses.

For example, in the situation of money being withdrawn from the ATM, accepting a simple "it will never happen again" response from your spouse — especially when they've proven more than once that they're not trustworthy around money — wouldn't be a good match for the situation. Your response to broken agreements and boundary violations should match your level of distress or the consequences the issue creates for you.

Signaling how you plan to take action

When you need to do something about repeated broken agreements or boundary violations, I recommend you let the other person know what you plan to do.

For example, you can let someone close to you know what you plan to do if they violate a boundary (or break an agreement) in the future. You should also let them know when you plan to take action, if a date or time frame is applicable in the situation.

Say your spouse has repeatedly promised to clean up a big pile of power tools sitting on top of the outdoor grill on your patio before the big July 4 cookout you're hosting at your house. It's now the middle of May, and the pile of power tools is still sitting there. You decide to try something different, and you ask your spouse when they think they can get those power tools off the patio. They give you a look (which I suggest you ignore) and say, "I'll get it done in the next two weeks. Now are you happy?"

You should ignore their tone and start by saying, "Yes, that would make me really happy!" Then add, "I need the patio to be clean and organized for the July 4 party. So, I just want to let you know that if the power tools are still sitting on the patio two weeks from now, I'll be getting some help to make sure the patio is clean and ready for the cookout."

No one can predict how your spouse will respond to your new approach, but you must stick to your talking points, which are exactly what you just said. (See Chapter 6 for more info on how to manage resistance and pushback.) Try your best not to get sidetracked or derailed into other topics. Your topic is getting the power tools off the patio. Period.

The next thing you should do is go directly to your calendar and mark it for two weeks and one day from the date of your conversation about getting the tools cleared out. That's the day you'll get help to clear those power tools off the patio if your spouse doesn't follow through.

Here are a few ways to tell another person how you plan to take a boundary to the next level:

>> Your sister repeatedly comes to your house without first checking with you to make sure it's okay, despite your multiple requests and a past agreement from her to honor the boundary. You tell her, "I need you to respect my boundary that you won't come to my home without my agreement that it's okay. If you come to my house in the future without discussing it with me, I may not (or won't) answer the door."

>> Your client purchased a three-month package for a certain number of classes with you that's valid for only three months. They have repeatedly canceled or rescheduled, and it's now two months past the three-month time frame. The client has one class remaining in their package. You send an email letting them know they have two weeks to use the remaining class, and after two weeks their remaining class will expire.

>> Your boyfriend has repeatedly broken an agreement that he won't use your bicycle. You tell him, "I'm repeating my boundary that nobody except me can use my bicycle. If you use my bike in the future, I will put a lock on it; and I will be the only person who knows the lock code."

Notice that each statement includes a description of the original boundary or agreement, and each is specific about how you plan to take action if the boundary is broken in the future.

When you let another person know how you plan to take action, your intention is self-protection and self-care. If your intention for creating a boundary is to punish or retaliate rather than create clarity or protect yourself, you're seeking revenge, not doing boundary work.

Some do's and don'ts for telling another person how you plan to take action include:

>> *Don't* tell another person how you plan to take a boundary to the next level unless you're sure, beyond a doubt, that you'll follow through with your plan. If you say what you'll do and you don't follow through, you've lost credibility with yourself and the other person, and you've also lost trust in yourself.

>> *Don't* tell another person how you plan to take a boundary to the next level when you're highly emotional, triggered, or flooded with negative feelings. Wait until you're in a calm, clear-headed state, and then have the conversation.

>> *Do* be specific and descriptive about your plan. For example, use clear and unambiguous descriptions, time frames, dates, and deadlines.

>> *Do* describe what you'll do rather than what the other person will do. For example, say, "I will put a lock on my bike," rather than, "You won't ride my bike." The second statement implies that you have the power to stop someone from riding your bike by telling them what they won't do. It's also a demand, and demands are harmful to adult relationships. (See Chapter 2 for more details about demands.)

>> *Do* take responsibility for any part you played in the broken agreement. For example, if you allow a person to repeatedly overstep a limit or break an agreement without saying or doing anything, you can say something like "I need to clean this up because I haven't held up my end of the agreement" or "I've allowed this to go on too long by not saying anything, and that's on me." Then you can describe how you're taking the agreement to the next level.

WARNING

If you're planning to take a boundary to the next level with someone who is threatening or dangerous, or has a history of harassing you, don't signal to them what you plan to do. In cases like this, it's best to proceed with your plan — putting in place any measures you need to take for your safety. If you have any doubts about what the best plan of action is, talk to a trusted friend, mentor, life coach, or therapist who has a good working knowledge of boundaries.

Avoiding engagement or private conversations with difficult people

In some situations involving very difficult people or chronic boundary pushers who play a significant role in your life — for example, a family member, client, professor, or supervisor — you can't easily limit contact or end the relationship. Depending on the situation, your options include trying to restrict or avoid contact as much as you can or interacting with them only when another person is present to serve as a kind of witness.

Over the years, I've heard my fair share of the stereotypical mother-in-law stories. In all fairness, many kind, sweet, and welcoming mothers-in-law exist, but they aren't the mothers-in-law people talk about when they're in a psychotherapist's or life coach's office.

Some exceptionally difficult relationships require you to limit or carefully manage your contact, including with in-laws. One woman decided that she wasn't willing to be alone in a room or have private telephone conversations with her mother-in-law any longer. As you can imagine, her boundaries didn't win her any popularity contests among family members.

REMEMBER

Winning popularity contests isn't the goal or purpose of boundaries. In fact, when you improve and level up your boundaries, you'll notice that you become unpopular with some people. Those people tend not to like boundaries. This is just one of the many perks of good boundaries!

Here are several ways to limit or avoid engaging with chronic boundary pushers:

>> Limit the amount of time you spend with them.

>> See them only in the company of other people — never alone, if possible.

>> Speak to them only by telephone. Start your conversation by saying, "I have 10 minutes (or however much time you're willing to give them). I have another commitment at [the exact time at the 11th minute]."

>> Communicate with them in writing only. If needed, copy (cc) or blind copy (bcc) anyone who needs to be kept updated about your communications.

>> Follow up in writing after every conversation that includes important information or an agreement.

Getting boundaries and agreements in writing

When it comes to making agreements and setting boundaries, you can't ever go wrong by putting them in writing. And when you're dealing with difficult people or chronic boundary pushers, following up verbal communications in writing is especially clarifying and effective.

Following up a verbal agreement with a written confirmation may feel too formal or too over-the-top to you. But imagine a scenario in the future where you make a verbal agreement with someone who has a reputation for not honoring agreements. You decide to skip the written follow-up confirming the agreement because you're worried about how they may respond.

The problem is, when you try to hold a repeat boundary violator accountable, they're likely to respond with something like:

>> I don't remember you saying that.

>> I didn't agree to that.

>> That's not what happened.

>> Oh, I didn't think you were serious.

>> That's ridiculous!

That's why it's best to send a follow-up email whenever you create an agreement or boundary — not just with difficult people, but with everyone.

TIP

Email is the preferred way to communicate in writing with difficult people, or with anyone with whom you're negotiating a legal matter, especially a divorce. If you ever need to produce communications between you and another person for a legal matter, emails are generally considered more credible and admissible than text messages.

I strongly recommend you follow up in writing in any of the following situations:

>> After you've created a spoken agreement or verbally expressed a boundary

>> After any verbal communications with someone who consistently misunderstands, forgets, or misinterprets communications

>> After any verbal communications with someone you believe may not have your best interest at heart or is trying to discredit you

>> After any communications with someone who is a chronic boundary pusher

>> Anytime you want to confirm or put in writing something you said, something the other person said, an agreement you made, or a boundary you communicated

Limiting contact or going no-contact

Limiting contact or going no-contact with someone is always an option, especially when you're dealing with repeat boundary violators. The only time it's not appropriate to limit contact or go no-contact with someone is when you have a specific agreement regarding your availability to them, or you're responsible for caring for them — for example, a patient, child, or older adult. However, even in these cases, you can arrange for their care if you need to limit or completely stop contact for a temporary period.

If the person you need to limit contact or go no-contact with is a family member, you'll probably face some pushback. You may even encounter strong disapproval. (See Chapter 6 for more information about how to manage boundary resistance or pushback.)

In many cultures and families (regardless of culture), not being available or not having contact with family members is simply unheard of. However, in some situations limiting contact or going no-contact — even with a family member — is not only rational and reasonable, but the most responsible action to take.

Here are several reasons you may decide to limit contact or go no-contact with another person when you're taking a boundary to the next level:

>> They're threatening, harassing, or verbally abusive to you, your family members, or your friends.

>> You struggle to hold a boundary during face-to-face or telephone conversations with them, so you limit all contact to email or text communications.

>> They've stolen money or personal belongings from you.

>> You want to send a strong message that you're fundamentally changing the nature of your relationship with them and the level of access they have to you.

>> They've recently betrayed or significantly deceived you, and you need space to gain clarity, create emotional safety, and begin to heal.

>> You've been in an emotionally abusive relationship for some time, and you need to go no-contact with the abusive person so you can restore your confidence in your reality and begin healing without being in their presence or under their influence.

>> The person, including a parent or family member, is abusive (emotionally, physically, or sexually) or violent.

TIP

Going no-contact with someone isn't just for repeated boundary violations or dangerous situations. You can limit contact or go no-contact anytime you feel a need to take a temporary pause, or you need space to sort out your thoughts and emotions. The person you go no-contact (or limited contact) with may not like your decision to create space. In fact, they may express their deep displeasure with your choice. But you have a right to limit contact or go no-contact with anyone. And in the end, it may be the most respectful, compassionate, and helpful choice you can make for yourself and the relationship.

Resting assured that ignoring communications may be self-care

If you're a naturally kind person or a people pleaser, it may feel unbearable to think about not acknowledging a text, email, or phone call from someone — even a boundary pusher. The problem with continuing to respond to someone who's proven that they can't respect your boundaries is:

>> You're rewarding them for contacting you each time you respond to them.

>> Because you're rewarding them by responding, you continue to receive communications from them.

If that's okay with you, you can certainly keep responding! But I'm thinking you'd like to experience something different, and that's why I want you to know that not responding to people who are being difficult, annoying, harassing, or threatening is your right. In fact, it may even be your duty to yourself if you've already told them not to contact you, or you've otherwise clearly communicated that you'll no longer be in contact with them.

When you ignore communications, you're not just letting the other person know what they can expect from you (no response); you're also giving yourself the gift of reducing drama, along with the calm you create when drama is reduced or eliminated. You're giving yourself freedom from the obligation to engage with someone you don't want to engage with. And that's a high-level form of self-care.

Protecting yourself online

One of the easiest and quickest ways to be a nuisance or to harass another person is to stalk or threaten them online. If you've recently been a victim of someone who harassed, stalked, or threatened you, take extra precautions to protect yourself online, including securing any accounts you access online.

Here are some best practices for protecting yourself online if you're being harassed, threatened, or stalked:

>> Consider temporarily pausing, suspending, or deleting social media accounts until the threatening behavior stops. If you're not ready to take a pause or delete your social media accounts, limit or temporarily stop posting. Don't share information that discloses your location or plans.

- » Change your passwords for email, bank, and social media accounts immediately. Change your passwords at least once a month until the threatening behavior has ended.

- » Scan your devices to detect any tracking software or spyware that may have been installed on them.

- » Install software that blocks others from spying on or tracking you on all your devices.

- » Block the threatening person on your phone, social media sites, or any other online platforms if possible.

- » If you have children who are on social media sites, block the threatening person from their accounts. People who threaten, harass, or stalk have no boundaries, and they may attempt to contact your children.

- » Change your security PINs, especially with banks and other financial institutions.

- » Place either a credit freeze or a lock on your accounts with credit bureaus to protect yourself from identify theft. You can also purchase an identity theft protection plan for added security.

- » Don't engage online with people you don't know. Anyone can set up a profile or email account, for example, using whatever name they choose.

Reporting unethical or illegal behavior

It's unfortunate, but sometimes the very people who are supposed to help, support, or protect others fail to do so. And sometimes they violate boundaries. You may have heard stories about professionals like doctors, therapists, clergy members, or law enforcement officers acting unethically, abusively, or even illegally. Or you may have been victimized by someone whose job or duty was to help or protect you.

There may be times when someone you know — including a family member — breaks the law or engages in unethical behavior that you feel you should report to law enforcement or a licensing board.

Some unethical or illegal situations that should be reported to a licensing board, law enforcement, or both include:

- » A medical or mental health practitioner engaging in a sexual relationship with a patient or client

- » A law enforcement officer physically or sexually abusing someone in their custody

>> An adult, including a parent, relative, sports coach, tutor, or teacher, engaging in sexual contact with a minor

>> A clergy member engaging in sexual contact with any member of the church, including adults or minors

>> A mental health treatment provider pressuring clients to attend multiple sessions per week for no apparent reason or attempting to exert a significant amount of influence or control in a client's life

REMEMBER

When referring to an adult sexually abusing a minor, never use the word *relationship* to describe the situation. If a high school coach sexually abused a teenager they coached, they did not have a relationship. When describing the sexual contact they had, it's more accurate to say the coach abused, molested, assaulted, or raped the minor. Consent cannot occur between an adult and a minor. Adults are responsible for refraining from sexually abusing minors and for protecting minors from sexual abuse. See Chapter 9 for more information about sexual boundary violations.

There are many reasons someone may choose not to report problematic or abusive behavior, including how often the behavior occurred, the relative seriousness of the incident or situation, or fear of retaliation. However, when you're weighing whether you want to report unethical or illegal behavior, keep in mind that there's a higher-than-average chance the person you're considering reporting has engaged in the behavior before. In other words, you're not the first person to know about the behavior (or to be a victim). And you likely won't be the last, especially if the behavior goes unreported.

It's true that some people can hold strong boundaries with a doctor or mental health professional who acts unethically, for example. But many people struggle to hold boundaries in these situations because they're caught off guard or feel obligated to comply with instructions or directions given by a person in authority.

Some people — minors or people with intellectual disabilities, for example — may not realize that a certain behavior is inappropriate or unethical. Or they may be unable to say *no* or tell anyone what happened. When you're deciding whether to report unethical or illegal behavior, remember that you're protecting others when you decide to report the behavior. In fact, you may feel it's your duty because of the power you have to potentially protect future victims.

REMEMBER

Ultimately, you get to decide whether you report someone for unethical or illegal behavior. No one can decide what's right for you.

If you're struggling with whether to report someone, talk to a person you trust who can listen and brainstorm your options with you. A mental health professional is an ideal person for this role. Most psychotherapists have experience with helping clients make these kinds of decisions, and most have had to make a few of their own.

If you decide to report someone for unethical or illegal behavior, know that you're helping potential future victims. You're also helping the person you reported by giving them an opportunity to face their mistakes and change their behavior.

Knowing When You Need Law Enforcement or Legal Help

Unfortunately, some boundary violations require the intervention of law enforcement or warrant consultation with an attorney.

Here's a partial list of situations that are best handled through a report to law enforcement:

>> Someone threatens to harm you or your children, or to destroy or take your personal property.

>> Someone commits physical violence against you, your children, your pets, or anyone in the immediate vicinity. If the violence is directed at you (or your children) and you're able to leave safely, that's the best first course of action.

>> You've gone no-contact with someone (see the earlier section "Limiting contact or going no-contact"), and they repeatedly come to your home, your workplace, or a family member's home.

>> A person you have a restraining order against violates the order.

>> You're being stalked or harassed, either in person or online.

>> Your identity is stolen (including by a family member or friend).

>> You need to retrieve or remove your belongings from a home you shared with a former partner who has threatened or abused you.

>> A former partner who has threatened or abused you needs to retrieve or remove their belongings from your home.

>> You're being exploited by someone who is demanding or taking money from you.

In each of these situations, keep detailed records of communications and all evidence of contact, including emails, voicemails, text messages, and security camera recordings.

TIP

Going to a police station or a courthouse can be frightening and intimidating. If you need to go to a police station (or any place that feels uncomfortable to you) to file a report, ask a friend or family member to go with you for extra support. Having another set of eyes and ears with you also helps you remember what was said or what they asked or recommended that you do.

You may need to consult an attorney if you're experiencing any of the following:

>> Your spouse or someone else repeatedly restricts your access to bank accounts or other financial accounts holding money that belongs to you (or is community property). Your attempts to get access to the accounts have been unsuccessful.

>> Someone attempts to get you to sign a contract or other legal document that you don't understand, and you're discouraged or blocked from talking to an attorney.

>> Your neighbor repeatedly engages in activities or behavior that's a nuisance or threatening. Attempts to resolve the situation have been unsuccessful.

>> You're experiencing repeated harassment (including sexual harassment) in the workplace. You've filed several complaints to report the harassment and no action has been taken.

>> You believe you were fired from your job because you refused to have a sexual relationship with a supervisor, employer, or owner of the business.

>> A family member or your spouse claims that certain financial accounts or assets (such as real estate) aren't your property, but you have strong reasons to believe that's not the case.

Getting Professional Help When You Struggle to Protect Yourself

If you realize you have a pattern of being taken advantage of, being exploited, or being in personal or professional relationships where your boundaries are repeatedly violated, I recommend you get professional help. Working with a mental health professional or experienced life coach helps you identify how you continue to fall into this pattern throughout your life and what to do about it.

Here are my do's and don'ts for finding a counselor, therapist, or life coach to work with if you struggle to protect yourself:

>> *Do* ask people in your support network for recommendations and referrals. Asking people you know and trust is usually the best and quickest way to find a high-quality referral.

>> *Do* talk to at least three potential candidates before committing to work with someone.

>> *Do* ask the prospective life coach or therapist questions about how they help people who want to improve their boundaries, and anything else you're curious about. The client-therapist relationship is an intimate, often long-term one, and you have a right to ask a prospective therapist any questions you have.

>> *Don't* base your decision about whom to work with on how much the provider charges. Cheapest isn't always the best. If you can afford to work with the person you feel most comfortable with, that person is the best choice. Life coaches and therapists who charge very low fees are more likely to be inexperienced, which means you may not get the best help, or it may take twice as long to get the results you want.

>> *Do* choose someone who is knowledgeable about trauma as well as personal and relationship boundaries. You can ask them about both when you interview them.

>> *Do* attend at least three sessions with your new therapist or life coach before deciding that they're not a good fit for you. Give yourself permission to transition to another provider if you don't feel like you can make progress with them.

REMEMBER

Whatever you do, don't blame yourself for struggling to protect yourself. It's highly likely that you came by these challenges honestly — meaning you weren't taught what self-protection looks like when you were growing up. (See Chapter 5 for more information about the connection between your boundaries as an adult, and what you learned about boundaries growing up.)

Find someone you trust to work with and focus on the vision you have for yourself. Think about what you want to create — for example, a more peaceful life where you feel protected and safe. You have the power to create this for yourself; you just may need a little help to get there.

6

The Part of Tens

IN THIS PART . . .

Explore outside-the-box options for giving yourself an extra layer of protection.

Recognize ten common myths about how boundaries work.

Know the signs that you may need professional help to take your boundaries to the next level.

Chapter **21**

Ten Out-of-the-Box Options for Extra Protection

When people hear the word *boundaries*, a look of irritation or dread often crosses their face. Most people find boundary work difficult and challenging. That's because sometimes it is! However, like most things in life, it's possible to interject playfulness, humor, and even fun into the serious work of setting boundaries.

In this chapter, I introduce you to some unconventional, out-of-the-box ideas for creating boundaries. Some may even sound a bit New Agey or woo-woo to you. Think of these options for extra protection like a buffet: You get to decide which ones you want to experiment with, and which ones you prefer to leave on the buffet table.

TIP

Experiment with these options, even if your first thought is that they're weird or odd. You never know what may happen from running these experiments, and they're all free!

Taking the Secret Service to the Party

This out-of-the-box option for extra protection came from a brainstorming session I had many years ago with a client who worked for a government agency that, for privacy's sake, shall remain nameless. Taking the Secret Service to a party was the perfect solution for this client, and it can work for you too.

For example, say that you're going to the annual office holiday party and the guy who tried to get you fired last year and take your job will be there. You're dreading being in the same room with him or accidentally running into him by the punch bowl, and you're wondering how you're going to get through the evening. You need reinforcements.

Before you leave your house to go to the party, you can imagine that you've got a complete Secret Service detail assigned just to you, like the President of the United States. These agents have poker faces, black suits, earpieces, and dark glasses. They hold both hands in front of them at all times — so they're ready to reach inside their jacket to grab their weapon in case of emergency.

Imagine these agents going with you to the party (or anywhere else you'd like to have extra protection). Every time you feel a bit wobbly you see them in your mind's eye standing around you, and you know that everything is going to be alright.

TIP

You can even send them to the venue to make sure that all is well before you get there. You'll feel safe knowing that you're in good hands.

Putting Yourself Under Glass

Say you're on your way to the annual summer visit to see your Aunt Grizelda. She's the one with icy laser-beam eyes, who gives you the once-over (or sometimes the twice-over) every time you arrive at her house. She peppers you with a burst of questions about how much money you made last year or where your partner went to school (to make sure they're "good enough" for you). Her questions aren't motivated by curiosity or interest, but rather by her need to categorize and size up everyone and everything.

Putting yourself under glass is a great option for visiting your Aunt Grizelda. Before you go into her library to take your place on the spotless white sofa covered in plastic to preserve its perfection, you imagine a very large glass mason jar or bell placed over yourself, with the rim resting on the floor.

Sitting under the clear glass, you can see Aunt G and she can see you. You imagine all her words and all her nosy questions bouncing off or sliding down the outside of the glass onto the floor. You look down around the edge of the glass and decide which words and which questions you'd like to consider or answer.

Enclosed inside your glass sanctuary, you can be with Aunt G in a way that feels calm, serene, and protected.

Dressing Up in Riot Gear

TIP

If you're in a situation where you must have contact with someone who's reliably difficult or a serial boundary violator, this strategy is for you. I've used dressing up in riot gear myself, during a brief period when I was working for someone who was, in my humble opinion, a complete nightmare.

To get the full effect of what this looks like, imagine a time — probably when you were watching the news — when you saw a swarm of law enforcement at the ready, holding a line of protection. They had special riot shields and helmets that included a tinted visor to keep out the sun and protect them from tear gas and projectiles. You may need this level of protection, and it can all be yours — in your mind's eye!

Imagining yourself dressed up in riot gear is an ideal option for interactions or situations with people who've proven themselves to be extremely difficult. As helpful as this out-of-the-box option for extra protection is, my advice is to create maximum distance between you and these types of folks as soon as possible.

REMEMBER

There may be times when you need to stay at a job or interact with someone who warrants this extra protection on a regular basis. But the sooner these terminal troublemakers are in your rearview mirror, the better.

Imagining Yourself in a Zen Bubble

This one is short and sweet.

Imagining yourself in a zen bubble is perfect for when you feel your agitation rising as you listen to a coworker complaining about the boss for the 1,629th time. Or when your brother is giving you the detailed play-by-play of last night's football game in his best sports commentator voice when he knows you can't stand football. You're tempted to chuck everything you know about the listening and speaking boundaries (see Chapters 10 and 11), and you need extra support to stay the course.

To create a peaceful inner calm, imagine a bubble all around you extending at least 3 feet from your body. If you want to get fancy, you can imagine bathing the inside of the bubble in your favorite zen-inducing color, or adding sparkles or an image of your favorite chilled-out being.

Breathe in. Breathe out. Ahhhhh.

Erecting a Titanium Partition

I've used this tool more times than I can easily recall, because it works. Erecting a titanium partition is perfect for times when you either feel the need for a bit of extra protection or suddenly begin to feel anxious or sad for no apparent reason.

For this one, you imagine a titanium (or another strong material of your choosing) partition in front of or around you. Ideally, this imaginary barrier is placed between you and the person you feel you need protection from. Or it can completely surround you if you're not sure where the "disturbance" is coming from. Once the partition is erected, you wait and see what happens. The results are often immediate. Within a few minutes the uncomfortable feeling can completely disappear.

The skeptics among us say this works because uncomfortable emotions and sensations are *impermanent* — meaning they were going to disappear anyway. And while I wholeheartedly agree that uncomfortable emotions always disappear eventually, if you want to experience the shift from discomfort to comfort sooner rather than later, why not give it a try?

Sending "Back Off!" Vibes

You can have lots of fun with this one when someone is crowding you a bit too much — but not so much that you absolutely must say something directly to them. You can also use "Back off!" vibes when you know the situation is temporary — like when you're traveling on the Tube in London and you'll be getting off at the next stop.

For this tactic, you look at the person hemming you in (or not, depending on your mood) and imagine telling them in a very firm voice, "Back off!" This silent command may or may not work, but it can feel good. Plus, it's a fun experiment to run. You never know.

REMEMBER

If someone (including someone you know) is too close to you and you can't easily create the needed space yourself, you can say, "I need more space. Would you back up a bit?" Your request for more space may not be well received due to the average person's lack of understanding of good boundaries. But if you need more space, ask for it. (See Chapter 8 for more information about physical boundaries.)

Using Jewelry, Crystals, or Rocks

Back in the late 1980s I often wore a beautiful clear quartz crystal necklace. I didn't necessarily believe it had magical healing powers, but I thought it was pretty. A chiropractor I went to at the time once asked me as I was lying face up on his table awaiting my treatment, "Why don't you just use your crystal?" Very funny, Dr. Werner. I wondered, was this one of the patient diagnostic questions he learned in chiropractic school?

Dr. Werner aside, many people feel an attraction to rocks, stones, gems, or certain types of jewelry. Whether these natural objects truly contain magical properties is something geologists and other scientists can sort out. In the meantime, if having an amethyst worry stone in your pocket or wearing a tourmaline bracelet to a meeting with your overbearing boss with narcissistic tendencies feels good, go for it!

Taking Along Darth Vader

Can you imagine having a real-life Darth Vader (from the epic *Star Wars* movies) as a bodyguard? That's exactly what this out-of-the-box extra protection tool invites you to do.

Lord Vader is a menacing, dark figure you wouldn't want to face in a lightsaber duel. On the other hand, having him on your side as a protector and bodyguard may be exactly what you need every now and then. Anytime you're feeling unsteady, unsafe, or even in danger, you can imagine him walking beside you. And since it's all about imagination and play, you can clone him and take a whole squad of Darth Vaders with you!

Arriving Early and Owning the Room

Arriving early and owning the room is a strategy that's particularly helpful when you're going to a meeting or event where you're feeling a bit less-than or out of your element.

Credit for this extra protection tool goes to one of my dearest friends, Gayle, who gave it to me many years ago. I was in a particularly contentious negotiation with the landlord of my office, who also happened to be a colleague. I was preparing to meet the landlord and the co-owner of the property at a local café to go over some of the sticking points of my lease, and I was feeling nervous and a bit unsure of myself.

Gayle advised me to get to the café at least 15 minutes early. I was to choose a table and the exact seat where I felt most comfortable and confident. Once I had the right location, table, and seat, I should get everything I needed for the meeting in front of me — documents, a list of my talking points, blank paper to take notes, a pen — and then make sure I had whatever beverages I needed. With the time remaining before the meeting got started, I was supposed to imagine receiving the best possible outcome.

I did just as Gayle suggested, and the meeting went very well. So well that today, more than a decade later, my former landlord and I have a very cordial and friendly relationship.

Thank you, Gayle.

Going to the Loo (Bathroom)

As my British friends know, "I'm going to the loo" is what you say when you're headed to the bathroom. Unlike the other options in this chapter, going to the loo happens in real life and not just in your mind. But it's too good not to include here as an option for extra protection.

Say you're with a friend or relative having lunch, and they've been talking non-stop for 15 minutes. You're feeling stressed and overwhelmed and you need a break. Go to the loo! (And if you're wondering how talking for 15 minutes without stopping is a boundary problem, see Chapter 10.)

Or maybe you're at a party and you're being followed around by someone who gets a bit too close to you or has a frightening habit of staring intently into your eyes as if they're trying to see into the deepest, darkest recesses of your mind. Kindly excuse yourself and go to the loo! (For more tips about navigating physical boundaries and how close other people can get to you, see Chapter 8.)

Taking a walk is an excellent substitute for going to the loo. It's not always an option, but if it's available and you love the outdoors, go for a nice, long, peaceful walk!

Chapter **22**

Ten Myths about Boundaries

The very mention of boundaries often elicits negative and undeserved reactions in many people. There are probably as many myths about boundaries as there are people who don't understand what they are or how they work. These myths originate from simply not knowing and not seeing the ways in which boundaries already exist and impact our everyday lives in profound ways.

In this chapter, I call out some of the most common myths and misunderstandings about boundaries, including that boundaries are selfish, that they're harmful to relationships, or that some people don't have the right to set boundaries.

Boundaries Are Selfish

Since nobody likes to be called selfish, we've discovered that one of the easiest ways to convince someone that they ought to behave in a certain way is to label their behavior selfish. This being the case, you can count on being called selfish at least once as you begin leveling up your boundaries skills.

For example, say you decide to end the open-door policy you've always had for your home office. You begin closing your office door and hanging a sign on it that says, "Making Big Money for the Family — SEE YOU AFTER 4!" Your family may call you selfish for imposing this unexpected and unwanted limit. But is it true that you're selfish? If you're using your listening boundary (see Chapter 11 for more details), you'll see that their claim that what you're doing is selfish is a perception, not a fact.

People are entitled to think that when you create space to do your work, you're being selfish. And you're entitled to believe that you're doing a great service to your family — and making lots of money so they can enjoy a vacation next summer — by protecting your focus time to do your genius work.

Healthy boundaries can never be selfish.

Creating a Boundary Means Telling Others What to Do

When you set boundaries or make requests, some people are going to believe you're telling them what to do.

For example, imagine you make a simple request like "Would you call me and let me know when your plane lands in Madagascar?" The person receiving the request responds, "Why are you telling me what to do?" Because you know how the listening boundary works (see Chapter 11), you can relax and even smile inside as you witness this massive listening boundary malfunction.

TIP

For every request, there are at least three responses: *Yes, no,* or *let's negotiate.*

Agreements are boundaries you create by making a request. You tried to create an agreement by asking a question, but your request was perceived as a demand. A question can never be a demand, and it can never mean you're telling another person what to do.

Boundaries Are New Age Garbage

This myth is fascinating because it seems to suggest that stop signs, walls, fences, lines on city streets, and your right to say no were all invented after the 1970s. It's both a misunderstanding of the meaning of boundaries and a matter of opinion. If someone wants to believe that boundaries are New Age garbage, more power to them! (If you want to have some fun with them, ask them if they'll give you their wallet.) They're entitled to their opinion, and you're entitled to yours.

This myth got me thinking: If boundaries aren't New Age garbage, what's the opposite of New Age garbage? Old Age treasure? I like it — let's go with it!

There's No Place for Boundaries in Intimate Relationships

This one is both a matter of opinion and often a matter of manipulation. Sometimes one person in a long-term intimate relationship will endorse this belief to get their spouse to do what they want them to do.

When you begin improving your boundaries, the people closest to you will notice. And they won't always be enthusiastic about the changes they see in you!

For example, say that during your 27-year marriage you've been dutifully washing your spouse's laundry or packing their lunch every morning before they head off to work. There's nothing wrong with doing your spouse's laundry or packing their lunch every day. However, you now realize that you stopped enjoying doing these favors around 25 years ago. And ever since then you've continued to do them because you worried about the message that changing your behavior would send to your spouse or you didn't think you had a right to change your mind.

REMEMBER

You always have a right to change your mind about anything. No exceptions.

But now that you're discovering more about yourself and about the way boundaries work, you see that you have a choice. So, you decide that you'll no longer do these two favors. When you tell your spouse, they say, "Your boundaries are hurting our intimacy."

If standing up for your freedom to change your mind is new behavior for you, you'll have a hard time staying with your reality and your right to stop doing your spouse's laundry and making their lunch. You may even think they're "right." But actually, your spouse is simply expressing their opinion.

Do you think it will help the intimacy of your relationship if you continue making your spouse's lunch and doing their laundry for the next 27 years when you don't want to? What if you allow your spouse to believe what they believe, and you allow yourself to believe what you believe?

Standing up for what you want and what you believe isn't easy. But it will save you from building up even more resentment or, worse, becoming physically ill from continuing to do something you hate to do.

Boundaries are a vital and necessary part of life, and life includes intimate relationships.

Women Don't Have a Right to Say No to Sex

I'm truly heartbroken to say that I've seen the consequences of this myth play out for women many times over many decades.

The myth that women don't have a right to say no to sex has deep and ancient roots in *patriarchal* (male-dominated) and *misogynistic* (prejudice against females) worldviews. These attitudes aren't necessarily gender-specific. It's as possible for a woman to hold misogynistic or patriarchal views as it is for a man. The myth that women owe their spouse sex is often found in certain religious communities or churches.

On the most basic level, believing that women don't have a right to say no to sex is an opinion or a belief. But the most important question is, what do you believe? If you believe you owe your spouse sex, this means you agree to have sex anytime they want sex. I can't speak for the 4 billion women on the planet. But the hundreds of women I've had the privilege of working with who've shared with me the intimate details of their lives tell me no. They don't agree to have sex with their partner anytime their partner wants to have sex. I'm open to the possibility that there are exceptions, but I've never encountered one.

At best this myth is a version of the juvenile and manipulative "If you love me, you'll let me." Yuck. If you find yourself on the receiving end of a pressure tactic like this one, you can simply say, "I hear that you think I owe you sex. I have a different opinion, and no."

REMEMBER

No person, regardless of their gender, owes another person access to their body. Ever.

If You've Made Mistakes in the Past, You Can't Set Limits

The myth that you can't set boundaries because you've made mistakes is more common than you may imagine for people who are drowning in guilt and remorse over something they did in the past.

Unfortunately, if you believe this myth, you're not only a victim of your own distorted thinking, but you're also running the risk of allowing others to violate your boundaries (since you don't have a right to stop them) or enabling people in your life with whom you must set limits.

Imagine that 5 minutes ago you yelled at your 16-year-old who has an alcohol problem. You told her that she's never going to amount to anything if she doesn't stop drinking. You feel awful for yelling and shaming her. Does this mean that when she asks you for the car keys so she can go to the liquor store, you should give them to her? Of course not!

When you don't set limits with people because you're operating under a misguided and incorrect belief that you don't have a right to set boundaries, you're not only doing yourself a disservice, but you're also missing an opportunity to demonstrate that you care about yourself and others by setting loving and appropriate limits.

Boundaries Are Something You Do to Another Person

You can't create a boundary that involves what another person will or won't do without their agreement. You can only create boundaries for yourself about what you will and won't do. Since the only two ways that boundaries can be created is when an individual person establishes their own boundaries or when two or more people create an agreement, there's no possible way that a boundary can be something done to another person.

REMEMBER

You can create boundaries for yourself, and you can create boundaries with others by making agreements.

Boundaries Are Punishment

Here's another myth that's pure perception, and a matter of opinion. When someone tells you that you're punishing them with your boundaries, it's usually both a thinking error (faulty thinking) and a manipulation designed to get you to backtrack on limits you're trying to set for your own well-being. (For more information about how to improve your thinking skills, see Chapter 14.)

Here are a few examples of situations in which someone may claim that your boundaries are punishing them:

>> You state your intention to begin a 30-day separation from your spouse because you need time apart to figure out how to handle a marital crisis, infidelity, mental health issue, or active addiction.

>> You're a business owner whose customer asks for a full refund for a service that was nonrefundable. As a courtesy, you issue a 50 percent refund.

>> After being told by your mother-in-law for the 100th time that she wishes her picture-perfect child had married their high school sweetheart rather than you (after 25 years of marriage), you tell your spouse that you will no longer be going to the annual Christmas party she hosts at her house.

>> You just got home from a 14-hour shift at the hospital and your spouse wants to watch *Titanic* (running time: 195 minutes). You say, "I would love to watch the movie with you after I've gotten some sleep."

In each of these cases, you're either taking care of yourself or sticking to an already established agreement.

REMEMBER

Everyone is entitled to their opinion. And you're entitled to yours.

People Who Have Boundaries Are Uptight

Sooner or later as you're improving your boundaries skills, someone is going to tell you that you're uptight. This (unsolicited) judgment is a subtle form of "Loosen up! What's your problem?" or "Can't you take a joke?"

I don't know about you, but I can definitely find uptight in myself — at least from time to time. And here's the beauty of you being able to find uptight in yourself if someone accuses you of this terrible offense: When someone says you're uptight or nerdy or a clean freak or a slow driver, and you can see that quality in yourself, then you and the other person are in complete agreement! No need to argue.

The bottom line is that people can believe that you and your boundaries are uptight or outrageous. You believe your boundaries are making your life orderly, calm, and sane. Each of you is entitled to your opinion. Case closed.

Family Members Get a Pass on Boundaries

There's a lot of truth in the adage that blood is thicker than water. This idea may be at the root of some people's belief that you get to run roughshod over your relatives' boundaries.

The family exception to boundaries can apply to anything from "borrowing" your sister's 7-carat ruby ring for a big date to expecting a family member to bail you out of jail for the fifth time for driving under the influence.

I'm reminded of a story I heard once about a man who was in a hurry to catch a plane to go to an important business meeting. He drove up to the entrance of the airport, stopped his car, got his suitcase out of the trunk, and walked into the terminal. He boarded his flight and left his car sitting in front of the entrance to the airport.

I doubt he was shocked to discover his car was gone when he returned four days later. He called his brother to come pick him up from the airport. His brother agreed, but when he got to the airport and told his car-abandoning brother how infuriated he was about being expected to pick him up after making such a dim-witted, short-sighted decision, his brother said, "Well, that's what families do!"

In so many words, his brother was saying that family members are entitled to get what they want from other family members — no exceptions — and that family members don't have a right to say *no*. No, family members aren't entitled to a free pass on personal boundaries.

TIP

Family members, spouses, employers, and others can't decide what your boundaries are. They get a pass on boundaries only if you give them one.

Chapter **23**

Ten Signs That You Need Professional Help

I f you struggle to protect yourself with good personal boundaries, you may stay in abusive or dangerous relationships that pose grave risks to you or your loved ones. Or you may find yourself in situations where others take advantage of you emotionally, sexually, or financially. You may be over-involved in other peoples' lives or even engage in dangerous or illegal activities or violate their boundaries.

In this chapter, I describe the red flags that signal you have problems with personal boundaries that you shouldn't ignore. If you can't create or maintain healthy personal or relationship boundaries and it's creating severe consequences in your life, you need to seek professional help.

You're in an Abusive Relationship

If you're in a relationship that's chronically abusive emotionally, physically, or sexually, not only do you need the professional help of a licensed mental health treatment provider, but you may also need legal help.

TIP

If you're not sure if what you're experiencing is abuse, review Chapters 7, 8, 9, and 10 for details about what constitutes emotional, physical, or sexual boundary violations.

Abuse can take many forms. Here are some of the most common that occur specifically in relationships:

>> You're called demeaning or shaming names on a regular basis.

>> You experience physical violence of any kind, including being grabbed, pushed, pinched, slapped, or held against your will.

>> Your online activities — including looking at your phone, email, or social media accounts — are monitored with or without your consent or knowledge.

>> You're "required" to share your whereabouts, who you're with, or details about your everyday activities on a regular basis.

REMEMBER

If you're in an abusive relationship, contact your local domestic violence hotline or the National Domestic Violence Hotline (800-799-7233).

You're Over-Involved in Others' Lives

I can't tell you how many stories I've heard over the years of people who never learned about or didn't care about staying inside their circle of control, or what they have power over. (For more information about the circle of control, see Chapter 16.) This boundary problem shows up most often in parent-adult child relationships but can also happen in other contexts like long-term committed relationships.

For example, some parents tell their adult children where to go to college, take an active (and unwanted) role in all the details of planning their children's weddings, and tell them how to parent their own children. These are the same parents who, when their kids were growing up, picked their friends, laid out their clothes for school each morning, and told them how to style their hair until they were seniors in high school.

These boundaryless parents almost always use money to influence and control their adult children. And sadly, this level of over-involvement creates stress, drama, and sometimes extreme dependency in their adult children. Parents' over-the-top intrusions into their adult children's lives often renders them unable to become confident, self-sufficient adults.

If you're one of these parents — or someone who's over-involved or too invested in another adult's life — chances are this is a learned behavior passed down to you from your parents. It's based on a false (and likely unconscious) belief that feeling peaceful and happy depends on your loved ones looking and behaving the way you need them to. This level of dependency makes you extremely anxious because you (and everyone else) don't have that much power.

Being unable to stay inside your circle of control severely damages your relationships, and ultimately you. If you know this is a problem for you, find a mental health provider who can help you get to the root of what's driving your behavior and help you set boundaries with yourself. Do it for yourself, and for those you love.

Someone Is Taking Advantage of You, and You Can't Set a Boundary

Exploitation can occur in many contexts and in many kinds of relationships. People who take advantage of others are skillful at detecting who is most vulnerable, including older people, single mothers struggling to make ends meet, trauma survivors, and people who are isolated or lonely.

You may be an older person who's being cared for by a family member or a paid caretaker who's taking money from you or stealing your belongings. Or maybe you met someone online who appeared to want an intimate relationship with you but is now asking for money or telling you dramatic or disturbing stories about how they need money to pay for a dying relative's medical bills, for example.

If you're older than 65 and you believe you're being taken advantage of, contact local adult protective services or a clergy member, doctor, or other professional you trust.

If you're being threatened (but you're not in immediate danger), go to your local police station to report the person who's threatening you. You should also find a mental health treatment provider who can help you work on boundaries or resolve any trauma you've experienced due to your current situation.

If you're being taken advantage of by an employer or supervisor in the United States, contact the Equal Employment Opportunity Commission (EEOC) at 800-669-4000 or info@eeoc.gov.

Your Partner Restricts Your Activities or Connections

Restricting another person's activities or their access to other people is extremely common in physically abusive or highly controlling relationships. If you're an adult and your partner, spouse, or anyone else tries to limit your access to activities or other people, you shouldn't discount or ignore this dangerous warning sign.

Here are some examples of restricting another person's activities or relationships:

» You're not allowed to leave your home when you want to.

» You're given an allowance or kept on a very strict budget for necessities like groceries, food, or clothing, including for your children.

» You're not allowed to use a phone or computer.

» You have access only to devices that track your activity or are only available to you during times when you're being monitored.

» You're not free to make decisions about where you go or when you go somewhere.

If someone is trying to restrict your activities or your connections to other people, ask a person you trust to contact the local domestic violence hotline or the National Domestic Violence Hotline (800-799-7233), or contact them yourself if possible. You should also find a licensed mental health treatment provider to work with. Many local domestic violence agencies offer free or low-cost group counseling or limited private counseling sessions.

You Engage in Unsafe Activities to Please Your Partner

When someone you're in a relationship with asks (or commands) you to engage in unsafe activities, their demands usually involve sexual contact. However, you may have been asked to participate in unsafe (or even illegal) activities such as deceiving others for the purpose of exploiting them, stealing, committing fraud, or selling drugs.

If your partner or anyone else pressures you to engage in unprotected sex or other sexual activities that feel uncomfortable or dangerous to you, you have the right to say no. See Chapter 9 for more information about sexual boundaries.

If being pressured or coerced is a chronic pattern in your life or in your relationships, you should seek help from a qualified mental health treatment provider or contact your local domestic violence hotline as soon as possible.

You've Been Accused of Sexual Misconduct

In most cases, the first time someone is accused of sexual misconduct or inappropriate sexual behavior, no significant formal or legal action is taken. However, if you've been accused of sexual misconduct of any kind, you should seek the counsel of a mental health treatment provider with specific knowledge and training related to sexual trauma and personal or professional boundaries.

There are two important reasons to seek professional help after a first-time accusation of sexual misconduct. The first is that you may need help identifying blind spots or other issues that contributed to your part in the situation that led to the accusation.

The second reason is that sexual misconduct allegations are sometimes false accusations. In these cases, it's helpful to have the support of an objective third party who can help you sort through your feelings about being unjustly accused and the consequences you may have experienced as a result.

WARNING

If you've been accused of sexual misconduct more than once (and they aren't false accusations), there's a higher-than-average chance you either lack good information about sexual boundaries or have a serious untreated mental health issue. You should seek out a licensed mental health professional who has specific training in treating people with sexual boundary problems. You also need to consult an attorney.

You Intentionally Put Yourself in Dangerous Situations

If you consider yourself to be a risk-taker, you may be more comfortable with (and more prone to) putting yourself in dangerous situations. Provided the risks you take don't expose you to extreme danger, your level of risk-taking may not be a problem for you.

However, if you repeatedly find that you put yourself in dangerous situations without understanding why or if there's a high likelihood that you'll experience significant harm, you need professional help.

Some people put themselves in dangerous situations because they suffered childhood abuse or trauma. For example, someone who was repeatedly sexually abused by a parent may later engage in behaviors like loitering near bus stops at night, hoping that someone will see them and try to pick them up. They may know that they're putting themself in danger and they may not fully understand why they're engaging in this high-risk behavior.

Dangerous behaviors like these are examples of trauma reenactment. *Trauma reenactment* occurs when an adult repeats actions, behaviors, or relationship patterns that closely resemble prior abuse, usually in childhood.

REMEMBER

Regardless of the reasons, if you're concerned about the frequency or the intensity with which you expose yourself to dangerous situations or people, find a mental health treatment provider who specializes in trauma to work with as soon as possible.

You're Being Stalked or Harassed

Stalking means being pursued, followed, or persecuted, and *harassment* means being pressured or intimidated, or receiving repeated unwanted communications from another person. Stalking and harassment can occur either online, offline (in person), or both.

If you're being stalked or harassed, contact the police department to explore your options for reporting the offending behavior. If you're experiencing harassment in the workplace in the United States, contact the EEOC (800-669-4000 or info@eeoc.gov).

TIP

Depending on the severity of the situation, you should also find a mental health treatment provider who has specific training for treating trauma.

You Repeatedly Violate Other People's Boundaries

If you've been told more than twice by more than two people that you're getting too close, asking too many questions, or touching someone too soon, you have a pattern of violating other people's boundaries.

If you carefully read the information presented in this book and follow the guidelines I suggest, you can make significant improvements to your personal and relationship boundaries. However, I also recommend that while you're exploring the fundamentals of personal boundaries, you also find a mental health treatment provider to work with.

There are likely specific reasons you repeatedly violate other people's boundaries, and you'll benefit from understanding how and why these patterns developed. Explanations can range from not learning good boundaries when you were growing up, to having a serious mental health disorder.

Chapter 5 explains that you learned about boundaries from your family as you grew up. If you're boundaryless, it's very likely because that's what your family modeled. It's not your fault that you had inadequate guidance about boundaries, but it's your responsibility now to discover how to identify, create, and maintain healthy personal and relationship boundaries, and how to protect others from your boundarylessness or offending behaviors.

You're Engaged in Illegal Behavior That Violates Boundaries

If you've engaged in illegal behavior that violates others' boundaries, you need to contact an attorney immediately to help you navigate any legal consequences you're facing. You also need to work with a mental health treatment provider who can help you get to the bottom of why you're engaging in illegal behavior and who can provide the support and resources you need to stop the behavior.

Attorneys, like licensed mental health treatment providers, are required to keep their clients' information confidential. However, be aware that in many states in the United States licensed mental health treatment providers are required to report some illegal behavior, including viewing child pornography. If you go to a therapist in a state with this requirement and disclose certain illegal behavior, your therapist may give you the option of reporting yourself to the local authorities, or the therapist will contact them directly. But don't let this requirement stop you from getting help. Discuss your concerns about disclosing certain information with your therapist so you can get the help you need.

In many instances, people who engage in illegal behavior that violates others' boundaries are survivors of childhood trauma. If your current problematic behavior mimics or is very similar to trauma you experienced as a child, it's not your fault that you were traumatized. But it is your responsibility now to avoid repeating what happened to you. Seek both legal and mental health counseling from a licensed professional to help you stop harming others or yourself.

Index

A

abrupt changes of subject, 212

abuse
- abusive or dangerous physical contact, 149–150
- carried shame, 83, 85–86
- claiming right to another person's body, 217
- failure of parents to give protection from, 83
- offensive and offending people, eliminating from life, 73–74
- professional help for abusive relationships, 363–364
- refusing privacy, 151
- reporting, 342–344
- trauma created from boundary violations, 137–139
- unwanted sexual experiences or contact, 163

accountability
- adding to action plan, 288–289
- follow-through, improving, 303
- in new agreements, 325–326, 328–329

accusations of sexual misconduct, 367

acknowledging without agreeing, 107

action plans
- accountability, adding to, 288–289
- agreements, knowing when you have, 294–296
- aligning with points of power, 287–290
- commitment to, honesty about, 290–294
- doubts, delaying action when having, 291–292
- examples of, 287
- overview, 87, 226, 285–286
- retaliatory or vengeful actions, avoiding, 296–299

agreement journal, 294, 317

agreements
- about sexual boundaries, 157
- boundary violations, 132–133, 135
- broken, 234, 305–306
- crafting effective requests, 289
- creating, 40–42
- creating outcomes with requests, 280
- egos and, 190
- ending, 132–133
- evaluating, 306–309
- failure to make, 304–305
- forgetting, 317
- getting in writing, 338–339
- to have conversations, 184–185
- knowing when you have, 294–296
- leading with, 188–191
- misunderstanding meaning of, 303–304
- negotiating, 295
- processing one incident or situation at a time, 234–236
- recommitting to original action or, 309–310
- resentment, eliminating, 128
- revised, starting over with, 311
- scanning for when listening, 204–205

aikido, 115–116

alarms, setting, 67–68

Angelou, Maya, 321

anger
- knowing what isn't working, 228–229
- in repetitive stories, identifying, 123
- resentment, 125–128
- signs of, 121–123

arousal, sexual, 168, 169

arriving early and owning the room, 353–354

asking for help, 116, 279–280

asking questions, 108–109, 208–209

assumptions, 39

authentic personal power, cultivating, 272–274

B

"Back off!" vibes, sending, 352–353

blaming others, 181, 193–194

body sensations, noticing, 133

boundary pushers and offenders, 129–133

boundary ruptures, 136, 137–139

boundary violations. See also repeated boundary violations
- in childhood, 137
- classifying, 134–136
- getting professional help, 345–346
- law enforcement or legal help for, 344–345

listening
- changing subject abruptly, 212

About the Author

Victoria Priya (formerly known as Vicki Tidwell Palmer) is a **Licensed Clinical Social Worker** (LCSW) and a Somatic Experiencing® Practitioner (SEP). Although no formal training programs that grant psychotherapists a certification in personal boundaries currently exist, Victoria was crowned "The Boundaries Queen" by a group of her clients several years ago. It's her humble belief that this honor establishes her boundaries creds in a way that no training, certification, or license ever could.

Victoria is the founder of The Radiant Threefold Path, host of *The Boundaries Queen, Radiant Threefold Path,* and the highly popular *Beyond Bitchy: Mastering the Art of Boundaries* (2018–2021) podcasts, and best-selling author of *Moving Beyond Betrayal.*

Victoria has trained and studied with leading relationship and trauma experts, including Pia Mellody, John and Julie Gottman, and Terry Real, Maggie Kline, as well as renowned spiritual teachers, including Ram Dass, the venerable Thich Nhat Hanh, and Byron Katie (in her nine-day School for The Work training).

She maintains an active private coaching practice in Houston, Texas. Victoria has been married for 37 years and is the proud mother of one son.

Dedication

This book is dedicated to you, dear reader. Without you, this book would not exist.

May you experience peace, freedom, and spaciousness. These are just three of the many paradoxical and hidden gifts of boundaries.

Author's Acknowledgments

Everything that comes into being is created through a mysterious merging of innumerable events, known and unknown. *Personal Boundaries For Dummies* is no exception.

When I unexpectedly received an email from Elizabeth Stilwell, an acquisitions editor on the *For Dummies* team at John Wiley & Sons, on June 28, 2023, I was stunned. And yet I could also see my part in how that event came to be.

I love sharing my knowledge and experience of how boundaries work. I've seen over and over in both my personal life and in my work with clients that healthy, respectful, and effective boundaries change lives.

I owe deep gratitude to many people who have had a part in the creation of this book. Many more than I can name. A special thanks to Donna Wright, the project editor, and Kelly Brillhart, the copy editor, who painstakingly (and patiently) edited the manuscript, and to my colleague Cynthia Schiebel for taking on the role of technical editor.

To my husband, Micheal, for his unwavering and generous support over the past 37 years — giving me the freedom to create what is near and dear to my heart so that I can help others. To my mother, Nancy Freshour Brown, and my father, John Edward Tidwell, for giving me life. And Pia Mellody for giving me a deep appreciation for boundaries, which she rightly calls a spiritual practice. To Lynn Grodzki for her constant, steady support and guidance for more than a decade, and Melissa Ford for giving me a new vision of my life and work and persistently inviting me to question the stories I make up about myself and others.

Special and deep thanks to Gayle Jamail for more than I can possibly say. To my former client, MG (she knows who she is), who was the first person to ask me to write a second book on boundaries for a broader audience so she could pass along to her friends and family the information, tools, and skills that helped her. MG, here's your book!

Lastly, I want to thank my clients, who have trusted me to walk beside them through difficult, dark times and the many invisible, sometimes excruciating initiations that all of us eventually face. Witnessing your courage and the resilience of the human spirit is a persistent source of awe, joy, and inspiration to me.

Publisher's Acknowledgments

Acquisitions Editor: Elizabeth Stilwell

Project Editor: Donna Wright

Copy Editor: Kelly Brillhart

Technical Editor:
Cynthia Schiebel, MEd, LPC, LCDC, BCC

Proofreader: Susan Hobbs

Production Editor: Pradesh Kumar

Cover Image: © mdyn/Adobe Stock Photos